AAT

Technican Level 4

Units 8, 9 & 16

Cost Management, Resource Allocation & Evaluating Activities

Workbook

1140/A01

FOULKS*lynch*

British Library Cataloguing-in-Publication Data

A catalogue record for this book is available from the British Library.

Published by Foulks Lynch Ltd
4, The Griffin Centre
Staines Road
Feltham
Middlesex
TW14 0HS

ISBN   0 7483 5114 0

Printed and Bound in Great Britain by Ashford Colour Press, Gosport, Hants.

© Foulks Lynch Ltd, 2001

Acknowledgements

We are grateful to the Association of Accounting Technicians, the Association of Chartered Certified Accountants, the Chartered Institute of Management Accountants and the Institute of Chartered Accountants in England and Wales for permission to reproduce past examination questions. The answers have been prepared by Foulks Lynch Ltd. The copyright to the questions remains with the examining body.

CONTENTS

PREFACE

This is the 2001 edition of the AAT workbook for Units 8, 9 and 16 - Cost Management, Resource Allocation and Evaluating Activities. The workbook includes the sample central and devolved assessments provided by the AAT.

The workbook has been produced to complement our Units 8, 9 and 16 textbook and it contains numerous practice questions and tasks designed to reflect and simulate the work place environment. These are arranged to match the chapters of the textbook, so that you can work through the two books together.

The workbook also contains practice central and devolved assessments to prepare you completely for the assessment procedures which form part of your course.

Fully comprehensive answers to all questions, tasks and assessments are provided, with the exception of those which are designated as being specifically for classroom work.

You will find that completion of all the elements of this workbook will prepare you admirably for the assessments which you must carry out to pass Units 8, 9 and 16. You are reminded that competence must be achieved in EACH section. You should therefore attempt and aim to complete EVERY task in EACH section. All essential workings should be included with your answer, where appropriate. An indication of how much time you should spend on each section is given for some questions. Where no time allocated is cited ask your tutor for advice.

Class Activities

A feature of this workbook is the section at the end comprising Activities which are specially designed for classroom use. The answers to these are not included in the workbook but are reproduced in the **College Kit** which is available to college lecturers who adopt our material.

College Kits

In addition to the Textbooks and Workbooks, Foulks Lynch offers colleges adopting our material the highly popular **'College Kits'**.

The College Kit for these units contains:

- additional Devolved and Central Assessment material in looseleaf form which can be photocopied to provide practice classwork for students (much of this additional Central Assessment material is taken from the AAT's own Central Assessments); and

- the looseleaf answers to the class examples from the Workbook.

These Kits are supplied at no extra cost and may be photocopied under the limited licence which is granted to adopting colleges.

PRESENT VALUE TABLE

Present value of 1 ie, $(1 + r)^{-n}$ where r = discount rate, n = number of periods until payment

Periods (n)	Discount rates (r)									
	1%	2%	3%	4%	5%	6%	7%	8%	9%	10%
1	0.990	0.980	0.971	0.962	0.952	0.943	0.935	0.926	0.917	0.909
2	0.980	0.961	0.943	0.925	0.907	0.890	0.873	0.857	0.842	0.826
3	0.971	0.942	0.915	0.889	0.864	0.840	0.816	0.794	0.772	0.751
4	0.961	0.924	0.888	0.855	0.823	0.792	0.763	0.735	0.708	0.683
5	0.951	0.906	0.863	0.822	0.784	0.747	0.713	0.681	0.650	0.621
6	0.942	0.888	0.837	0.790	0.746	0.705	0.666	0.630	0.596	0.564
7	0.933	0.871	0.813	0.760	0.711	0.665	0.623	0.583	0.547	0.513
8	0.923	0.853	0.789	0.731	0.677	0.627	0.582	0.540	0.502	0.467
9	0.914	0.837	0.766	0.703	0.645	0.592	0.544	0.500	0.460	0.424
10	0.905	0.820	0.744	0.676	0.614	0.558	0.508	0.463	0.422	0.386
11	0.896	0.804	0.722	0.650	0.585	0.527	0.475	0.429	0.388	0.350
12	0.887	0.788	0.702	0.625	0.557	0.497	0.444	0.397	0.356	0.319
13	0.879	0.773	0.681	0.601	0.530	0.569	0.415	0.368	0.326	0.290
14	0.870	0.758	0.661	0.577	0.505	0.442	0.388	0.340	0.299	0.263
15	0.861	0.743	0.642	0.555	0.481	0.417	0.362	0.315	0.275	0.239

Periods (n)	Discount rates (r)									
	11%	12%	13%	14%	15%	16%	17%	18%	19%	20%
1	0.901	0.893	0.885	0.877	0.870	0.862	0.855	0.847	0.840	0.833
2	0.812	0.797	0.783	0.769	0.756	0.743	0.731	0.718	0.706	0.694
3	0.731	0.712	0.693	0.675	0.658	0.641	0.624	0.609	0.593	0.579
4	0.659	0.636	0.613	0.592	0.572	0.552	0.534	0.516	0.499	0.482
5	0.593	0.567	0.543	0.519	0.497	0.476	0.456	0.437	0.419	0.402
6	0.535	0.507	0.480	0.456	0.432	0.410	0.390	0.370	0.352	0.335
7	0.482	0.452	0.425	0.400	0.376	0.354	0.333	0.314	0.296	0.279
8	0.434	0.404	0.376	0.351	0.327	0.305	0.285	0.266	0.249	0.233
9	0.391	0.361	0.333	0.308	0.284	0.263	0.243	0.225	0.209	0.194
10	0.352	0.322	0.295	0.270	0.247	0.227	0.208	0.191	0.176	0.162
11	0.317	0.287	0.261	0.237	0.215	0.195	0.178	0.162	0.148	0.135
12	0.286	0.257	0.231	0.208	0.187	0.168	0.152	0.137	0.124	0.112
13	0.258	0.229	0.204	0.182	0.163	0.145	0.130	0.116	0.104	0.093
14	0.232	0.205	0.181	0.160	0.141	0.125	0.111	0.099	0.088	0.078
15	0.209	0.183	0.160	0.140	0.123	0.108	0.095	0.084	0.074	0.065

CUMULATIVE PRESENT VALUE OF £1

This table shows the present value of £1 per annum, receivable or payable at the end of each year for *n* years

Present (n)	Interest rates (r)									
	1%	2%	3%	4%	5%	6%	7%	8%	9%	10%
1	0.990	0.980	0.971	0.962	0.952	0.943	0.935	0.926	0.917	0.909
2	1.970	1.942	1.913	1.886	1.859	1.833	1.808	1.783	1.759	1.736
3	2.941	2.884	2.829	2.775	2.723	2.673	2.624	2.577	2.531	2.487
4	3.902	3.808	3.717	3.630	3.546	3.465	3.387	3.312	3.240	3.170
5	4.853	4.713	4.580	4.452	4.329	4.212	4.100	3.993	3.890	3.791
6	5.975	5.601	5.417	5.242	5.076	4.917	4.767	4.623	4.486	4.355
7	6.728	6.472	6.230	6.002	5.786	5.582	5.389	5.206	5.033	4.868
8	7.652	7.325	7.020	6.733	6.463	6.210	5.971	5.747	5.535	5.335
9	8.566	8.162	7.786	7.435	7.108	6.802	6.515	6.247	5.995	5.759
10	9.471	8.983	8.530	8.111	7.722	7.360	7.024	6.710	6.418	6.145
11	10.37	9.787	9.253	8.760	8.306	7.887	7.499	7.139	6.805	6.495
12	11.26	10.58	9.954	9.385	8.863	8.384	7.943	7.536	7.161	6.814
13	12.13	11.35	10.63	9.986	9.394	8.853	8.385	7.904	7.487	7.103
14	13.00	12.11	11.30	10.56	9.899	9.295	8.745	8.244	7.786	7.367
15	13.87	12.85	11.94	11.12	10.38	9.712	9.108	8.559	8.061	7.606

Present (n)	Interest rates (r)									
	11%	12%	13%	14%	15%	16%	17%	18%	19%	20%
1	0.901	0.893	0.885	0.877	0.870	0.862	0.855	0.847	0.840	0.833
2	1.713	1.690	1.668	1.647	1.626	1.605	1.585	1.566	1.547	1.528
3	2.444	2.402	2.361	2.322	2.283	2.246	2.210	2.174	2.140	2.106
4	3.102	3.037	2.974	2.914	2.855	2.798	2.743	2.690	2.639	2.589
5	3.696	3.605	3.517	3.433	3.352	3.274	3.199	3.127	3.058	2.991
6	4.231	4.111	3.998	3.889	3.784	3.685	3.589	3.498	3.410	3.326
7	4.712	4.564	4.423	4.288	4.160	4.039	3.922	3.812	3.706	3.605
8	5.146	4.968	4.799	4.639	4.487	4.344	4.207	4.078	3.954	3.837
9	5.537	5.328	5.132	4.946	4.772	4.607	4.451	4.303	4.163	4.031
10	5.889	5.650	5.426	5.216	5.019	4.833	4.659	4.464	4.339	4.192
11	6.207	5.938	5.687	5.453	5.234	5.208	4.836	4.656	4.486	4.327
12	6.492	6.194	5.918	5.660	5.421	5.197	4.988	4.793	4.611	4.439
13	6.750	6.424	6.122	5.842	5.583	5.342	5.118	4.910	4.715	4.533
14	6.982	6.628	6.302	6.002	5.724	5.468	5.229	5.008	4.802	4.611
15	7.191	6.811	6.462	6.142	5.847	5.575	5.324	8.092	4.876	4.675

SAMPLE

SIMULATIONS

TECHNICIAN STAGE

NVQ/SVQ LEVEL 4 IN ACCOUNTING

SPECIMEN CENTRAL ASSESSMENT

CONTRIBUTING TO THE MANAGEMENT OF COSTS AND THE ENHANCEMENT OF VALUE (UNIT 8)

Time allowed – 2 hours plus 15 minutes' reading time

◆ FOULKS*lynch*

SECTION 1 (Suggested time allocation: 70 minutes)

Data

You are employed as an Accounting Technician by Original Holidays Limited. Original Holidays commenced business one year ago as a tour operator specialising in arranging holidays to the small island of Zed. Recent newspaper reports have stated that the cost of hotel bedrooms per night in Zed has been increasing over the last twelve months due to its government refusing to allow further hotels to be built despite increasing demand from tourists.

The managing director of Original Holidays, Jane Armstrong, is concerned that this will affect the profitability of the company's operations to the island. She asked Colin Ware, the financial accountant, to provide data showing the nightly cost of a bedroom charged to Original Holidays over the last four quarters. Colin's response is reproduced below.

MEMO

To: Jane Armstrong	Date: 5 January 20X8
From: Colin Ware	
Subject: Nightly cost per bedroom	

Thank you for your recent enquiry concerning the cost per night of a bedroom in Zed. I have analysed the amounts paid per quarter over the last twelve months and divided that amount by the number of bedrooms hired per night. The nightly cost per bedroom is as follows:

	Quarter 1	Quarter 2	Quarter 3	Quarter 4
Cost per night	£102.400	£137.760	£134.480	£68.921

(Note: all figures in pounds to 3 decimal places.)

On receiving the memo, Jane noticed that the cost to Original Holidays per bedroom per night had actually been falling over the last three quarters and has asked for your help in reconciling this with the newspaper reports. You obtain the following information:

- Over several years, there has been a consistent seasonal variation in the cost of bedrooms per night. According to the marketing manager, these are:

	Quarter 1	Quarter 2	Quarter 3	Quarter 4
Seasonal variations *as percentage of trend*	– 20%	+5%	+40%	– 25%

- A financial newspaper provides you with the following exchange rates between the UK pound and the Zed franc:

Quarter 1	Quarter 2	Quarter 3	Quarter 4
2,000 francs	2,000 francs	2,800 francs	3,000 francs

◈ FOULKS*lynch*

Task 1.1

(a)   Using the quarterly exchange rates given, identify the actual nightly cost per bedroom in Zed francs for each quarter.

(b)   Using the information provided by the marketing manager, identify the trend in costs in Zed francs for each quarter.

(c)   Identify the quarterly percentage increase in the cost of a bedroom per night in Zed francs and express this as an annual percentage to 2 decimal places.

(d)   Forecast the cost in British pounds of a bedroom per night for the first quarter of next year using the exchange rate for the fourth quarter.

Data

On receiving your analysis of the cost per bedroom per night, Jane Armstrong expresses concern that the company's existing reporting system does not provide sufficient information to monitor operations. She shows you a copy of the operating statement for the third quarter prepared using the existing system. The statement excludes marketing, administrative and other head-office overheads and is reproduced below.

Original Holidays Operating Statement for the 3rd Quarter – 20X7

	Budget	Actual
Number of holidays	6,000	7,800
	£	£
Turnover	1,800,000	2,262,000
Accommodation	840,000	1,048,944
Air transport	720,000	792,000
Operating profit	240,000	421,056

Jane has shared her concerns with Colin Ware, the financial accountant. He has suggested that a standard costing report, reconciling standard cost to actual cost, would provide more meaningful information for management. To demonstrate to Jane Armstrong the improved quality of a standard costing system of reporting, Colin asks you to reanalyse the operating statement for the third quarter. To help you, he provides you with the following information:

- The accommodation is a variable cost. Its usage variance is nil.

- Air transport is a fixed cost and relates to the company's own 105-seat aircraft.

- The budget provided for 80 return flights in the quarter with each flight carrying 75 tourists. This volume was used to calculate the fixed overhead absorption rate when costing individual holidays.

- Due to operational difficulties, the aircraft only undertook 78 return flights, carrying a total of 7,800 passengers in quarter 3.

Task 1.2

(a)   Using the budgeted data, calculate the standard absorption cost per holiday.

(b)   Using your answer to part (a), calculate the standard absorption cost of 7,800 holidays.

(c)   Calculate the following variances:

      (i)   material price variance for the accommodation
      (ii)   fixed overhead expenditure variance for the air transport
      (iii)   fixed overhead volume variance for the air transport
      (iv)   fixed overhead capacity variance for the air transport
      (v)   fixed overhead efficiency variance for the air transport.

(d)   Prepare a statement reconciling the budgeted (or standard) absorption cost to the actual cost.

(e)   Identify the single most important reason for the increase in the actual profit.

Task 1.3

Write a memo to Jane Armstrong *briefly* explaining what the following variances attempt to measure and giving ONE possible reason why each variance might have occurred:

- the fixed overhead expenditure variance
- the fixed overhead capacity variance
- the fixed overhead efficiency variance.

◈ FOULKS*lynch*

SECTION 2 (Suggested time allocation: 50 minutes)

Data

Diamond Ltd is a retail jeweller operating 30 branches in similar localities. Common accounting policies operate throughout all branches, including a policy of using straight-line depreciation for fixed assets.

All branches use rented premises. These are accounted for under 'other costs' in the operating statement. Fixed assets are predominantly fixtures and fittings.

Each branch is individually responsible for ordering stock, the authorising of payments to creditors and the control of debtors. Cash management, however, is managed by Diamond's head office with any cash received by a branch being paid into a head office bank account twice daily.

You are employed in the head office of Diamond Ltd as a financial analyst monitoring the performance of all 30 branches. This involves calculating performance indicators for each branch and comparing each branch's performance with company standards. Financial data relating to Branch 24 is reproduced below.

Diamond Ltd – Branch 24 –Year ended 31 December 20X7

Operating statement	£'000	£'000	Operating net assets at year end	£'000	£'000
Turnover		720.0	*Fixed assets*		
Opening stock	80.0		Cost		225.0
Purchases	340.0		Accumulated depreciation		(90.0)
Closing stock	(60.0)				
			Net book value		135.0
		360.0			
Gross profit		360.0	*Working capital*		
Wages and salaries	220.6		Stocks	60.0	
Depreciation	45.0		Debtors	96.0	
Other costs	36.8		Creditors	(51.0)	105.0
		302.4	*Net assets*		240.0
Operating profit		57.6			

Task 2.1

Prepare a statement showing the following performance indicators for Branch 24:

(a)   the return on capital employed
(b)   the gross profit margin as a percentage
(c)   the asset turnover
(d)   the sales (or net profit) margin as a percentage
(e)   the average age of debtors in months
(f)   the average age of creditors in months
(g)   the average age of the closing stock in months.

Data

The financial director of Diamond Ltd is Charles Walden. He is concerned that branch 24 is not performing as well as the other branches. All other branches are able to meet or exceed most of the performance standards laid down by the company.

Charles is particularly concerned that branches should achieve the standards for return on capital employed and the asset turnover. He also feels that managers should try to achieve the standards laid down for working capital management. The relevant standards are:

- return on capital employed   40%
- asset turnover   4 times per annum
- average age of debtors   0.5 months
- average age of creditors   3 months
- average age of closing stock   1 month

Charles Walden has recently attended a course on financial modelling and scenario planning. Charles explains that scenario planning shows the likely performance of a business under different assumed circumstances. It requires an understanding of the relationship between the different elements within the financial statements and how these change as the circumstances being modelled change. As an example, he tells you that if the volume of branch turnover was to increase then the cost of sales would also increase but that all other expenses would remain the same as they are fixed costs.

He believes scenario planning would be particularly helpful to the manager of Branch 24, Angela Newton. Charles had previously discussed the performance of the branch with Angela and emphasised the importance of improving the asset turnover and maintaining control of working capital. However, Angela raised the following objections:

- turning over assets is not important, making profit should be the main objective
- Branch 24 has been in existence for two years less than all the other branches.

Task 2.2

Charles Walden asks you to write a memo to Angela Newton. Your memo should:

(a)   show the return on capital employed that Branch 24 would have achieved had it been able to achieve the company's asset turnover during the year to 31 December 1997 while maintaining prices and the existing capital employed

(b)   show the return on capital employed and the asset turnover for the year if Branch 24 had been able to achieve the company's standards for the average age of debtors, the average age of creditors and the average age of finished stock while maintaining its existing sales volume

(c)   *using the data in task 2.1 and your solution to task 2.2a*, address the issues raised by Angela Newton.

CONTRIBUTING TO THE MANAGEMENT OF COSTS
AND THE ENHANCEMENT OF VALUE
(UNIT 8)

SPECIMEN CENTRAL ASSESSMENT
SUGGESTED ANSWERS

SECTION 1

Task 1.1

		Quarter 1	Quarter 2	Quarter 3	Quarter 4
	UK cost (£)	102.400	137.760	134.480	68.921
	Exchange rate	2,000	2,000	2,800	3,000
(a)	Zed cost (F)	204,800	275,520	376,544	206,763
	Seasonal variations†	−20%	5%	40%	−25%
(b)	Trend unit cost (F)	256,000	262,400	268,960	275,684
	Increase (F)		6,400	6,560	6,724
(c)	Increase (%)	2.5% 2.5% 2.5%			
	Annual rate = $(1.025)^4 - 1 = 10.38\%$				

† Seasonal variations are expressed as a percentage of the trend. If the trend is 100% and the seasonal variation −20% then the forecast actual is 80%. Deriving the trend from the actual, therefore, involves a 25% adjustment (20%/80%) and not a 20% adjustment.

(d)	Trend cost, quarter 4 (F)	275,684
	Add 2½%	6,892
	Trend forecast (F)	282,576
	Seasonal adjustment (−20%)	(56,515)
	Forecast cost (F)	226,061
	Exchange rate	3,000
	Forecast cost (£)	£75.35

Task 1.2

			£
(a)	Accommodation (variable cost)	*£840,000/6,000*	140
	Air transport (fixed cost)	*£720,000/6,000*	120
	Standard absorption cost per holiday		260
(b)	Standard absorption cost for 7,800 holidays	*£260 × 7,800*	£2,028,000

(c) Cost variances:

(i)		Material price variance	*(140 − 134.48) × 7,800*	£43,056 (F)
(ii)		Fixed overhead expenditure variance	*720,000 − 792,000*	£72,000 (A)
(iii)		Fixed overhead volume variance	*(7,800 − 6,000) × £120*	£216,000 (F)
(iv)		Fixed overhead capacity variance	*(78 − 80) × 75 × £120*	£18,000 (A)
(v)		Fixed overhead efficiency variance	*(100 − 75) × 78 × £120*	£234,000 (F)

(d)

Original Holidays Ltd – Cost Reconciliation Statement 3rd Quarter 20X7

	£
Standard absorption cost for 7,800 holidays	2,028,000
Material price variance	43,056 (F)
Fixed overhead expenditure variance	72,000 (A)
Fixed overhead capacity variance	18,000 (A)
Fixed overhead efficiency variance	234,000 (F)
Actual absorption cost	1,840,944

(e)   The single most important reason for the increased profit is the more intensive use of the aircraft. This is represented by the favourable fixed overhead efficiency variance of £234,000.

Task 1.3

MEMO

To: Jane Armstrong   Date: 5 January 20X8

From: Accounting Technician

Subject: Fixed overhead variances

Fixed overheads behave differently from variable costs such as accommodation. Over the relevant range, fixed costs remain the same irrespective of activity. The only way they can, therefore, change is if the price paid for those overheads changes. This is what the fixed overhead expenditure variance measures. For quarter 3, this was an adverse variance of £72,000. This might have been due to increased costs of parking the aircraft when not being used.

The fixed overhead capacity variance is a measure of asset usage. If it is favourable, the aircraft would have been used more than budgeted, if adverse, less than budgeted. The adverse variance in the case of Original Holidays has been identified as arising from operational difficulties. It represents the loss of the two flights compared with budget. This would have arisen if the aircraft had to be taken out of service to await spare parts which were not readily available.

Finally, the fixed overhead efficiency variance is a measure of productivity. It measures how intensively the aircraft was being used while it was operating rather than standing idle. For each of the 78 return flights actually operated, 100 passengers (7,800 passengers divided by 78 flights) were carried compared with the budget of 75. This explains the favourable variance.

SECTION 2

Task 2.1

Diamond Ltd
Performance Report – Branch 24
Year ended 31 December 20X7

(a)	Return on capital employed	*57.6/240.0*	24%
(b)	Gross profit margin	*360.0/720.0*	50%
(c)	Asset turnover	*720.0/240.0*	3 times
(d)	Sales margin	*57.6/720.0*	8%
(e)	Average age of debtors	*(96.0/720.0) × 12*	1.6 months
(f)	Average age of creditors	*(51.0/340/0) × 12*	1.8 months
(g)	Average age of stock	*(60.0/360.0) × 12*	2.0 months

Task 2.2

WORKINGS

£

(a)	Revised turnover	*£240,000 × 4*	960,000
	Cost of sales = 50%		480,000
	Gross profit		480,000
	Fixed costs		302,400
	Operating profit		177,600
	Revised return on capital employed	*177,600/240,000*	74%

£

(b)	Revised working capital		
	Revised debtors	*(0.5 × 720,000)/12*	30,000
	Revised stock	*(1 × 360,000)/12*	30,000
	Revised creditors	*(3 × 340,00)/12*	(85,000)
	Revised working capital		(25,000)
	Add fixed assets		135,000
	Revised capital employed		110,000
	Return on capital employed	*57,600/110,000*	52%
	Asset turnover	*720,000/110,000*	6.5

(c)

MEMO

To: Angela Newton   Date: 5 January 20X8

From: Financial analyst

Subject: Branch 24 performance indicators

Charles Walden has asked me to write to you concerning the performance indicators of Branch 24 and the extent of improvement possible if the branch was able to achieve the performance standards established by the company.

Had Branch 24 been able to achieve the same asset turnover as other branches, the return on capital employed would have been 74%, comfortably in excess of the standard return on capital employed.

Likewise, had the branch controlled its working capital at standard levels, not only would the return on capital employed have been 52% but it would also have achieved an asset turnover of 6.5 times.

You are quite correct to emphasise the need for profitability. If the asset turnover can be improved while maintaining the existing level of net assets, then turnover will increase. If the cost of this increased turnover is less than its value, then this will lead to both increased profits and an increase in the return on capital employed.

The suggestion that your performance might be less than other branches because your branch has been established for less time may be valid. From the financial data related to your branch, it would appear that Branch 24 was only opened two years ago. (The annual depreciation is £45,000 and the accumulated depreciation is £90,000.) If other branches have been established longer, then the accumulated depreciation will be greater, leading to a lower net book value and a lower capital employed. It is also possible that the older fixtures and fittings would have been purchased at a lower price, resulting in the annual depreciation charge also being less and hence increasing operating profit.

TECHNICIAN STAGE

NVQ/SVQ LEVEL 4 IN ACCOUNTING

SPECIMEN CENTRAL ASSESSMENT

CONTRIBUTING TO THE PLANNING AND ALLOCATION OF RESOURCES
(UNIT 9)

Time allowed – 2 hours plus 15 minutes' reading time

SECTION 1 (Suggested time allocation: 50 minutes)

Data

Star Fuels is a multinational oil company selling oil for industrial and domestic purposes through a network of distributors. Distributors purchase fuel oil from Star Fuels and then sell it on to their own customers.

A regular complaint of the distributors is that they either have to pay for the fuel on delivery to their storage tanks or be charged interest on a daily basis on the amount owed. This problem could be reduced if the distributors were able to forecast their demands more accurately.

You are employed as the Assistant Management Accountant to Northern Fuel Distributors Ltd, a major distributor of Star Fuel's fuel oils. You recently attended a meeting with Mary Lamberton, a member of Star Fuel's central staff. At the meeting, she demonstrated a statistical software package used for estimating the demand for fuel oil. The user enters sales volumes per period and the package then calculates the least-squares regression equation for the data. This is in the form $y = a + bx$ where x is the time period, y is the forecast and a and b are terms derived from the original data. Following further inputs by the user, the package can also estimate seasonal variations. Two forms of seasonal variation are calculated: the first calculates the seasonal variance as an absolute amount, the second as a percentage.

One week after the meeting, your copy of the software arrives at the head office of Northern Fuel Distributors Ltd and you immediately set about testing its capability. Purely for the purpose of testing, you assume seasonal variations occur quarterly. You enter this assumption along with the sales turnover figures for fuel oil for the last 20 quarters. Within moments, the software outputs the following information.

Regression line:

$$y = \text{£}2,000,000 + \text{£}40,000x$$

Seasonal variations

Quarter	A	B	C	D
Amount	+£350,000	+£250,000	−£400,000	−£200,000
Percentage	+15%	+10%	−15%	−10%

Quarter A refers to the first quarter of annual data, B to the second quarter, C to the third and D to the fourth. The pattern then repeats itself. In terms of the specific data you input, seasonal variation A refers to quarter 17, B to quarter 18, C to quarter 19 and D to quarter 20.

Actual sales turnover for quarters 17 to 20 was as follows:

Quarter	17	18	19	20
Sales turnover	£3,079,500	£3,002,400	£2,346,500	£2,490,200

Task 1.1

Making use of the formula derived by the software package, calculate the forecast sales turnover for quarters 17 to 20 using:

(a)   the absolute seasonal variations
(b)   the percentage seasonal variations.

Task 1.2

(a)   From your answers to Task 1.1, determine which method of calculating seasonal variations gives the best estimate of actual sales turnover.

(b)   Having identified the preferred method, use that method to forecast the sales turnover for quarters 21 to 24.

Task 1.3

Write a memorandum to your Managing Director. The memorandum should:

(a)   explain what is meant by seasonal variations and seasonally adjusted data. Illustrate your explanation with examples relevant to Northern Fuel Distributors

(b)   suggest why your chosen method of seasonal adjustment might be more accurate

(c)   show how an understanding of seasonal variations and seasonally adjusted data can help Northern Fuel Distributors to be more efficient

(d)   identify TWO weaknesses within your approach to forecasting undertaken in Tasks 1.1 and 1.2.

SECTION 2 (Suggested time allocation: 70 minutes)

Data

It is 1 March and Professor Pauline Heath has just taken up her new appointment as the head of the postgraduate business studies department in a new university. Due to unfilled vacancies throughout the current academic year, the department has had to rely on part-time academic staff. The cost of part-time staff who are self-employed is coded to account number 321, while those who are taxed under the pay-as-you-earn system are charged to account code 002. Both types of staff enter their claims within ten days of each month-end and these then appear in the management reports of the subsequent month. There are also unfilled clerical and administrative staff vacancies.

The university has a residential conference centre, which the department makes use of from time to time. Sometimes this is because the department's allocated rooms are all in use and sometimes because the department teaches at weekends. The charge for the use of the centre is coded to account 673. An alternative to using the conference centre is to hire outside facilities at local hotels, in which case the expenditure is coded to account 341.

The main forms of income are tuition fees and a higher education grant from the government. The extent of this grant is known before the commencement of the academic year and is payable in two parts, one-third at the end of December and the balance at the end of April.

One of Professor Heath's first tasks was to check the enrolments for the current year. The financial and academic year commenced on 1 September and is subdivided into three terms, each lasting four months. The Autumn term commenced on 1 September and the Spring term on 1 January. All courses commence at the beginning of the Autumn term, the MBA and MSc courses lasting three terms and the diploma course two terms.

The departmental administrator has presented Professor Heath with the enrolment data for the current academic year. Whilst absorbing this information, she has also received the latest management accounts for the department. Both sets of information are reproduced below.

Professor Heath is experiencing difficulties understanding the latest management report. She has written a memo to the university's finance director expressing her anxieties about the presentation of the report and its detailed contents.

Enrolment data – current academic year	Fee (£)	Enrolments	Income (£)
MBA – three terms	3,500	160	560,000
MSc – three terms	3,200	80	256,000
Diploma Course – two terms	1,200	100	120,000
			936,000

DEPARTMENT OF POSTGRADUATE BUSINESS STUDIES
MONTHLY MANAGEMENT REPORT – FEBRUARY

Code	Account heading	Annual budget	6 months to 28 February			Budget remaining
			Actual	Budget	Variance	
	EXPENSES					
001	Full-time academic	600,000	230,000	300,000	70,000	370,000
002	Part-time academic	84,000	48,000	42,000	-6,000	36,000
003	Clerical and administration	84,000	36,000	42,000	6,000	48,000
218	Teaching and learning material	30,000	0	15,000	15,000	30,000
321	Teaching and research fees	20,000	19,000	10,000	-9,000	1,000
331	Agency staff (clerical and administrative)	300	2,400	150	-2,250	-2,100
341	External room hire	1,000	400	500	100	600
434	Course advertising (press)	26,000	600	13,000	12,400	25,400
455	Postage and telephone recharge	8,000	1,200	4,000	2,800	6,800
673	Internal room hire	24,000	14,000	12,000	-2,000	10,000
679	Central services recharge	340,000	170,000	170,000	0	170,000
680	Rental light and heat recharge	260,000	130,000	130,000	0	130,000
		1,477,300	651,600	738,650	87,050	825,700
	INCOME					
802	Tuition fees	900,000	936,000	900,000	-36,000	-36,000
890	Higher education grant	750,000	250,000	250,000	0	500,000
		1,650,000	1,186,000	1,150,000	-36,000	464,000
	Net surplus/deficit	172,700 -361,700		534,400	411,350	-123,050

Task 2.1

(a)   Rearrange the account headings into a more meaningful form for managers. This should include columnar headings for any financial data you feel is appropriate but you DO NOT need to include any figures.

(b)   Briefly justify your proposals.

Task 2.2

In her memo, Professor Heath states that the current form of report does not help her manage her department. Identify the strengths and weaknesses apparent in the current system, other than the presentational ones covered in task 2.1, and make and justify outline proposals that will help her manage the department.

Task 2.3

Referring to the detailed financial data under the heading of INCOME above, reproduce the actual income to date in a form consistent with accounting principles.

All workings should be shown.

CONTRIBUTING TO THE PLANNING AND ALLOCATION OF RESOURCES
(UNIT 9)

SPECIMEN CENTRAL ASSESSMENT
SUGGESTED ANSWERS

SECTION 1

Task 1.1

Quarter	Season	Trend variance £	Absolute (absolute) £	Forecast variance £	Percentage (percentage) %	Forecast £
17	A	2,680,000	350,000	3,030,000	115	3,082,000
18	B	2,720,000	250,000	2,970,000	110	2,992,000
19	C	2,760,000	-400,000	2,360,000	85	2,346,000
20	D	2,800,000	-200,000	2,600,000	90	2,520,000

Task 1.2

Quarter	Actual £	Forecast (absolute) £	Error Forecast £	Forecast (percentage) £	Error Forecast £
17	3,079,500	3,030,000	49,500	3,082,000	-2,500
18	3,002,400	2,970,000	32,400	2,992,000	10,400
19	2,346,500	2,360,000	-13,500	2,346,000	500
20	2,490,200	2,600,000	-109,800	2,520,000	-29,800

(a) Examining the residual errors from using the two different methods of measuring seasonal variations, the percentage seasonal variation always results in a lower error than the absolute variation. On the basis of the sample of four quarters, the percentage seasonal variation thus appears to be the more accurate method for calculating seasonal variations.

(b)

Quarter	Season	Trend £	Seasonal Variation %	Forecast £
21	A	2,840,000	115	3,266,000
22	B	2,880,000	110	3,168,000
23	C	2,920,000	85	2,482,000
24	D	2,960,000	90	2,664,000

Task 1.3

MEMO

To: The Managing Director   Date: June 1997

From: The Assistant Management Accountant

Subject: Seasonal variations and seasonally adjusted data

Seasonal variations are regular, predictable and consistent changes in activity that occur over a period of time, normally one year. For oil distribution, the demand will be higher in winter months than summer months, and this is reflected in the seasonal variations for Northern Fuel Distributors. Quarter A is likely to include the winter months, with demand being 115% of the average quarter. Quarter C, with demand only being 85% of the average quarterly demand, is likely to include mainly summer months.

Seasonally adjusted data is the actual data from which the seasonal variations have been removed. It comprises two elements: the trend, or general direction in which the data is moving, plus any random variations. For example, the forecast seasonal variation for quarter 17 was $15/115 \times £3,082,000$ or $+£402,000$. Deducting this from the actual demand of £3,079,500 leaves an underlying figure of £2,677,500. As the trend was forecast as £2,680,000, the random error is -£2,500. Possible reasons for this error might be an unusually mild winter or insufficient stock of fuel to meet customers' needs. Provided that these random variations are small, the seasonally adjusted data allows the general direction of the demand for fuel oil over time to be seen.

Seasonal variations can be viewed in two ways: as an absolute amount or as a percentage. Doubling the activity being considered is likely to double the seasonal variation. Therefore, when the trend is either an increasing or decreasing one, measuring seasonal variations as a percentage is likely to be more accurate. As the demand for Northern Fuel Distributors' fuel oil is increasing through time, the percentage method has been used to forecast demand.

An awareness of seasonal variations and seasonally adjusted data enables future trends to be determined, along with variations about that trend. Not only does this help Northern Fuel Distributors to forecast future profits, but it also helps in stock control. By accurate forecasting of demand, excessive stocks are minimised. This helps cash flow in two ways: it reduces cash tied up in stocks and minimises the interest charged on amounts owing to Star Fuels.

There are, however, limitations to the forecasting technique demonstrated. First, the assumption implicit in linear regression is that demand is a linear function of time. Secondly, it assumes that demand is based only on time, whereas there might be other variables influencing demand (such as other competitors and the prices they charge for their energy). Thirdly, the data used was measured in monetary terms. Part of any increased demand may be due to rising prices rather than increased volume. It might, therefore, be better to measure demand in litres rather than value. Fourthly, quarterly measurement may hide peaks and troughs of demand; forecasting by the week is likely to reduce this problem.

◈ FOULKS*lynch*

SECTION 2

Task 2.1

(a)   **Rearrangement of account headings**

	Actual this month	Budget this month	Variance this month	Actual to date	Budget to date	Variance to date	Annual budget	Budget remaining
Tuition fees								
Higher education grant								
TOTAL REVENUE								
Full-time academic								
Part-time academic								
Teaching and research fees								
DIRECT LABOUR COST								
Teaching and learning material								
OTHER DIRECT COURSE COSTS								
Clerical and administration								
Agency staff (clerical)								
SUPPORT COSTS								
Rental light and heat recharge								
External room hire								
Internal room hire								
ACCOMMODATION COSTS								
Course advertising (press)								
Postage and telephone recharge								
OTHER OVERHEADS								
DEPARTMENTAL CONTRIBUTION								
Central services recharge								
DEPARTMENTAL SURPLUS/DEFICIT								

(b)   **Justification**

Budgets serve a variety of purposes, including planning, controlling and acting as authority to incur expenditure. In the original format, the monthly management report produced accounting information in the order of the financial accounting codes. This may not be the appropriate order for the user. For example, Professor Heath is unlikely to be interested in whether part-time staff are on the payroll or invoice the university for their services. Within the constraints of the existing system, accounts have been brought together by function. This makes clear the total expenditure on lecturing, other direct course costs, the cost of support services and the cost of accommodation. Again, it is only likely to be a detail for an operating manager whether room hire is an internal or an external charge. Rearranging the account headings in this format begins to show Professor Heath where expenses are being incurred and should help her control expenditure. It will also highlight the net effect of favourable variances - such as the saving in staff costs resulting from the vacancies - being balanced by the adverse variances on similar functional expense headings such as part-time academic staff.

The revised management report has introduced monthly data. In the original format, the only way monthly information could be derived was by comparing this month's year-to-date figures with those of the previous month. If control is to be effective, the extent of any variance should be clear, unambiguous and timely. Introducing monthly budget, actual and variance columns helps in this task.

The 'budget remaining' figure has been retained. This represents the difference between the annual budget and expenditure to date and shows how much further authorised expenditure is possible under the various account headings. Finally, in the variance columns, the direction of the variance should be made clearer. If actual expenditure was different from budgeted, the absolute variance should be shown, followed by (A) where expenditure was in excess of the budget and (F) where it was below budget. The reverse should apply to revenues, with (F) representing revenues greater than budget and (A) revenues less than budget.

Task 2.2

The main strength of the current system is that it identifies the amount of the budget yet to be consumed under the various accounting headings. In that sense, it is fulfilling its authorisation role. However, to begin to manage the department effectively, Professor Heath needs to know the sources of income and why expenses are being incurred, and this is not being provided by the current system.

At the moment, the university is viewing the department as the activity, whereas the department comprises several activities in the form of different courses. In the private sector, these would probably be called products. Currently, the department supports three products, the two degree courses and the diploma course. Although these all bring in revenue, they also consume expenses, and so it is important to know what contribution each product makes to the overall departmental surplus. The first priority is therefore to extend the coding and account-heading system to enable expenditure by course to be recorded. Some costs such as the teaching materials can be directly attributable to individual courses, while other costs – such as lecturers – may have to be apportioned.

Consideration should also be given to introducing some form of flexible budgeting as a control mechanism - although this will be of only limited use because of the high proportion of fixed costs within any teaching department. Nevertheless, it would explain whether the increased revenue has arisen because fees have been greater than budgeted or the number of students is higher than planned. In addition, the introduction of flexible budgeting would emphasise the effect of contribution on the well-being of the department.

Two further weaknesses of the current system appear to be the arbitrary way that the budget is divided into calendar months and the failure to accrue expenses. For many expenses, it appears that the budget is merely divided by twelve to derive the monthly figure. Some form of profiling is called for. For example, course advertising is likely to be greatest towards the end of the academic year as courses are marketed for the subsequent year. There is also a need to accrue expenses – in particular, the current report fails to accrue for part-time staff salaries. Yet a further weakness is the lack of information about the number of students and other non-financial but relevant management information.

Task 2.3

Course	Revenue £	Number of terms	Number of months	Six months' revenue £
MBA	560,000	3	12	280,000
M Sc	256,000	3	12	128,000
Diploma	120,000	2	8	90,000
				498,000
Government grant (£750,000 pa)				375,000
Revenue for six months				873,000

TECHNICIAN STAGE

NVQ/SVQ LEVEL 4 IN ACCOUNTING

SAMPLE SIMULATION

EVALUATING CURRENT AND PROPOSED ACTIVITIES (UNIT 16)

Time allowed – 4 hours

DATA AND TASKS

INSTRUCTIONS

This simulation is designed to test your ability to evaluate current and proposed activities.

The situation and the tasks for you to follow are set out on pages 24 – 26.

You are allowed **four hours** to complete your work.

Your answers should be set out in the answer booklet provided. If you require additional answer pages, ask the person in charge.

A high level of accuracy is required. Check your work carefully before handing it in.

Correcting fluid may be used but it should be used in moderation. Any errors should be crossed out neatly and clearly. The use of pencils for your written answers is not acceptable.

You should read the whole simulation before commencing work so as to gain an overall picture of what is required.

THE SITUATION

Your name is Sally Parkin and you are employed as a financial analyst with the Midtown Enterprise Agency. The agency provides technical, marketing and financial assistance to small- and medium-sized business in Midtown and surrounding areas.

Each company which registers with the agency is assigned a counsellor who attends board meetings and offers advice and guidance. Companies registered with the agency can also call on its services at any time.

One company regularly calling on the services of the agency is Questking Ltd. Neil Henderson, a counsellor employed by the Midtown Enterprise Agency, was allocated Questking Ltd as a client some 12 months ago. Since becoming involved with Questking you have made several visits to the company and have access to the company's accounting procedures manual.

Organisations involved in the simulation

Midtown Enterprise Agency
Questking Ltd

Personnel involved in the simulation

Financial analyst to the agency	Yourself, Sally Parkin
Counsellor responsible for Questking Ltd	Neil Henderson
Managing Director of Questking Ltd	Helen Johnson
Production Director of Questking Ltd	Tony Anderson
Marketing Director of Questking Ltd	Ann Fowler
Company Secretary of Questking Ltd	John Peters

The company's products and organisation

Questking Ltd has four divisions. Division A is located on a separate site and produces and sells a modem used in computers. This is its only product. Divisions B, C and D share the same site. This site comprises a single factory where divisions B, C and D are located plus a central office block containing the personnel, finance and administration functions. Division B makes four products, P1, P2, P3 and P4. Divisions C and D each make a single product.

THE TASKS TO BE COMPLETED

Before commencing the tasks read the extract from the accounting procedures manual of Questking Ltd on pages 36 and 39, the memo from your colleague, Neil Henderson, on page 26 and the agenda for the board meeting on page 28 of this booklet.

Suggested answer formats are provided in the answer booklet but you may prefer to use another format with which you are familiar. Blank pages are provided on pages 52 and 53 of the answer booklet.

1   Refer to the memo from Ann Fowler, the marketing director, on page 31 (annex 2) and annex 1.1 on page 29 of this booklet.

- Identify those costs which would be saved and those costs which would still be incurred if Division C was to be closed.

- Use your findings to identify the change in Questking Ltd's profit if Division C is closed.

- Prepare brief notes to Neil Henderson stating and justifying your recommendation for the future of Division C.

- Using the data in annex 1.1 on page 29, identify ONE limitation to your recommendation.

You should provide your answer on page 41 of the answer booklet where the budget for Division C has been reproduced and a possible answer format provided.

2   Refer to the memo from Tony Anderson, the production director, on page 32 and the budget for Division B shown as annex 1.3 on page 30 of this booklet.

- Calculate a revised production schedule which will maximise the profits of Division B for the forthcoming year.

- Identify the total contribution made by your proposal.

- Show the change in profit compared with the proposal by Tony Anderson.

- Suggest ONE commercial reason why your proposal might not be accepted.

There is space for your workings and a possible format on page 41 of the answer booklet.

3   Refer to the letter on pages 33 and 34 from Neil Henderson to Helen Johnson, the managing director of Questking Ltd and the budget for Division A shown as annex 1.2 on page 29 of this booklet.

- Calculate the existing quarterly fixed and unit variable costs included in the cost of labour.

- Identify the existing total cost of fixed production overheads per quarter.

- Calculate the existing quarterly break-even point using the fixed costs directly attributable to Division A.

- Use your answer to identify the quarter in which Division A would begin to adversely affect Questking's overall profit, assuming current trends continue.

- Recalculate the quarterly break-even point using the revised costings proposed by Neil Henderson.

- Show the change in profit for the year if Neil Henderson's proposals are accepted and recommend whether or not his proposal should be accepted.

Your answer should be prepared on pages 43 and 44 of the answer booklet.

◇ FOULKS*lynch*

4   Refer to that part of Neil Henderson's memo on page 24 relating to the order from Past Computers Ltd and the memo from Ann Fowler, the marketing director which is reproduced on page 35 of this booklet.

- Use the data given in annex 1.2 on page 29 concerning fixed production overhead absorbed and unabsorbed and the explanation of accounting policies shown on pages 38 and 39 of this booklet to calculate the maximum capacity of Division A and any surplus capacity.

- Use your findings to evaluate the special order from Past Computers detailed in the memo from Ann Fowler, the marketing director, which is reproduced on page 35 of this booklet. You should also refer to the memo from Neil Henderson on page 27 of this booklet to evaluate the three options identified and make a recommendation whether or not to accept the special order.

- Write a memo to Neil Henderson. Your memo should summarise the profitability of the three options, suggest which option to take and identify ONE non-financial, commercial factor which should also be considered.

An outline memo is provided on pages 46 and 47 of your answer booklet.

5   Refer to the memo from John Peters, the company secretary, reproduced on page 36, the contract document on page 37 and the extract from the accounting procedures manual on pages 38 and 39 of this booklet.

- Evaluate the proposal using the net present value technique.
- Justify your treatment of the £80,000 sales proceeds of the existing machine.

For your evaluation you may wish to use the form used by the Midtown Enterprise Agency for evaluating clients' investment proposals, a copy of which appears on pages 48 and 49 of the answer booklet.

MIDTOWN ENTERPRISE AGENCY

INTERNAL MEMO

Date: 1 December

To: Sally Parkin

From: Neil Henderson

Subject: Board meeting at Questking Ltd

I have just received the agenda and other papers for the board meeting at Questking Ltd to be held on 12 December.

Unfortunately, I will be away from the office working with another client for the next 8 days. As you have helped Questking in the past, would you be good enough to read through the documents and prepare notes for me to use at the board meeting.

The possibility of a contract with Past Computers really cannot wait until the board meeting. If we are going to accept the contract we ought not to delay it as the company would be a prestigious customer.

Because of this, I guess that Questking will want to accept the contract even if it does make a loss.

There appears to be three options:

- source the full contract from internal production
- subcontract the whole order to Bright Processors Ltd.
- a mixture of in-house production and subcontracting.

Can you therefore write me a memo evaluating these three options for me to read when I return to the office. As I need this information before the board meeting, you should use the existing cost data for Division A and NOT my proposed changes.

Many thanks.

Quest*k*ing Ltd

Mill Road, Midtown MX14 8XY

29 November

To members of the board of directors

BOARD MEETING

The next board meeting will take place in the board room at Mill Road on 12 December at 10.00am. A buffet lunch will be served at 12.30 pm.

Chair: Helen Johnson, Managing Director
Board members: Tony Anderson – Production Director
                                  Ann Fowler – Marketing Director
                                  John Peters – Company Secretary

In attendance   Neil Henderson – Midtown Enterprise Agency

AGENDA

1	Apologies for absence	
2	Minutes of the previous meeting	to be tabled
3	Matters arising from the minutes	
4	Consideration of the budget for the next financial year	annex 1.1 – 1.3
5	The future of Division C	annex 2
6	Fire at Modern Supplies Ltd – implications for Questking Ltd	annex 3
7	The strategic development of Division A	annex 4
8	Special order from Past Computers Ltd	annex 5
9	Possible contract with Meldreth plc	annex 6 – 7
10	Any other business	

John Peters
Company Secretary

Annex 1.1

QUESTKING LTD – COMPANY BUDGETED PROFIT STATEMENT FOR NEXT YEAR

Division		A £	B £	C £	D £	Total £
Turnover		1,500,000	2,170,000	2,240,000	1,950,500	7,860,500
Material		660,000	609,000	789,000	690,400	2,748,400
Labour		357,000	310,200	524,100	387,100	1,578,400
Light, heat and power		80,000	120,000	150,000	90,000	440,000
Rent		50,000	160,000	200,000	120,000	530,000
Rates		30,000	240,000	300,000	180,000	750,000
Sales commission		75,000	108,500	112,000	97,525	393,025
Selling expenses		60,000	88,000	140,800	83,400	372,200
Central overheads:	Personnel	34,000	64,000	102,400	62,100	262,500
	Finance	18,000	48,000	76,800	46,575	189,375
	Administration	22,000	96,000	42,500	21,400	181,900
Profit/(loss)		114,000	326,300	(197,600)	172,000	414,700

Annex 1.2

DIVISION A DIVISIONAL BUDGETED PROFIT FOR NEXT YEAR BY QUARTER

		Quarter 1	Quarter 2	Quarter 3	Quarter 4	Total
Units produced and sold		9,000	8,000	7,000	6,000	30,000
		£	£	£	£	£
Turnover		450,000	400,000	350,000	300,000	1,500,000
Material		198,000	176,000	154,000	132,000	660,000
Labour		97,500	92,000	86,500	81,000	357,000
Fixed production overhead absorbed		36,000	32,000	28,000	24,000	120,000
Gross profit		118,500	100,000	81,500	63,000	363,000
Sales commission		22,500	20,000	17,500	15,000	75,000
Fixed production overhead unabsorbed		4,000	8,000	12,000	16,000	40,000
Selling expenses		15,000	15,000	15,000	15,000	60,000
Central overheads:	Personnel	8,500	8,500	8,500	8,500	34,000
	Finance	4,500	4,500	4,500	4,500	18,000
	Administration	5,500	5,500	5,500	5,500	22,000
Profit/(loss)		58,500	38,500	18,500	(1,500)	114,000

◈ **FOULKS**lynch

Annex 1.3

DIVISION B BUDGETED PROFIT STATEMENT
FOR NEXT YEAR BY PRODUCT

Product		P1	P2	P3	P4	Total
Units		1,900	2,600	2,000	1,500	8,000
		£	£	£	£	£
Turnover		380,000	650,000	600,000	540,000	2,170,000
Material		114,000	195,000	120,000	180,000	609,000
Labour		45,600	93,600	144,000	27,000	310,200
Light, heat and power		28,500	39,000	30,000	22,500	120,000
Rent		20,000	10,000	100,000	30,000	160,000
Rates		30,000	15,000	150,000	45,000	240,000
Sales commission		19,000	32,500	30,000	27,000	108,500
Selling expenses		20,900	28,600	22,000	16,500	88,000
Central overheads:	Personnel	15,200	20,800	16,000	12,000	64,000
	Finance	11,400	15,600	12,000	9,000	48,000
	Administration	22,800	31,200	24,000	18,000	96,000
Net profit/(loss)		52,600	168,700	(48,000)	153,000	326,300

Annex 2

Quest*k*ing Ltd

Internal Memo

To: Helen Johnson, Managing Director

From: Ann Fowler, Marketing Director

Date: 20 November

Subject: Future of Division C

I note from the budget for next year that Division C will, yet again, be reporting a loss. Given that the board of directors agreed at its last meeting to concentrate on improving the profitability of Questking Ltd, it is now time that we considered closing down Division C. If Division C was to be closed down, there would be an immediate increase in company profit of £197,600.

I think it would be a good idea to discuss the future of Division C at our next board meeting.

Annex 3

Questking Ltd

Internal Memo

To: Helen Johnson, Managing Director

From: Tony Anderson, Production Director

Date: 23 November

Subject: Fire at Modern Suppliers Ltd

You have probably read newspaper reports about the recent fire at Modern Suppliers Ltd. This has serious implications for Division B. Modern Suppliers are the sole manufacturers of the raw material used in all the products made by Division B. I have checked elsewhere and there is no acceptable substitute.

Yesterday, the sales director of Modern Suppliers Ltd wrote to me. Apparently, the factory which supplied us was totally destroyed and it will be at least a year before production recommences. He is, however, able to obtain limited supplies from their other factory. Unfortunately, the maximum they can supply to Division B is 26,800 kg over the next twelve months.

This means we will need to rearrange production. In summary, the original budget for next year showed a total output of 8,000 units which was to generate a profit of £326,300 for Division B. The individual product profitability and raw material usage was:

Product	P1	P2	P3	P4	Total
Units	1,900	2,600	2,000	1,500	8,000
Raw Materials (kg)	7,600	13,000	8,000	12,000	40,600
Net profit/(loss)	£52,600	£168,700	(£48,000)	£153,000	326,300
Unit profit/(loss)	£27.68	£64.88	(£24)	£102	£40.79

As you can see, there is insufficient raw material to keep to the original budget. Product P3 continues to make a loss and so I propose that we stop its manufacture. Given that the budgeted sales volumes are the maximum we can realistically sell, I suggest that the production schedule for next year should be determined by product profitability. The revised production schedule and divisional profitability will then be:

	Production Units	Unit profit	Total profit	Material per unit	Material used	Material remaining
Material available						26,800 kg
Product P4	1,500	£102.00	£153,000	8 kg	12,000 kg	14,800 kg
Product P2	2,600	£64.88	£168,688	5 kg	13,000 kg	1,800 kg
Product P1	450	£27.68	£12,456	4 kg	1,800 kg	nil

I would be grateful if we could agree this proposal at the next board meeting.

Annex 4

MIDTOWN ENTERPRISE AGENCY
18 The Quadrant
Midtown Science Park
Midtown MX14 1YZ

25 November

Ms Helen Johnson
Managing Director
Questking Ltd
Mill Road
Midtown
MX14 8XY

Dear Helen,

Future Strategy of Division A

At the last board meeting, you asked me to make proposals for the future development of Division A. Division A makes modems enabling users of personal computers to connect to the Internet. Initially, Division A was a market leader but competitors have recently introduced faster modems. This accounts for the decreasing demand for the output of the division. Clearly, if this problem is not addressed then Division A will soon be no longer viable.

There are two options available to Questking Ltd. These are:

- do nothing and close down the division when it becomes no longer profitable
- develop a new modem.

I have spoken to both Tony Anderson, your production director, and the technical experts at the enterprise agency. If you choose to develop a new modem, this will involve considerable development time and could not be introduced for at least two years even if development work started immediately. By then, Division A may have become a drain on the resources of Questking Ltd.

Given your wish to remain in the modem market, the first option is not recommended. It is possible, however, to improve the profitability of Division A's existing operations until the new modem is ready to be marketed.

I have been looking at Division A's costs. The factory employees are paid a relatively low basic wage which is then supplemented by a piecework payment for every modem produced. Sales staff are also paid a relatively low salary plus a commission of 5% on selling price. My proposal involves paying both groups a higher basic remuneration but lower commissions and piecework payments.

I have discussed this with John Peters, your company secretary, who showed me Division A's budget for the first quarter of next year. My proposals are to:

- pay production workers a total of £280,000 per year as basic wages plus £3 for each modem produced

- pay sales staff an additional salary but to reduce their commission to 2%. The effect of this would be to increase selling expenses to £100,000 per year but to reduce the amount paid as sales commission.

Continued

◈ FOULKS*lynch*

Reproduced below is Division A's proposed budget for the first quarter and the budget as it would appear if my proposals are accepted.

Division A Budget for quarter 1	Original budget	Revised budget
Units produced and sold	9,000	9,000
	£	£
Turnover	450,000	450,000
Material	198,000	198,000
Labour [1]	97,500	97,000
Fixed production overhead absorbed	36,000	36,000
Gross profit	118,500	119,000
Sales commission [2]	22,500	9,000
Fixed production overhead unabsorbed	4,000	4,000
Selling expenses [3]	15,000	25,000
Central overheads:		
Personnel	8,500	8,500
Finance	4,500	4,500
Administration	5,500	5,500
Net profit	58,500	62,500

		£
1	Labour	
	Wages per quarter £280,000/4	70,000
	Piecework 9,000 modems × £3	27,000
	Total	97,000
2	Sales commission £450,000 × 2%	9,000
3	Selling expenses £100,000/4	25,000

I would suggest that this proposal is added to the agenda for the next meeting of the board of directors.

Yours sincerely

Neil Henderson

Neil Henderson
Counsellor

Annex 5

Quest*k*ing Ltd

Internal Memo

To: Helen Johnson, Managing Director

From: Ann Fowler, Marketing Director

Date: 26 November

Subject: Special order from Past Computers

I have recently been having discussions with the directors of Past Computers Ltd. Past Computers sell computers and software as a total package to the general public through newspaper advertisements. They are prepared to purchase 12,000 of the current modems manufactured by Division A if we can guarantee delivery of that number over the next twelve months and make a small modification to the modem. The modification involves the adding of an additional printed circuit. Past Computers feels there is a demand for the modified modems if they are already installed in the computers as part of the all-inclusive price.

Past Computers are prepared to purchase the 12,000 modified modems for £44 each. I know this is less than our price for next year but there will be some savings in costs. Because this is a centrally negotiated order, there will be no sales commission payable. In addition, we will not have to use our normal packaging and this will reduce the cost of materials by £1 per modem.

Even with these savings, however, it looks as though the contract will make a loss. Looking at Division A's budget for next year, revenue is planned to be £1.5 million, sales volume 30,000 and profit £114,000. This makes the unit selling price £50.00 and unit profit £3.80. The £6.00 reduction in selling price is greater than the unit profit and so the loss per unit will be £2.20 before paying for the cost of the modification.

Although there will be no additional cost of labour for the modification, there is the cost of the additional printed circuit. These currently cost £18.00 each. Fortunately we have 9,000 of the printed circuits in stock which were used on last year's model and have no further use other than being sold for scrap for £36,000. According to the stock records, these 9,000 items cost £16 each - a saving of £2 compared with buying from the manufacturer.

If the cost of making the modems ourselves involves too great a loss, there is one other option. We could sub-contract the work to Bright Processors Ltd. We have used them in the past when we had insufficient capacity to meet demand and we found them extremely reliable. I have spoken to their sales manager who tells me they would be prepared to make the modified modem for £46 providing we gave them a minimum order of 1,000 modified modems. Although this would result in a loss of £24,000 on the contract, that appears less than making the modified modem ourselves.

As you are aware, I have been trying to sell to Past Computers for several years and this is the first time they have been prepared to place an order. It might, therefore, be worthwhile accepting the order as a loss-leader in order to establish a basis for future custom.

Annex 6

Quest*k*ing Ltd
Internal Memo

To: Helen Johnson, Managing Director

From: John Peters, Company Secretary

Date: 27 November

Subject: Possible contract with Meldreth plc

Since preparing the budget for Division D, an opportunity has arisen to bid for a four year contract to provide Meldreth plc with timers. A copy of their terms is enclosed with this memo. If we gain the contract, it will be necessary to purchase a machine costing £480,000. Division D has a machine which is no longer suitable for its needs. This can be sold for £80,000. The machine will have no further use after four years and its realisable value will be negligible. The net investment is, therefore, only £400,000. The supplier can also deliver the machine in the second week of January, well before the date required to commence the contract although after our accounting year end of 31 December.

As Questking Ltd has no other assets on which it claims capital allowances, another advantage will be the tax saving from the writing down allowance given by the Inland Revenue of 25%. Corporation tax at 33% will then be payable at the end of the following year.

There will be no further finance required as Meldreth will pay for the timers on delivery and we will not keep any form of stock ourselves. As £400,000 is beyond the spending limit of the manager of Division D, I have carried out a financial appraisal.

You will notice that Meldreth plc requires us to reduce prices by 20% on the preceding year's price after the first year. Although this seems excessive, I am reliably informed by the manager of Division D that material costs will also fall at a similar rate over those years. Because the 20% reduction in selling price is matched by the 20% reduction in material prices, I have ignored both reductions in my appraisal. Labour cost per unit will be £20 in the first year although subsequent wages increases are likely to be a compound 3% per year. Again, I have ignored this as the amount is so small.

		£
Unit profit:	Selling price – year 1	120
	Materials – year 1	60
	Labour – year 1	20
	Reapportioned overheads – including depreciation	20
		——
	Unit profit	20
		——

	£
Yearly profit (£20 × 8,000 timers)	160,000
Add: 25% capital allowances (£480,000/4)	120,000
	————
	280,000
Corporation tax at 33%	92,400
	————
Annual profit	187,600
	————

$$\text{Return on investment} = \frac{£187,600}{£400,000} = 46.9\%$$

As the return of 46.9 is greater than our required return of 25%, I recommend that we bid for the contract.

Meldreth plc

Midtown Industrial Estate
Midtown MX15 2MZ
Tel: 0199 984235

Invitation to Tender

The company and its suppliers

Meldreth plc is a major provider of industrial washing machines. Our leading market position has arisen from a policy of continuous improvement and Total Quality Management. Approved suppliers must demonstrate a similar commitment.

Approved suppliers must agree to flexible deliveries in support of our Just in Time stock procedures. In exchange for this commitment, Meldreth plc undertakes to pay suppliers within 24 hours of delivery.

The contract

The contract is for four years and involves supplying the company with 8,000 timers in each of those years. For the purpose of this contract, the year will be from 1 January to 31 December and deliveries in the first year are to commence from 1 February.

The price paid per timer in the first year will be £120.00. Efficiency gains are to be expected in subsequent years and so the company will only pay 80% of the previous year's price in the subsequent 3 years.

Suppliers wishing to bid for this contract should notify Meldreth plc by 1 January.

◈ **FOULKS***lynch*

Extract from Questking's accounting procedures manual

2.1	**Budget Assumptions**

- In preparing divisional budgets for the forthcoming year, divisional accountants should identify all assumptions concerning trends and provide explanations in writing for any increase or decrease in sales volume compared with the current year.

- Divisions should assume no change in stocks, enabling production and sales to be the same.

- Divisions should plan for no change in selling prices or input costs during the year.

2.2   Developing the divisional budget

- Budgets should use the standard layout reproduced below to assist future consolidation.

- Material and labour should be treated as varying with production and sales volume except in the case of Division A where there is a fixed element to the labour cost. Sales commission is to be payable as a percentage of selling price and not units sold.

- All other expenses are to be treated as fixed costs.

- Budgets should be prepared for each quarter of the forthcoming year if sales and production levels vary between quarters. If sales and production are constant throughout the year, a single, annual budgeted profit statement is sufficient.

- Where divisions make more than one product, a budgeted profit statement should be prepared for each product.

2.3   Fixed overheads

- Fixed production overhead is to comprise the following: light, heat and power; rent; and rates. These should be absorbed on the basis of *maximum* possible volume. Division A should use the actual costs incurred last year, adjusted for any known or likely changes. Divisions B, C and D will have fixed production overhead apportioned to them on the basis of floor area.

- Selling expenses comprise the salaries of sales staff employed by each division plus all other selling and marketing expenses unique to the division. Company-wide selling and marketing expenses will be recharged to divisions through the central administration charge.

- Central fixed overheads comprise the costs of personnel, finance and administration. These are apportioned to all divisions using a formula which takes account of the number of staff, the number of purchase invoices, the number of sales invoices and technical estimates.

- It has not proven possible to calculate depreciation for each division due to divisions making use of each other's plant, machinery and equipment. A company-wide depreciation charge of £80,000 has been calculated for the current year. This will be charged to divisions as part of the apportioned administration charge.

2.4   Pro forma budgeted profit statement for next year

- Turnover
- Material
- Labour
- Light, heat and power
- Rent
- Rates
- Sales commission
- Selling expenses
- Personnel
- Finance
- Administration
- Profit.

3   Account year-end

The accounting year-end for Questking Ltd is 31 December.

4   Capital investments

- All capital expenditure above £20,000 must be approved by the board of directors.

- All investments should be evaluated using net present value techniques discounted at the company's cost of capital of 25%.

- Three digit discount tables, reproduced below, should be used in determining net present values.

- Any initial capital outlay should be shown as taking place at the beginning of the first year.

- Operating cashflows should be treated as occurring at the year-end.

- The nine month delay in paying any corporation tax should be treated as a one year delay for investment purposes.

Discount rate end of year	10%	15%	20%	25%	30%	35%
1	0.909	0.870	0.833	0.800	0.769	0.741
2	0.826	0.756	0.694	0.640	0.592	0.549
3	0.751	0.658	0.579	0.512	0.455	0.406
4	0.683	0.572	0.482	0.410	0.350	0.301
5	0.621	0.497	0.402	0.328	0.269	0.223
6	0.564	0.432	0.335	0.262	0.207	0.165
7	0.513	0.376	0.279	0.210	0.159	0.122
8	0.467	0.327	0.233	0.168	0.123	0.091
9	0.424	0.284	0.194	0.134	0.094	0.067
10	0.386	0.247	0.162	0.107	0.073	0.050

TECHNICIAN STAGE

SIMULATION ANSWER BOOKLET

EVALUATING CURRENT AND PROPOSED ACTIVITIES
(UNIT 16)

ANSWER (TASK 1)

Analysis of costs

	Division C budget £	Costs saved £	Costs not saved £
Turnover	2,240,000		
Material	789,000		
Labour	524,100		
Light, heat and power	150,000		
Rent	200,000		
Rates	300,000		
Sales commission	112,000		
Selling expenses	140,800		
Personnel	102,400		
Finance	76,800		
Administration	42,500		
Loss	(197,600)		

Change in profits

Recommendation

Limitation to the recommendation (one example only)

ANSWER (TASK 2)

WORKINGS

Revised production schedule

	Production units	Material used kg	Material balance kg	Unit contribution £	Total contribution £
Material available			26,800		
Product P1/P2/P3/P4					
Product P1/P2/P3/P4					
Product P1/P2/P3/P4					
Product P1/P2/P3/P4					_____
Revised contribution					
Proposed contribution					_____
Increase in profit					_____

A commercial limitation to the above analysis

ANSWER (TASK 3)

Calculation of existing fixed and variable costs of labour

	Quarter 1	Quarter 2	Quarter 3	Quarter 4
Units produced and sold	9,000	8,000	7,000	6,000
Labour (£)	97,500	92,000	86,500	81,000

Calculation of existing quarterly cost of fixed production overheads

Calculation of existing unit contribution

FOULKS*lynch*

	Quarter 1	Quarter 2	Quarter 3	Quarter 4

ANSWER (TASK 3, continued)

Calculation of existing direct fixed costs

Break-even point using existing direct fixed costs =

Break-even quarter =

Calculation of revised unit contribution

Calculation of revised direct fixed costs =

Break-even point using revised direct fixed costs =

Change in profit

Recommendation

ANSWER (TASK 4)

Calculation of maximum capacity

Surplus capacity =

Workings for special order

ANSWER (TASK 4, continued)

MIDTOWN ENTERPRISE AGENCY

INTERNAL MEMO

Date:

To:

From:

Subject:

_____

_____

_____

_____

_____

_____

_____

_____

_____

_____

_____

_____

_____

_____

_____

_____

_____

ANSWER (TASK 4, continued)

ANSWER (TASK 5)

MIDTOWN ENTERPRISE AGENCY
Investment Proposal

Calculation of operating cashflows

End of year	Demand units a	Selling price b	Cash received c a × b	Material Unit d	Material Total e a × d	Labour Unit f	Labour Total g a × f	Net cash flow h c–e–g
		£	£	£	£	£	£	£
1								
2								
3								
4								
5								
6								
7								
8								
9								

Note: complete as many years as there are operating cashflows

ANSWER (TASK 5, continued)

<table>
<tr><td colspan="2" align="center">**Calculation of capital allowances**</td></tr>
<tr><td></td><td align="right">£</td></tr>
<tr><td>Capital cost
Writing down allowance – year 1</td><td align="right">—</td></tr>
<tr><td>Balance
Writing down allowance – year 2</td><td align="right">—</td></tr>
<tr><td>Balance
Writing down allowance – year 3</td><td align="right">—</td></tr>
<tr><td>Balance
Writing down allowance – year 4</td><td align="right">—</td></tr>
<tr><td>Balance
Writing down allowance – year 5</td><td align="right">—</td></tr>
<tr><td>Balance
Writing down allowance – year 6</td><td align="right">—</td></tr>
<tr><td>Balance
Writing down allowance – year 7</td><td align="right">—</td></tr>
<tr><td>Balance
Writing down allowance – year 8</td><td align="right">—</td></tr>
<tr><td>Balance
Writing down allowance – year 9</td><td align="right">—</td></tr>
<tr><td>Balance</td><td align="right">—</td></tr>
</table>

Notes:

**Approved plant and machinery are entitled to a 25% writing down allowance.
The number of years' allowances should equal the number of years' cashflows.**

The final year's allowance is equal to the balance outstanding.

ANSWER (TASK 5, continued)

Calculation of taxable profit

End of year	Profit before depreciation £	Capital allowances £	Taxable profit £	Corporation tax @ 33% £	Payable in year
1					
2					
3					
4					
5					
6					
7					
8					
9					

Investment appraisal

End of year	Operating NCF £	Corporation tax £	Net cashflow £	Discount factors	Discounted cashflow £
1					
2					
3					
4					
5					
6					
7					
8					
9					

Present value of inflows
Capital cost

Net present value

Note: complete as many years as there are operating cashflows

Recommendation

Justification of treatment of the £80,000 sales proceeds of existing machine:

If using this paper please indicate the task you are answering.

_____

_____

_____

_____

_____

_____

_____

_____

_____

_____

_____

_____

_____

_____

_____

_____

_____

_____

_____

_____

_____

_____

If using this paper please indicate the task you are answering.

_____

_____

_____

_____

_____

_____

_____

_____

_____

_____

_____

_____

_____

_____

_____

_____

_____

_____

_____

_____

_____

_____

EVALUATING CURRENT AND PROPOSED ACTIVITIES
(UNIT 16)

SIMULATION
SUGGESTED ANSWERS

ANSWER (TASK 1)

Analysis of costs

	Division C budget £	Costs saved £	Costs not saved £
Turnover	2,240,000		
Material	789,000	789,000	
Labour	524,100	524,100	
Light, heat and power	150,000		150,000
Rent	200,000		200,000
Rates	300,000		300,000
Sales commission		112,000	112,000
Selling expenses		140,800	140,800
Personnel	102,400		102,400
Finance	76,800		76,800
Administration	42,500		42,500
Loss	(197,600)	1,565,900	871,700

Change in profits

	£
Turnover lost if Division C is closed	2,240,000
Direct costs saved if Division C is closed	1,565,900
Contribution lost if Division C is closed	674,100

Recommendation

- In the short term, Division C is contributing £674,100 to Questking's budgeted profit.

- The costs saved if Division C is closed include not only the variable costs but also the direct fixed costs.

- The central fixed overheads have been apportioned and so will still have to be met if the division was closed.

- Closing the division down would cause profits to fall by the amount of its contribution.

- It is therefore recommended that Division C is not closed in the short term.

Limitation to the recommendation (one example only)

- Possible saving in some of the central fixed overheads such as depreciation or light, heat and power. However, the cost for the whole company for light, heat and power is only £440,000 which is less than the division's contribution. In the short term it will not be possible to make savings in the cost of rent and rates.

- Longer term, however, it might be possible to rent out part of the factory or use the space occupied by Division C to develop a new division which would generate a larger contribution. Longer term, it might also be possible to reduce some of the central fixed overheads relating to personnel, finance and administration.

ANSWER (TASK 2)

WORKINGS

Division B: Contribution per unit of limiting factor

	P1 £	*P2* £	*P3* £	*P4* £
Turnover	380,000	650,000	600,000	540,000
Material	114,000	195,000	120,000	180,000
Labour	45,600	93,600	144,000	27,000
Sales commission	19,000	32,500	30,000	27,000
Contribution	201,400	328,900	306,000	306,000
Sales volume	1,900	2,600	2,000	1,500
Contribution per unit	£106.00	£126.50	£153.00	£204.00
Material per unit (kg)	4.00	5.00	4.00	8.00
Contribution per kg	£26.50	£25.30	£38.25	£25.50
Order of preference	②	④	①	③

Revised production schedule

	Production units	*Material used* kg	*Material balance* kg	*Unit contribution* £	*Total contribution* £
Material available			26,800		
P3	2,000	8,000	18,800	153.00	306,000
P1	1,900	7,600	11,200	106.00	201,400
P4[1]	1,400	11,200	0	204.00	285,600
Revised contribution					793,000
Proposed contribution[2]					682,600
Increase in profit					110,400

Notes:

1    $11,200/8 = 1,400$

2   Proposed contribution

	Production units	*Unit contribution* £	*Total contribution* £
P4	1,500	204.00	306,000
P2	2,600	126.50	328,900
P1	450	106.00	47,700
			682,600

A commercial limitation to the above analysis

The plan involves no production or sales of product P2 and only limited sales of product P4. This gap in the product range may cause customers to look elsewhere or tempt other suppliers to enter the market. These longer-term implications should, therefore, be considered before making a final decision.

ANSWER (TASK 3)

Calculation of existing fixed and variable costs of labour

	Quarter 1	Quarter 2	Quarter 3	Quarter 4
Units produced and sold	9,000	8,000	7,000	6,000
Labour (£)	97,500	92,000	86,500	81,000
Change in volume		-1,000	-1,000	-1,000
Change in labour cost		-5,500	-5,500	-5,500
Piecework per unit (£)		5.50	5.50	5.50
Total cost of labour (£)	97,500	92,000	86,500	81,000
Total Piecework cost (£)	49,500	44,000	38,500	33,000
Fixed cost of labour (£)	48,000	48,000	48,000	48,000

Calculation of existing quarterly cost of fixed production overheads

Annex 1.1		*or*	Annex 1.2	
Central overheads per year:	£		(Data for first quarter)	£
Light, heat and power	80,000		Fixed production overhead absorbed	36,000
Rent	50,000		Fixed production overhead unabsorbed	4,000
Rates	30,000			
Total	160,000		Total per quarter	40,000
Quarterly cost (£160,000/4)	£40,000			

Calculation of existing unit contribution

	Quarter 1
Units produced and sold	9,000
	£
Turnover	450,000
Material	198,000
Piecework cost of labour	49,500
Sales commission	22,500
Total contribution	180,000
Unit contribution (£)	20.00

◆ FOULKS*lynch*

ANSWER (TASK 3, continued)

Calculation of existing direct fixed costs

		£
Total fixed production overhead		40,000
Selling expenses		15,000
Labour fixed cost		48,000
Total direct fixed costs		103,000

Break-even point using existing direct fixed costs (£103,000/£20)   5,150

Break-even quarter
Quarter 1 of the following year

Calculation of revised unit contribution

	Quarter 1
Units produced and sold	9,000
	£
Turnover	450,000
Material	198,000
Piecework cost of labour	27,000
Sales commission	9,000
Total contribution	216,000
Unit contribution	24.00

Calculation of revised direct fixed costs

	£
Total fixed production overhead	40,000
Selling expenses (£100,000/4)	25,000
Labour fixed cost (£280,000/4)	70,000
Total revised direct fixed costs	135,000

Break-even point using revised direct fixed costs (£135,000/£24)   5,625

Change in profit

	£		£
Total contribution (30,000 × £20)	600,000	Total contribution (30,000 × £24)	720,000
Direct fixed costs (£103,000 × 4)	412,000	Direct fixed costs (£135,000 × 4)	540,000
Contribution	188,000	Contribution	180,000

Recommendation

Implementing the revised plan will reduce profits by £8,000 and is, therefore, not recommended, although the difference is relatively small. This apparent inconsistency arises because the proposed changes involve higher fixed costs which become more significant when volume decreases – as it does in quarters 2, 3 and 4.

FOULKS*lynch*

ANSWER (TASK 4)

	£	Units
Total direct fixed production overhead absorbed in year	120,000	30,000
Overhead unabsorbed	40,000	
	160,000	

$\therefore$ 120,000/160,000 of capacity =   30,000 units

$\therefore$ Maximum capacity = 30,000 × $\dfrac{160,000}{120,000}$ =   40,000 units

$\therefore$ **Surplus capacity =**   **10,000 units**

Workings for special order

		£
Existing marginal costs		
Material	£198,000/9,000	22.00
Labour	£49,500/9,000	5.50
		27.50
Material saving		1.00
Revised marginal cost		26.50
Contract price		44.00
Unit contribution		17.50

◇ FOULKS*lynch*

ANSWER (TASK 4, continued)

MIDTOWN ENTERPRISE AGENCY

INTERNAL MEMO

Date: 1 December
To: Neil Henderson
From: Sally Parkin
Subject: Special order

As requested in your memo of 1 December, I have evaluated the three options. My detailed analysis is as follows:

Make all 12,000

	Units	£	£
Contribution	12,000	17.50	210,000
Contribution loss from existing sales	2,000	20.00	(40,000)
Opportunity cost of the additional material			
in stock	9,000		(36,000)
Cost of additional material purchased	3,000	18.00	(54,000)
Contribution			80,000

Make 10,000 and subcontract 2,000

	Units	£	£
Contribution on 10,000	10,000	17.50	175,000
Subcontract loss (cost £46, selling price £44)	2,000	2.00	(4,000)
Opportunity cost of additional material in stock	9,000		(36,000)
Cost of additional material purchased	1,000	18.00	(18,000)
Contribution			117,000

Subcontract all 12,000

	Units	£	£
Loss on contract	12,000	2.00	24,000

On this basis I recommend that we manufacture 10,000 units and subcontract the extra 2,000 to Bright Processors Ltd.

Other issues (one only)

There are a number of non-financial issues which should be considered before accepting my recommendation. These include:

- the possibility of Past Computers discovering that we are partly sourcing the contract from Bright Processors. Past Computers may decide to deal directly with Bright Processors

- uncertainty about the exact demand for the modems made by Division A. For example if demand was to fall by 2,000 compared to budget, the whole order could be sourced internally to give a contribution of £120,000.

ANSWER (TASK 5)

MIDTOWN ENTERPRISE AGENCY
Investment Proposal

Calculation of operating cashflows

End of year	Demand units a	Selling price b	Cash received c a × b	Material Unit d	Material Total e a × d	Labour Unit f	Labour Total g a × f	Net cash flow h c–e–g
		£	£	£	£	£	£	£
1	8,000	120.00	960,000	60.00	480,000	20.00	160,000	320,000
2	8,000	96.00	768,000	48.00	384,000	20.60	164,800	219,200
3	8,000	76.80	614,400	38.40	307,200	21.22	169,760	137,440
4	8,000	61.44	491,520	30.72	245,760	21.86	174,880	70,880

Calculation of capital allowances

	£
Capital cost	480,000
Writing down allowance – year 1	120,000
Balance	360,000
Writing down allowance – year 2	90,000
Balance	270,000
Writing down allowance – year 3	67,500
Balance	202,500
Balancing allowance	202,500

Calculation of taxable profit

End of year	Profit before depreciation £	Capital allowances £	Taxable profit £	Corporation tax @ 33% £	Payable in year
1	320,000	120,000	200,000	66,000	2
2	219,200	90,000	129,200	42,636	3
3	137,440	67,500	69,940	23,080	4
4	70,880	202,500	-131,620	-43,435	5

FOULKS*lynch*

Investment appraisal

End of year £	Operating NCF £	Corporation tax £	Net cashflow £	25% factors £	Discounted cashflow £
1	320,000		320,000	0.800	256,000
2	219,200	66,000	153,200	0.640	98,048
3	137,440	42,636	94,804	0.512	48,540
4	70,880	23,080	47,800	0.410	19,598
5		(43,435)	43,435	0.328	14,247
					436,433
Cost					480,000
NPV					(43,567)

Recommendation

With a negative net present value, the proposal should be rejected.

Justification of treatment of the £80,000 sales proceeds of existing machine:

The sales proceeds from the existing machine are a source of finance. They do not reduce the real cost of the machine and so its capital cost remains at £480,000.

COVERAGE OF PERFORMANCE CRITERIA

The following performance criteria are covered in this simulation. An indication of which performance criteria are covered by the individual tasks is given in brackets following the task assessment criteria (see below).

Element	PC Coverage
16.1	**Prepare cost estimates**
(i)	• The extent of the information to be contained within estimates is agreed with those who commission them.
(ii)	• Appropriate staff are consulted about technical aspects and any special features of work activity and projects which impact upon costs.
(iii)	• Current material, labour and other variable costs are identified and future trends assessed.
(iv)	• Estimates account for the effect of possible variations in capacity on fixed overhead rates.
(v)	• Estimates are prepared in an approved form and presented to the appropriate people within an agreed timescale.
16.2	**Recommend ways to improve cost ratios and revenue generation**
(i)	• Information relevant to estimating current and future costs and revenue is identified and used as the basis of analysis.
(ii)	• Critical factors which may affect costs and revenue are analysed using appropriate accounting techniques and clear conclusions are drawn from the analysis.
(iii)	• The views of appropriate specialists are gathered and used to inform analysis and any conclusions drawn.
(iv)	• The assumptions made and the degree of accuracy which exists in conclusions are clearly stated.
(v)	• Potential options and solutions are identified and evaluated for their contribution to improving cost ratios and revenue generation.
(vi)	• Recommendations to inform decisions are based on clearly stated conclusions drawn from an accurate analysis of all relevant information.
(vii)	• Recommendations are presented to the appropriate people in a clear and concise way and are supported with a clear rationale.

ASSESSMENT CRITERIA

Assessors must refer to the Standards of Competence for Accounting and be guided by the performance criteria when evaluating candidates' work.

Task 1   *One error* may be allowed in the analysis of costs. The recommendation requested in the task may be implied. To be assessed as competent, candidates should identify one valid justification or one limitation. (16.1 (i) – (iii), 16.1 (v), 16.2 (i) – (iv), 16.2 (vi), 16.2 (vii)).

Task 2   *One error* may be allowed in the calculation of contribution. The use of unit profit or the failure to recognise limiting factors in preparing the revised production schedule are fundamental errors and are not allowed. Failure to identify the proposed contribution from the schedule proposed by the production director (annex 3) or to suggest one commercial reason why the revised schedule might be rejected may be condoned. (16.1 (i) – (iii), 16.1 (v), 16.2 (i) – (vii)).

Task 3   Candidates must be able to calculate at least either the fixed and variable labour costs or the quarterly cost of fixed production overheads. In calculating the existing break-even point, one further error of either arithmetic or classification is allowed. A failure to identify the quarter when the contribution becomes negative may be condoned. *One error* is allowed in calculating the revised unit contribution and *one error* is allowed in calculating the revised fixed costs. In calculating the change in profit, the treatment of fixed costs as though they are variable costs is a fundamental error and may not be allowed. (16.1 (i) – (v), 16.2 (i) – (vii)).

Task 4   The calculation of total capacity must be conceptually correct although an arithmetic error may be condoned. In the calculation of the revised unit contribution, *one error* is allowed. *Two errors* are allowed in calculating the contribution when internally producing the special order and *two errors* are allowed in calculating the contribution from the partially subcontracted option. The wholly subcontracted option may be implied. (16.1 (i) – (iii), 16.1 (v), 16.2 (i) – (vii)).

Task 5   *One error* is allowed in the calculation of the operating cashflows. The same error over more than one year counts as *one error*. Providing candidates have calculated the capital allowances, either – but not both – of the following errors may be condoned: (i) the calculation of more than four years' writing down allowances (ii) the calculation of four years allowances but no balancing allowance.

There are four possible conceptual errors in the calculation of taxable profit: (i) the inclusion of depreciation, (ii) the omission of capital allowances (iii) the calculation of taxable profit and (iv) the failure to recognise the timing delay. No conceptual errors are allowed in the calculation of net present value. Providing candidates have made no more than two conceptual errors overall, a failure to recognise that the sales proceeds are irrelevant may be condoned. (16.1 (i) – (iii), 16.1 (v), 16.2 (i) – (vii)).

OVERALL ASSESSMENT

Candidates may be allowed to make further minor errors, providing such errors do not suggest a fundamental lack of understanding. Candidates must not be penalised more than once for an error. If a candidate transfers an incorrect figure to another task or part of task, this is not counted as a further error.

Assessors should be aware that there are several different, equally acceptable ways of presenting the solutions to the tasks.

General

- It is expected that work will be neatly and competently presented.
- Pencil is not acceptable.
- Liquid correcting fluid may be used but it should be used in moderation.

Discretion

In having regard to the above criteria, the assessor is entitled in marginal cases to exercise discretion in the candidate's favour. Such discretion shall only be exercised where other criteria are met to above the required standard and, in the opinion of the assessor, the assessment overall demonstrates competence and would be of an acceptable standard in the workplace.

◆ FOULKS*lynch*

CHAPTER QUESTIONS

Chapters 1 – 2

INTRODUCTORY PRINCIPLES

---

1 Activity

Task 1

Distinguish between, and give examples of, direct costs and indirect costs.

Task 2

The valuation of finished goods stocks and work-in-progress in a company manufacturing a range of products requires costs to be collected and classified according to the functions of the organisation.

(a) Describe the procedures necessary to collect the indirect costs of a manufacturing company

(b) Explain the procedures used to ascertain the cost of stocks and work-in-progress in such organisations.

---

2 Activity

Prepare a report for the Managing Director of your company explaining how costs may be classified by their behaviour, with particular reference to the effects both on total and on unit costs.

Your report should:

(a) say why it is necessary to classify costs by their behaviour;

(b) be illustrated by sketch graphs within the body of the report.

---

3 Activity

A management accountant has calculated the following data from the monthly output of a factory that makes a single product. Output (X) is measured in hundreds of units and total cost (Y) in hundreds of £ sterling.

Month	1	2	3	4	5	6	7	8	9	10	11	12

Output (in hundreds of units)

	40	35	32	36	45	37	43	39	42	38	40	41

Total cost (in hundreds of £ sterling)

	120	110	109	115	129	112	122	117	120	116	118	122

$\Sigma X = 468$ $\quad$ $\Sigma Y = 1,410$ $\quad$ $\Sigma XY = 55,206$ $\quad$ $\Sigma X^2 = 18,398$ $\quad$ $\Sigma Y^2 = 166,028$

A standard computer program has calculated the linear regression of total costs on output to be the following equation:

$$\text{TOTAL COST} = 59.8 + (1.48 * \text{OUTPUT})$$

Task 1

Explain the meaning of the terms '59.8' and '1.48' in the regression equation.

Task 2

Plot a scatter diagram of the data, including the equation.

Task 3

Predict the total costs of the factory next month, given that output is planned to be 4,400 units.

Chapter 3

OVERHEADS

---

1 Activity

PTS Ltd is a manufacturing company which uses three production departments to make its product. It has the following factory costs which are expected to be incurred in the year to 31 December 20X2:

		£
Direct wages	Machining	234,980
	Assembly	345,900
	Finishing	134,525

		£
Indirect wages and salaries	Machining	120,354
	Assembly	238,970
	Finishing	89,700

	£
Factory rent	12,685,500
Business rates	3,450,900
Heat and lighting	985,350
Machinery power	2,890,600
Depreciation	600,000
Canteen subsidy	256,000

Other information is available as follows:

	Machining	Assembly	Finishing
Number of employees	50	60	18
Floor space occupied (m^2)	1,800	1,400	800
Horse power of machinery	13,000	500	6,500
Value of machinery (£'000)	250	30	120
Number of labour hours	100,000	140,000	35,000
Number of machine hours	200,000	36,000	90,000

Task 1

Prepare the company's overhead analysis sheet for 20X2.

Task 2

Calculate appropriate overhead absorption rates (to two decimal places) for each department.

2   Activity

The Utopian Hotel is developing a cost accounting system. Initially it has been decided to create four cost centres: Residential and Catering deal directly with customers whilst Housekeeping and Maintenance are internal service cost centres.

The following overhead details have been estimated for the next period:

	Residential £	Catering £	House-keeping £	Mainten-ance £	Total £
Consumable materials	14,000	23,000	27,000	9,000	73,000
Staff costs	16,500	13,000	11,500	5,500	46,500
Rent and rates					37,500
Contents insurance					14,000
Heating and lighting					18,500
Depreciation on equipment etc					37,500
					227,000

The following information is also available:

	Residential £	Catering £	House-keeping £	Mainten-ance £	Total £
Floor area (m^2)	2,750	1,350	600	300	5,000
Value of equipment etc	£350,000	£250,000	£75,000	£75,000	£750,000
Number of employees	20	20	15	5	60

In the period it is estimated that there will be 2,800 guest-nights and 16,000 meals will be served. Housekeeping works 70% for Residential and 30% for Catering, and Maintenance works 20% for Housekeeping, 30% for Catering and 50% for Residential.

Task 1

Prepare an overhead statement showing clearly allocations and apportionments to each cost centre.

Task 2

Calculate appropriate overhead absorption rates for Residential and Catering.

Task 3

Calculate the under/over absorption of overheads if actual results were as follows:

    Residential: 3,050 guest-nights with overheads of £144,600.
    Catering: 15,250 meals with overheads of £89,250.

Task 4

Comment briefly on possible future developments in the Utopian hotel's cost accounting system.

3   Activity

Duo Ltd makes and sells two products, Alpha and Beta. The following information is available:

	Period 1	Period 2
Production (units)		
Alpha	2,500	1,900
Beta	1,750	1,250
Sales (units)		
Alpha	2,300	1,700
Beta	1,600	1,250

Financial data:

	Alpha £	Beta £
Unit selling price	90	75
Unit variable costs		
Direct materials	15	12
Direct labour (£6/hr)	18	12
Variable production overheads	12	8

Fixed costs for the company in total were £110,000 in period 1 and £82,000 in period 2. Fixed costs are recovered on direct labour hours.

Task 1

Prepare profit and loss accounts for period 1 and for period 2 based on marginal cost principles.

Task 2

Prepare profit and loss accounts for period 1 and for period 2 based on absorption cost principles.

Task 3

Comment on the position shown by your statements.

4   Activity

Having attended a course on activity based costing (ABC) you decide to experiment by applying the principles of ABC to the four products currently made and sold by your company. Details of the four products and relevant information are given below for one period:

Product	A	B	C	D
Output in units	120	100	80	120
Costs per unit	£	£	£	£
Direct material	40	50	30	60
Direct labour	28	21	14	21
Machine hours (per unit)	4	3	2	3

The four products are similar and are usually produced in production runs of 20 units and sold in batches of 10 units.

The production overhead is currently absorbed by using a machine hour rate, and the total of the production overhead for the period has been analysed as follows:

	£
Machine department costs (rent, business rates, depreciation and supervision)	10,430
Set up costs	5,250
Stores receiving	3,600
Inspection/quality control	2,100
Materials handling and dispatch	4,620

You have ascertained that the 'cost drivers' to be used are as listed below for the overhead costs shown:

Cost	Cost driver
Set up costs	Number of production runs
Stores receiving	Requisitions raised
Inspection/quality control	Number of production runs
Materials handling and dispatch	Orders executed

The number of requisitions raised on the stores was 20 for each product and the number of orders executed was 42, each order being for a batch of 10 of a product.

Task 1

Calculate the total costs for each product if all overhead costs are absorbed on a machine hour basis.

Task 2

Calculate the total costs for each product, using activity based costing.

Task 3

Calculate and list the unit product costs from your figures in Task 1 and Task 2 above, to show the differences and to comment briefly on any conclusions which may be drawn which could have pricing and profit implications.

Chapters 4 – 5

PRESENTATION OF INFORMATION

---

1   Activity

A local weekly newspaper sells about half a million copies a week in a region of about 100 square miles. Market research indicates that the readership profile is as follows:

Age	%	Annual income (£'000)	%	Sex	%
Under 25	10	Under 10	10	Male	50
25 - 34	15	10 – 15	10	Female	50
35 - 44	20	15 – 20	25		
45 - 54	20	20 – 25	25	Region	%
55 - 64	20	25 – 30	20		
65+	15	Over 30	10	Rural	10
				Suburban	30
Total	100	Total	100	Town	60

You are working with a marketing colleague on the design of a sample survey to find out (i) current strengths and weaknesses of the paper and (ii) whether the introduction of colour, leisure and/or business supplements etc would increase sales and by how much.

Task 1

Considering the information requirements, recommend a method for collecting the data (eg, by post, telephone, personal interviews etc), giving reasons.

Task 2

Design and explain a suitable practical sampling scheme that would achieve the objectives.

DO NOT ATTEMPT TO WRITE A QUESTIONNAIRE.

---

2   Activity

The unit sales of a brand for 20X1 and 20X2 were as follows:

	Jan	Feb	Mar	Apr	May	Jun	Jul	Aug	Sept	Oct	Nov	Dec
20X1	29	30	30	34	37	39	40	40	40	45	49	52
20X2	54	55	55	55	50	46	43	41	40	40	42	44

The brand has been supported by two weeks of television advertising every March and September. From April 20X2 there has been heavy price-cutting by its competitors.

Task 1

Calculate for 20X2:

(a)   cumulative monthly sales, and
(b)   moving annual totals.

Task 2

Plot a Z-chart for this period.

Task 3

What do these data show?

---

3   Activity

As the result of a takeover, the performance of three brands – A, B and C – is being reviewed. The unit sales for the last nine quarters is shown below. Contribution is 10 pence per unit.

Quarterly sales (thousand units)

| Brand | *20X0* | | | | *20X1* | | | | *20X2* |
	Q1	*Q2*	*Q3*	*Q4*	*Q1*	*Q2*	*Q3*	*Q4*	*Q1*
A	40	33	60	104	56	45	80	136	72
B	78	63	101	158	81	59	98	162	80
C	400	290	460	700	335	240	380	575	270

Task

Analyse these data and write a management report of your main findings, including at least five clear points.

Note: no technical statistical analysis is required but graphs, diagrams or simple tables may be included as necessary.

Chapters 6 – 7

TIME SERIES AND INDEX NUMBERS

1   Activity

Annual sales of Brand Y over the last eleven years have been as follows:

Unit sales of Brand Y, 20X0 – 20X10 (thousands)

20X0	20X1	20X2	20X3	20X4	20X5	20X6	20X7	20X8	20X9	20X10
50	59	46	54	65	51	60	70	56	66	76

Task 1

Calculate a **three-year** moving average trend.

Task 2

Plot the series and the trend on the same graph.

Task 3

Produce a sales forecast for 20X11, stating any assumptions.

2   Activity

The sales of Yelesol ice cream for the last twelve quarters have been as follows:

		Sales (thousand units)	Moving annual total (thousand units)
20X1	Q_4	14	–
20X2	Q_1	16	–
			100
	Q_2	30	
			104
	Q_3	40	
			104
	Q_4	18	
			108
20X3	Q_1	16	
			112
	Q_2	34	
			108
	Q_3	44	
			108
	Q_4	14	
20X4			112
	Q_1	16	
			120
	Q_2	38	–
	Q_3	52	–
	Q_4		

Task 1

Calculate a centred moving average.

Task 2

Plot a graph of the data and the centred moving average.

Task 3

Find the average quarterly seasonal variations.

Task 4

Calculate sales forecasts for the next two quarters.

---

3 Activity

The data below refers to Average Earnings Index numbers in Great Britain for different sectors of industry, 20X1 = 100, and the Retail Price Index, 20X0 = 100.

Date	Whole economy	Production industries	Service industries	Retail price index
20X1	100.0	100.0	100.0	107.0
February 20X2	104.6	104.9	104.4	111.5
May 20X2	107.5	108.1	107.2	115.0
August 20X2	109.1	109.2	108.7	115.8
November 20X2	112.8	112.9	112.7	118.5
February 20X3	114.0	114.3	113.7	120.2
May 20X3	118.5	118.2	118.6	126.2
August 20X3	120.9	119.7	121.1	128.1
November 20X3	123.8	123.7	123.0	130.0
February 20X4	124.7	125.2	123.8	130.9
May 20X4	128.1	129.2	127.1	133.5
August 20X4	130.8	130.2	130.4	134.1
November 20X4	130.8	131.8	129.7	135.6

(Source: Employment Gazette, January 20X5)

Task 1

Using 20X1 = 100 as base throughout, deflate the Production Industries Index and comment briefly on the **real** (inflation-adjusted) change in its average earnings over the period 20X2 – X4.

Task 2

A retired person from the Service Industries had an index-linked pension of £5,000 a year, starting in May 20X2 and uprated each November in line with the average earnings index for that sector. Find the pension rates for November in each of the years 20X2, 20X3, 20X4 and comment on their value in real terms.

Chapters 8 – 10
BUDGETS

---

1 Activity

One of the most common uses of a microcomputer spreadsheet package is the preparation of budgets and their subsequent comparison with actual performance.

Task

Show, using a screen layout, how a spreadsheet may be used to prepare a production budget and a raw material purchases budget.

You should:

(a)   state the assumptions made regarding stock levels and production requirements
(b)   show a screen layout, using the full width (ie, a double page spread) of your answer book
(c)   indicate the use of formulae on the screen layout where appropriate.

---

2 Activity

An ice cream manufacturer is in the process of preparing budgets for the next few months, and the following draft figures are available:

Sales forecast

June	6,000 cases
July	7,500 cases
August	8,500 cases
September	7,000 cases
October	6,500 cases

A case has a standard cost of £15 and a standard selling price of £25.

Each case uses 2½ kgs of ingredients and it is policy to have stocks of ingredients at the end of each month to cover 50% of next month's production. There are 5,800 kgs in stock on 1 June.

There are 750 cases of finished ice cream in stock on 1 June and it is policy to have stocks at the end of each month to cover 10% of the next month's sales.

Task 1

Prepare a production budget (in cases) for the months of June, July, August and September.

Task 2

Prepare an ingredients purchase budget (in kgs) for the months of June, July and August.

Task 3

Calculate the budgeted gross profit for the quarter June to August.

Task 4

Describe briefly what advantages there would be for the firm if it adopted a system of flexible budgeting.

3   Activity

D Ltd is preparing its annual budgets for the year to 31 December 20X4. It manufactures and sells one product, which has a selling price of £150. The marketing director believes that the price can be increased to £160 with effect from 1 July 20X4 and that at this price the sales volume for each quarter of 20X4 will be as follows:

	Sales volume
Quarter 1	40,000
Quarter 2	50,000
Quarter 3	30,000
Quarter 4	45,000

Sales for each quarter of 20X5 are expected to be 40,000 units.

Each unit of the finished product which is manufactured requires four units of component R and three units of component T, together with a body shell S. These items are purchased from an outside supplier. Currently prices are:

Component R	£8.00 each
Component T	£5.00 each
Shell S	£30.00 each

The components are expected to increase in price by 10% with effect from 1 April 20X4; no change is expected in the price of the shell.

Assembly of the shell and components into the finished product requires 6 labour hours: labour is currently paid £5.00 per hour. A 4% increase in wage costs is anticipated to take effect from 1 October 20X4.

Variable overhead costs are expected to be £10 per unit for the whole of 20X4; fixed production overhead costs are expected to be £240,000 for the year, and are absorbed on a per unit basis.

Stocks on 31 December 20X3 are expected to be as follows:

Finished units	9,000 units
Component R	3,000 units
Component T	5,500 units
Shell S	500 units

Closing stocks at the end of each quarter are to be as follows:

Finished units	10% of next quarter's sales
Component R	20% of next quarter's production requirements
Component T	15% of next quarter's production requirements
Shell S	10% of next quarter's production requirements

Task 1

Prepare the following budgets of D Ltd for the year ending 31 December 20X4, showing values for each quarter and the year in total:

(a)   sales budget (in £s and units)
(b)   production budget (in units)
(c)   material usage budget (in units)
(d)   production cost budget (in £s).

Task 2

Sales are often considered to be the principal budget factor of an organisation.

Explain the meaning of the 'principal budget factor' and, assuming that it is sales, explain how sales may be forecast making appropriate reference to the use of statistical techniques and the use of microcomputers.

---

4   Activity

There is a continuing demand for three sub-assemblies – A, B and C – made and sold by MW Ltd. Sales are in the ratios of A 1, B 2, C 4 and selling prices are A £215, B £250, C £300. Each sub-assembly consists of a copper frame onto which are fixed the same components but in differing quantities as follows:

Sub-assembly	Frame	Component D	Component E	Component F
A	1	5	1	4
B	1	1	7	5
C	1	3	5	1
Buying in costs, per unit	£20	£8	£5	£3

Operation times by labour for each sub-assembly are:

Sub-assembly	Skilled hours	Unskilled hours
A	2	2
B	1½	2
C	1½	3

The skilled labour is paid £6 per hour and the unskilled £4.50 per hour. The skilled labour is located in a machining department and the unskilled labour in an assembly department. A five-day week of 37½ hours is worked and each accounting period is for four weeks.

Variable overhead per sub-assembly is A £5, B £4 and C £3.50. At the end of the current year, stocks are expected to be as shown below but because interest rates have increased and the company utilises a bank overdraft for working capital purposes, it is planned to effect a 10% reduction in all finished sub-assemblies and bought-in stocks during Period 1 of the forthcoming year.

Forecast stocks at current year end:

Sub-assembly			
A	300	Copper frames	1,000
B	700	Component D	4,000
C	1,600	Component E	10,000
		Component F	4,000

Work-in-progress stocks are to be ignored.

Overhead for the forthcoming year is budgeted to be production £728,000, selling and distribution £364,000 and administration £338,000. These costs, all fixed, are expected to be incurred evenly throughout the year and are treated as period costs.

Within Period 1 it is planned to sell one thirteenth of the annual requirements which are to be the sales necessary to achieve the company profit target of £6.5 million before tax.

Task 1

Prepare budgets in respect of Period 1 of the forthcoming year for:

(a)   sales, in quantities and value

(b)   production, in quantities only

(c)   materials usage, in quantities

(d)   materials purchased, in quantities and value

(e)   manpower budget, ie, number of people needed in each of the machining department and the assembly department.

Task 2

Discuss the factors to be considered if the bought-in stocks were to be reduced to one week's requirements – this has been proposed by the purchasing officer but resisted by the production director.

---

5   Activity

The Arcadian Hotel operates a budgeting system and budgets expenditure over eight budget centres as shown below. Analysis of past expenditure patterns indicates that variable costs in some budget centres vary according to Occupied Room Nights (ORN) whilst in others the variable proportion of costs varies according to the number of visitors (V).

The budgeted expenditures for a period with 2,000 ORN and 4,300 V were as follows:

Budget centre	Variable costs vary with:	Budgeted expenditure £	Partial cost analysis Budget expenditure includes: £
Cleaning	ORN	13,250	£2.50 per ORN
Laundry	V	15,025	£1.75 per V
Reception	ORN	13,100	£12,100 fixed
Maintenance	ORN	11,100	£0.80 per ORN
Housekeeping	V	19,600	£11,000 fixed
Administration	ORN	7,700	£0.20 per ORN
Catering	V	21,460	£2.20 per V
General overheads	–	11,250	all fixed

In period 9, with 1,850 ORN and 4,575 V, actual expenditures were as follows:

Budget centre	Actual expenditure £
Cleaning	13,292
Laundry	14,574
Reception	13,855
Maintenance	10,462
Housekeeping	19,580
Administration	7,930
Catering	23,053
General overheads	11,325

Task 1

Prepare a flexible budget for period 9.

Task 2

Show the individual expenditure variance for each budget centre.

Task 3

Discuss briefly the advantages that a budgeting system brings to the Arcadian Hotel.

Chapters 11 – 12

STANDARD COSTING AND VARIANCES

1	Activity

Task 1

Explain the difference between a fixed and flexible budget, stating which is more appropriate for budgetary control.

Task 2

Explain how the standard direct labour cost would be determined when a standard costing system is in use.

The following details have been extracted from the standard cost card of Product X which is manufactured by the XYZ chemical company which uses an absorption costing system:

	£
Direct materials	8.40
Direct labour	7.60
Variable overhead	3.90
Fixed overhead	5.10
	25.00

The fixed overhead charged to each unit of the product is based on a monthly production of 2,000 units.

During October 20X3, the actual production amounted to 2,150 units and costs incurred were as follows:

	£
Direct materials	18,100
Direct labour	14,980
Variable overhead	8,160
Fixed overhead	9,950

Task 3

Calculate the following total cost variances:

(a) direct materials
(b) direct labour
(c) variable overhead
(d) fixed overhead.

2   Activity

PQ Ltd has two production departments – machining and assembly. Two of its main products are the Major and the Minor, the standard data for which are as follows:

	Per unit	
	Major	*Minor*
Direct materials:		
Material @ £15 per kg	2.2 kgs	1.4 kgs
Direct labour:		
Machining department @ £6 per hour	4.8 hrs	2.9 hrs
Assembly department @ £5 per hour	3.6 hrs	3.1 hrs
Machining time	3.5 hrs	0.9 hrs

The overhead rates for the period are as follows:

Machining department	*Assembly department*
£16.00 per machine hour	£9.50 per labour hour

Task 1

Calculate the standard production cost for each product showing clearly, as a sub total, the standard prime cost.

During the period, actual results for labour were as follows:

	Major	*Minor*
Production	650 units	842 units
Direct labour:		
Machining department	2,990 hrs costing £18,239	2,480 hrs costing £15,132
Assembly department	2,310 hrs costing £11,700	2,595 hrs costing £12,975

Task 2

Calculate the direct labour total variance and the rate and efficiency variances for each product and each department.

Task 3

Explain briefly what information the above variances provide for management.

3   Activity

The following standard costs of production have been calculated by a chemist of ARF Ltd for one tonne of chemicals:

400kg of material A @ £2.50 per kg
600kg of material B @ £4.00 per kg
20 hours of labour @ £6.00 per hour

The management accountant of the company advises you that in addition to the above, further overhead costs are expected as follows:

Variable overhead	£4.00 per labour hour
Fixed overhead	£500,000 per month.

The planned production for April 20X2 was 4,500 tonnes of the finished chemical.

Task 1

Prepare the production cost budget of the company for April 20X2 using marginal costing principles.

During April the actual production was 5,000 tonnes of the finished product and the costs incurred were:

		£
Material A		4,870,000
Material B		13,125,000
Direct labour		580,000
Variable overhead		437,000
Fixed overhead		475,000

Task 2

Calculate:

(a)   the direct material total variance
(b)   the direct labour total variance
(c)   the variable production overhead total variance; and
(d)   the fixed production overhead total variance (based on marginal costing principles).

---

4   Activity

JM Ltd uses absorption costing principles for its variance analysis.   The flexible budget for production overhead for the company, which makes one product, shows a budgeted monthly expenditure of £72,000 for an output of 3,000 tonnes and of £108,000 for an output of 7,000 tonnes.   The standard overhead absorption rate for absorption purposes is £18 per tonne.   During the month of April, the company incurred overhead expenditure of £105,750 (£52,000 variable and £53,750 fixed) for an output of 5,500 tonnes.

Task 1

Calculate the following:

(a)   budgeted variable overhead cost per tonne
(b)   total budgeted fixed cost per month
(c)   budgeted output per month on which the standard overhead rate is based
(d)   budgeted overhead allowance for the actual output in April
(e)   the total overhead absorbed for the month of April
(f)   variable production overhead expenditure variance for the month of April
(g)   fixed production overhead expenditure variance for the month of April
(h)   fixed production overhead volume variance for the month of April.

Task 2

Explain why it is advantageous to use flexible budgets for costs classified as production overhead expenses.

Task 3

State the name of two typical production costs which would be classified as variable production overhead expenses.

Task 4

Explain the terms 'attainable standard' and 'ideal standard' and state, with reasons, which ought to be used when setting operational performance standards.

◆ FOULKS_lynch_

5   Activity

SK Ltd makes and sells a single product 'Jay' for which the standard cost is as follows:

		£ per unit
Direct materials	4 kilograms @ £12 per kg	48
Direct labour	5 hours @ £7 per hour	35
Variable production overhead	5 hours @ £2 per hour	10
Fixed production overhead	5 hours @ £10 per hour	50
		143

The variable production overhead is deemed to vary with the hours worked.

Overhead is absorbed into production on the basis of standard hours of production and the normal volume of production for the period just ended was 20,000 units (100,000 standard hours of production).

For the period under consideration, the actual results were:

Production of 'Jay'	18,000 units
	£
Direct material used – 76,000 kgs at a cost of	836,000
Direct labour cost incurred – for 84,000 hours worked	604,800
Variable production overhead incurred	172,000
Fixed production overhead incurred	1,030,000

Task 1

Calculate and show, by element of cost, the standard cost for the output for the period.

Task 2

Calculate and list the relevant variances in a way which reconciles the standard cost with the actual cost.

Note: fixed production overhead sub-variances of capacity and volume efficiency (productivity) are *not* required.

Task 3

Comment briefly on the usefulness to management of statements such as that given in your answer to (b) above.

Chapters 13 – 14

IMPROVING PERFORMANCE

1 Activity

As senior product management accountant you have been informed by the MD that 'something drastic has to be done about quality'. In his view, quality is the responsibility of your department and he has suggested that you take a tougher line with those responsible for quality problems, raise quality standards, increase inspection rates, and give greater authority to quality control inspectors.

Task 1

Evaluate the suggestions made by the MD.

Task 2

State what additional or alternative proposals you would offer.

2 Activity

The directors of a family-owned retail department store were shocked to receive the following profit statement for the year ended 31 January 20X0:

	£'000	£'000	£'000
Sales		5,000	
Less: Cost of sales		3,398	
		——	1,602
Wages – Departments	357		
Office	70		
Restaurant	26		
	——	453	
Delivery costs		200	
Departmental expenses		116	
Salaries – Directors and management		100	
Directors' fees		20	
Sales promotion and advertising		120	
Store capacity costs ie, rent, rates and energy		488	
Interest on bank overdraft		20	
Discounts allowed		25	
Bad debts		15	
Miscellaneous expenses		75	
		——	1,632
Net loss			(30)

Management accounting has not been employed but the following breakdown has been extracted from the financial records:

	Departments				Restaurant
	Ladies' wear	Men's wear	General	Toys	
	£'000	£'000	£'000	£'000	£'000
Sales	800	400	2,200	1,400	200
Purchases	506	220	1,290	1,276	167
Opening stock	90	70	200	100	5
Closing stock	100	50	170	200	6
Wages	96	47	155	59	26
Departmental expenses	38	13	35	20	10
Sales promotion and advertising	10	5	30	75	–
Floor space occupied	20%	15%	20%	35%	10%

The directors are considering two separate proposals which are independent of each other:

(1)   Closing the Toys Department
(2)   Reducing selling prices on Ladies' Wear and Men's Wear by 5% in the hope of boosting sales.

Task 1

Present the information for the year to 31 January 20X0 in a more meaningful way to aid decision making. Include any statistics or indicators of performance which you consider to be useful.

Task 2

Show and explain the change in profit for a full year if the Toys Department were closed and if all other costs remain the same.

Task 3

Show for the Ladies' Wear and Men's Wear Departments, if selling prices are reduced by 5% and unit costs remain the same:

(a)   the increase in sales value (to the nearest thousand pounds) that would be required for a full year to maintain the gross profits, in £s, earned by each of these Departments, and

(b)   the increase in (a) above expressed as a percentage of the sales for each Department to 31 January 20X0.

Task 4

State your views on both the proposals being considered by the directors and recommend any alternative action you think appropriate.

Chapters 15 – 16

DECISION MAKING PRINCIPLES

1   Activity

A wholesaler buys a perishable commodity at £30 per case and sells it at £60 per case. Daily demand is uncertain, and any unsold cases at the end of the day are given without charge to a local charity and so represent a loss to the wholesaler.

Past records suggest that the pattern of demand is as follows:

	Daily demand	
Number of cases		Probability
20		0.20
21		0.40
22		0.30
23		0.10

The wholesaler wishes to know the amounts of stock to be purchased each day in order to maximise long-run profitability.

Task 1

Construct a conditional and expected profit table for the commodity.

Task 2

Advise the wholesaler of the best amount of stock to be purchased each day.

Task 3

Discuss briefly what assumptions the wholesaler might make regarding stock levels if there was no prior knowledge of the demand pattern.

2   Activity

A summary of a manufacturing company's budgeted profit statement for its next financial year, when it expects to be operating at seventy five per cent of capacity, is given below:

	£	£
Sales:		
9,000 units at £32		288,000
Less:		
Direct materials	54,000	
Direct wages	72,000	
Production overhead:		
Fixed	42,000	
Variable	18,000	
		186,000
Gross profit		102,000
Less:		
Administration, selling and distribution costs:		
Fixed	36,000	
Varying with sales volume	27,000	
		63,000
Net profit		39,000

Task 1

(a)   Calculate the breakeven point in units and in value.

(b)   Draw a contribution volume (profit volume) graph on graph paper.

(c)   Ascertain from your graph answer to (b) above, what profit could be expected if the company operated at full capacity.

It has been estimated that:

(a)   if the selling price per unit were reduced to £28, the increased demand would utilise 90% of the company's capacity without any additional advertising expenditure, and

(b)   to attract sufficient demand to utilise full capacity would require a 15% reduction in the current selling price and a £5,000 special advertising campaign.

Task 2

Present a statement showing the effect of the two alternatives compared with the original budget and to advise management which of the three possible plans ought to be adopted ie, the original budget plan or (a) above or (b) above.

An independent market research study shows that by spending £15,000 on a special advertising campaign, the company could operate at full capacity and maintain the selling price at £32 per unit.

Task 3

(a)   Advise management whether this proposal should be adopted, and
(b)   state any reservations you might have.

3   Activity

You are the management accountant of a publishing and printing company which has been asked to quote for the production of a programme for the local village fair. The work would be carried out in addition to the normal work of the company. Because of existing commitments, some weekend working would be required to complete the printing of the programme. A trainee accountant has produced the following cost estimate based upon the resources required as specified by the production manager:

			£
Direct materials	– paper (book value)		5,000
	– inks (purchase price)		2,400
Direct labour	– skilled	250 hours @ £4.00	1,000
	– unskilled	100 hours @ £3.50	350
Variable overhead		350 hours @ £4.00	1,400
Printing press depreciation		200 hours @ £2.50	500
Fixed production costs		350 hours @ £6.00	2,100
Estimating department costs			400
			13,150

You are aware that considerable publicity could be obtained for the company if you are able to win this order and the price quoted must be very competitive.

The following notes are relevant to the cost estimate above:

(1)   The paper to be used is currently in stock at a value of £5,000. It is of an unusual colour which has not been used for some time. The replacement price of the paper is £8,000, whilst the scrap value of that in stock is £2,500. The production manager does not foresee any alternative use for the paper if it is not used for the village fair programmes.

(2)   The inks required are not held in stock. They would have to be purchased in bulk at a cost of £3,000. 80% of the ink purchased would be used in printing the programmes. No other use is foreseen for the remainder.

(3)   Skilled direct labour is in short supply, and to accommodate the printing of the programmes, 50% of the time required would be worked at weekends for which a premium of 25% above the normal hourly rate is paid. The normal hourly rate is £4.00 per hour.

(4)   Unskilled labour is presently under-utilised, and at present 200 hours per week are recorded as idle time. If the printing work is carried out at a weekend, 25 unskilled hours would have to occur at this time, but the employees concerned would be given two hours time off (for which they would be paid) in lieu of each hour worked.

(5)   Variable overhead represents the cost of operating the printing press and binding machines.

(6)   When not being used by the company, the printing press is hired to outside companies for £6.00 per hour. This earns a contribution of £3.00 per hour. There is unlimited demand for this facility.

(7)   Fixed production costs are those incurred by and absorbed into production, using an hourly rate based on budgeted activity.

(8)   The cost of the estimating department represents time spent in discussions with the village fair committee concerning the printing of its programme.

Task 1

Prepare a revised cost estimate using the opportunity cost approach, showing clearly the minimum price that the company should accept for the order. Give reasons for each resource valuation in your cost estimate.

◈ FOULKS*lynch*

Task 2

Explain why contribution theory is used as a basis for providing information relevant to decision making.

Task 3

Explain the relevance of opportunity costs in decision making.

4 Activity

Z plc operates a single retail outlet selling direct to the public. Profit statements for August and September 20X6 are as follows:

	August £	September £
Sales	80,000	90,000
Cost of sales	50,000	55,000
Gross profit	30,000	35,000
Less:		
Selling and distribution	8,000	9,000
Administration	15,000	15,000
Net profit	7,000	11,000

Task 1

Use the high and low points technique to identify the behaviour of:

(a) cost of sales
(b) selling and distribution costs, and
(c) administration costs.

Task 2

Using graph paper, draw a contribution breakeven chart and identify the monthly breakeven sales value, and area of contribution.

Task 3

Assuming a margin of safety equal to 30% of the breakeven value, calculate Z plc's annual profit.

Z plc is now considering opening another retail outlet selling the same products. Z plc plans to use the same profit margins in both outlets and has estimated that the specific fixed costs of the second outlet will be £100,000 per annum.

Z plc also expects that 10% of its annual sales from its existing outlet would transfer to this second outlet if it were to be opened.

Task 4

Calculate the annual value of sales required from the new outlet in order to achieve the same annual profit as previously obtained from the single outlet.

Task 5

Briefly describe the cost accounting requirements of organisations of this type.

Chapters 17 – 18

DECISION MAKING TECHNIQUES

---

1   Activity

The management of Springer plc is considering next year's production and purchase budgets.

One of the components produced by the company, which is incorporated into another product before being sold, has a budgeted manufacturing cost as follows:

	£
Direct material	14
Direct labour (4 hours at £3 per hour)	12
Variable overhead (4 hours at £2 per hour)	8
Fixed overhead (4 hours at £5 per hour)	20
Total cost	54 per unit

Trigger plc has offered to supply the above component at a guaranteed price of £50 per unit.

Task 1

Considering cost criteria only, advise management whether the above component should be purchased from Trigger plc. Any calculations should be shown and assumptions made, or aspects which may require further investigation should be clearly stated.

Task 2

Explain how your above advice would be affected by each of the two **separate** situations shown below.

(a)   As a result of recent government legislation if Springer plc continues to manufacture this component the company will incur additional inspection and testing expenses of £56,000 per annum, which are not included in the above budgeted manufacturing costs.

(b)   Additional labour cannot be recruited and if the above component is not manufactured by Springer plc the direct labour released will be employed in increasing the production of an existing product which is sold for £90 and which has a budgeted manufacturing cost as follows:

	£
Direct material	10
Direct labour (8 hours at £3 per hour)	24
Variable overhead (8 hours at £2 per hour)	16
Fixed overhead (8 hours at £5 per hour)	40
	90 per unit

All calculations must be shown.

The production director of Springer plc recently said:

'We must continue to manufacture the component as only one year ago we purchased some special grinding equipment to be used exclusively by this component. The equipment cost £100,000, it cannot be resold or used elsewhere and if we cease production of this component we will have to write off the written down book value which is £80,000.'

Task 3

Draft a brief reply to the production director commenting on his statement.

2   Activity

For the next period DNP Ltd has prepared the following budgeted information for its three products:

	Product A	Product B	Product C
Sales volume (units)	8,750	12,500	5,000
Selling price per unit	£80	£64	£100
Variable cost per unit	£20	£23	£35
Fixed costs attributable to products (£'000)	65	140	95
Apportioned general fixed costs (£'000)	280	320	200

Task 1

Prepare a statement showing the budgeted profit for *each* product *and* for DNP Ltd in total.

Task 2

Because of increased competition, consideration is being given to the elimination of product C.

Prepare a statement showing the budgeted profit for products A and B and for DNP Ltd in total, assuming that product C is eliminated and that the sales of products A and B remain the same and that general fixed costs fall by 10%.

Task 3

Comment on the position revealed by your two statements.

3   Activity

BSE Veterinary Services is a specialist laboratory carrying out tests on cattle to ascertain whether the cattle have any infection. At present, the laboratory carries out 12,000 tests each period but, because of current difficulties with the beef herd, demand is expected to increase to 18,000 tests a period, which would require an additional shift to be worked.

The current cost of carrying out a full test is:

	£ per test
Materials	115
Technicians' wages	30
Variable overhead	12
Fixed overhead	50

Working the additional shift would:

(a)   require a shift premium of 50% to be paid to the technicians on the additional shift

(b)   enable a quantity discount of 20% to be obtained for all materials if an order was placed to cover 18,000 tests

(c)   increase fixed costs by £700,000 per period.

The current fee per test is £300.

Task 1

Prepare a profit statement for the current 12,000 capacity.

Task 2

Prepare a profit statement if the additional shift was worked and 18,000 tests were carried out.

Task 3

Comment on THREE other factors which should be considered before any decision is taken.

4   Activity

Three products – X, Y and Z – are made and sold by a company; information is given below:

		Product X £	Product Y £	Product Z £
Standard costs				
Direct materials		50	120	90
Variable overhead		12	7	16

Direct labour:	Rate per hour £	Hours	Hours	Hours
Department A	5	14	8	15
Department B	6	4	3	5
Department C	4	8	4	15

Total fixed overhead for the year was budgeted at £300,000.

The budget for the current financial year, which was prepared for a recessionary period, was based on the following sales:

Product	Sales in units	Selling price per unit £
X	7,500	210
Y	6,000	220
Z	6,000	300

However, the market for each of the products has improved and the Sales Director believes that without a change in selling prices, the number of units sold could be increased for each product by the following percentages:

Product	Increase
X	20%
Y	25%
Z	33 ⅓%

When the Sales Director's views were presented to a management meeting, the Production Director declared that although it might be possible to sell more units of product, output could not be expanded because he was unable to recruit more staff for Department B, there being a severe shortage of the skills needed by this department.

Task 1

Show in the form of a statement for management, the unit costs of each of the three products and the total *profit* expected for the current year based on the original sales figures.

Task 2

State the profit if the most profitable mixture of the products was made and sold, utilising the higher sales figures and the limitation on Department B.

Task 3

Identify and comment on **three** possible problems which may arise if the mixture in Task 2 above were to be produced.

---

5   Activity

Z Ltd is a retailer with a number of shops selling a variety of merchandise. The company is seeking to determine the optimum allocation of selling space in its shops. Space is devoted to ranges of merchandise in modular units, each module occupying seventy square metres of space. Either one or two modules can be devoted to each range. Each shop has seven modular units.

Z Ltd has tested the sale of different ranges of merchandise and has determined the following sales productivities:

Sales per module per week

	1 Module £	2 Modules £
Range A	6,750	6,250
Range B	3,500	3,150
Range C	4,800	4,600
Range D	6,400	5,200
Range E	3,333	3,667

The contribution (selling price – product cost) percentages of sales of the five ranges are as follows:

        Range A 20%
        Range B 40%
        Range C 25%
        Range D 25%
        Range E 30%

Operating costs are £5,600 per shop per week and are apportioned to ranges based on an average rate per module.

Task 1

Determine the allocation of shop space that will optimise profit, clearly showing the ranking order for the allocation of modules.

Task 2

Calculate the profit of each of the merchandise ranges selected in Task 1 above, and of the total shop.

Task 3

Define the term 'limiting factor', and explain the relevance of limiting factors in planning and decision-making.

Chapters 19 – 20

PRICING AND COST ESTIMATION

---

1   Activity

A small manufacturing company has fixed overheads of £1,480 a week. Other costs and the number of units produced are shown for the last 15 weeks.

Week	Materials £	Power, transport and miscellaneous £	Production units
1	1,700	1,445	85
2	1,280	819	64
3	1,000	500	50
4	760	289	38
5	800	320	40
6	1,460	1,066	73
7	1,820	1,656	91
8	1,200	720	60
9	1,640	1,345	82
10	2,000	2,000	100
11	2,400	2,880	120
12	2,800	3,920	140
13*	420	88	21
14*	300	45	15
15*	400	80	20

*indicates holiday period   *(Source: internal company records)*

The company receives £65 per unit in sales revenue.

Task 1

Plot a graph of total costs and revenue against production.

Task 2

Find where the company breaks even.

Task 3

Assuming the company could produce the same amount each week, recommend how many units each week it should manufacture and explain why.

2   Activity

You have just taken up the position as the first full-time accountant for a jobbing engineering company. Previously the accounting work had been undertaken by the company's auditors who had produced the following summarised profit and loss statement for the financial year which ended on 31 March of this year.

	£	£	£
Sales			2,400,000
Direct material		1,000,000	
Direct labour:			
Grinding department	200,000		
Finishing department	260,000	460,000	
Production overhead:			
Grinding	175,000		
Finishing	208,000	383,000	
Administration costs		118,500	
Selling costs		192,000	2,153,500
Net profit			246,500

The sales manager is currently negotiating a price for an enquiry for a job which has been allocated number 878 and he has been given the following information by his staff:

Preferred price to obtain a return of 16 $\frac{2}{3}$ % on selling price	£22,656
Lowest acceptable price	£18,880

These prices have been based on the following estimated costs for proposed Job 878:

	£	£
Direct material		9,000
Direct labour:		
Grinding department 400 hours @ £5	2,000	
Finishing department 300 hours @ £6	1,800	3,800
		12,800
Add: 47.5% to cover all other costs		6,080
Total cost		18,880

The sales manager seeks your advice about the validity of the method he is using to quote for Job 878.

The company is currently busy with a fairly full order book but the Confederation of British Industry has forecast that a recession is imminent for the engineering industry.

Task 1

Criticise the method adopted for estimating the costs which are used as the basis for quoting prices for jobs.

Task 2

Suggest a better method of estimating job costs and calculate a revised job cost and price, based on the information available, to give to the sales manager.

Task 3

Suggest how you would propose to improve the accounting information to assist with controlling costs and providing information for pricing purposes.

---

3   Activity

A printing and publishing company has been asked to provide an estimate for the production of 100,000 catalogues, of 64 pages (32 sheets of paper) each, for a potential customer.

Four operations are involved in the production process; photography, set-up, printing and binding.

Each page of the catalogue requires a separate photographic session. Each session costs £150.

Set-up would require a plate to be made for each page of the catalogue. Each plate requires four hours of labour at £7 per hour and £35 of materials. Overheads are absorbed on the basis of labour hours at an hourly rate of £9.50.

In printing, paper costs £12 per thousand sheets. Material losses are expected to be 2% of input. Other printing materials will cost £7 per 500 catalogues. 1,000 catalogues are printed per hour of machine time. Labour and overhead costs incurred in printing are absorbed at a rate of £62 per machine hour.

Binding costs are recovered at a rate per machine hour. The rate is £43 per hour and 2,500 catalogues are bound per hour of machine time.

A profit margin of 10% of selling price is required.

Task 1

Determine the total amount that should be quoted for the catalogue job by the printing and publishing company.

Task 2

Calculate the additional costs that would be charged to the job if the labour efficiency ratio achieved versus estimate in set-up is 90%.

Chapters 21 – 22

INVESTMENT APPRAISAL

---

1 Activity

The Management Services Division of a company has been asked to evaluate the following proposals for the maintenance of a new boiler with a life of seven years.

PROPOSAL 1

The boiler supplier will make a charge of £13,000 per year on a seven-year contract.

PROPOSAL 2

The company will carry out its own maintenance estimated at £10,000 per annum now, rising at 5% per annum with a major overhaul at the end of year 4 costing an additional £25,000.

The discount rate is 10% and all payments are assumed to be made at year ends.

Task 1

Calculate the maintenance cost for each year if the company provides its own maintenance.

Task 2

Calculate the present value of the cost of maintenance, if the company carries out its own maintenance.

Task 3

Calculate the present value of the supplier's maintenance contract.

Task 4

Recommend, with reasons, which proposal should be adopted.

---

2 Activity

A company is planning a capital investment for which the following cashflows have been estimated:

Time	Net cashflow £
Now	– 10,000
At the end of year 1	+ 500
At the end of year 2	+ 2,000
At the end of year 3	+ 3,000
At the end of year 4	+ 4,000
At the end of year 5	+ 5,000
At the end of year 6	+ 2,500
At the end of year 7	+ 2,000
At the end of year 8	+ 2,500

The company has a cost of capital of 15%.

Task 1

Calculate the net present value of the investment.

Task 2

Calculate the approximate Internal Rate of Return of the investment.

Task 3

Comment on whether the investment should be initiated and what other factors should be considered.

---

3   Activity

An oil well is currently producing annual (year-end) cash flows of £0.5 million. The best geological evidence suggests that the well has reserves that will last for another 10 years, at the present rate of extraction. A special pump could be installed, at a cost of £0.75 million, that could double the rate of extraction but halve the life of the well. After the well had been exhausted, this special pump could be sold for £100,000. The immediate introduction of the special pump is now being considered. Last year's earnings have just been distributed and the existing equipment has no resale value.

Task 1

Tabulate the annual effect on earnings over the next ten years of introducing the special pump.

Task 2

Compare the net present value of the options if the cost of capital to the company is 8% per annum and explain the answer.

Task 3

Find whether the pump should be installed if the cost of capital were to be 12%, giving reasons.

PRACTICE CENTRAL ASSESSMENT ACTIVITIES

QUESTIONS

◆ **FOULKS**_lynch_

ASSESSMENT ACTIVITIES – CONTENTS

AAT Assessments

These assessment activities have been taken from the December 1996 to December 2000 Central Assessments set by the AAT. The assessments have been divided into Sections as follows:

UNIT 8 – SECTION 1 – JUNE 1997

SECTION 1 (Suggested time allocation: 70 minutes)

Data

Malton Ltd operates a standard marginal costing system. As the recently appointed management accountant to Malton's Eastern division, you have responsibility for the preparation of that division's monthly cost reports. The standard cost report uses variances to reconcile the actual marginal cost of production to its standard cost.

The Eastern division is managed by Richard Hill. The division only makes one product, the Beta. Budgeted Beta production for May 1997 was 8,000 units although actual production was 9,500 units.

In order to prepare the standard cost report for May, you have asked a member of your staff to obtain standard and actual cost details for the month of May. This information is reproduced below.

	Unit standard cost				Actual details for May	
	Quantity	*Unit price*	*Cost per Beta £*		*Quantity*	*Total cost £*
Material	8 litres	£20	160	Material	78,000 litres	1,599,000
Labour	4 hours	£6	24	Labour	39,000 hours	249,600
Standard marginal cost			184	Total cost		1,848,600

Task 1.1

(a) Calculate the following:

   (i) the material price variance
   (ii) the material usage variance
   (iii) the labour rate variance
   (iv) the labour efficiency variance (sometimes called the utilisation variance).

(b) Prepare a standard costing statement reconciling the actual marginal cost of production with the standard marginal cost of production.

Data

After Richard Hill has received your standard costing statement, you visit him to discuss the variances and their implications. Richard, however, raises a number of queries with you. He makes the following points:

- an index measuring material prices stood at 247.2 for May but at 240.0 when the standard for the material price was set

- the Eastern division is budgeted to run at its normal capacity of 8,000 units of production per month but during May it had to manufacture an additional 1,500 Betas to meet a special order agreed at short notice by Malton's sales director

- because of the short notice, the normal supplier of the raw material was unable to meet the extra demand and so additional materials had to be acquired from another supplier at a price per litre of £22

- this extra material was not up to the normal specification, resulting in 20% of the special purchase being scrapped *prior* to being issued to production

- the work force could only produce the special order on time by working overtime on the 1,500 Betas at a 50% premium.

◈ FOULKS*lynch*

Task 1.2

(a)   Calculate the amounts within the material price variance, the material usage variance and the labour rate variance which arise from producing the special order.

(b)   (i)   Estimate the revised standard price for materials based on the change in the material price index.

          (ii)   For the 8,000 units of normal production, use your answer in (b)(i) to estimate how much of the price variance calculated in task 1.1 is caused by the general change in prices.

(c)   Using your answers to part (a) and (b) of this task, prepare a revised standard costing statement. The revised statement should subdivide the variances prepared in task 1.1 into those elements controllable by Richard Hill and those elements caused by factors outside his divisional control.

(d)   Write a *brief* note to Richard Hill justifying your treatment of the elements you believe are outside his control and suggesting what action should be taken by the company.

UNIT 8 – SECTION 1 – DECEMBER 1997

SECTION 1 (Suggested time allocation: 70 minutes)

Data

You have recently accepted an appointment as the accountant to Debussy Limited, a small family firm manufacturing a specialised fertiliser. The fertiliser is produced using expensive ovens which need to be kept at a constant temperature at all times, even when not being used. Because of this, the power which provides the heating does not vary with changes in production output and so its costs are viewed as being fixed.

The managing director, Claude Debussy, is concerned that the existing accounting system is not providing adequate information for him to run the business. By way of example, he shows you the accounts for the year ended 30 November 1997. An extract from those accounts showing budgeted and actual results is reproduced below.

	Annual Budget 12,000		Annual Results 13,000		Quarter 4 Budget 3,000		Quarter 4 Results 2,400	
Units produced (tonnes)								
	£	£	£	£	£	£	£	£
Material		144,000		188,500		36,000		35,280
Labour		192,000		227,500		48,000		42,240
Fixed overheads:								
Lease of machinery	60,000		60,000		15,000		15,000	
Rent	40,000		40,000		10,000		10,000	
Rates	56,000		64,000		14,000		16,000	
Insurance	48,000		52,000		12,000		13,000	
Power	120,000	324,000	140,000	356,000	30,000	81,000	36,000	90,000
Total expenses		660,000		772,000		165,000		167,520

Extract from the Profit and Loss Account of Debussy Ltd for the year ended 30 November 1997

Claude Debussy draws your attention to the high level of fixed overheads and how these are absorbed using labour hours.

'I do not fully understand the fixed overhead figures for the fourth quarter,' he explained. 'The way they are presented in the accounts does not help me to plan and control the business. It is no good blaming the production workers for the increase in fixed overheads as we have been paying them £8 per hour – the same amount as agreed in the budget – and they have never worked any overtime.'

Claude Debussy turns to you for advice. He is particularly interested in understanding why the fixed overheads have increased in the fourth quarter despite production falling. He is also interested in knowing how many labour hours were planned to be worked and how many hours were actually worked in that quarter.

Task 1.1

(a)   For the fourth quarter, calculate the following information for Claude Debussy:

      (i)   the labour hours budgeted to be worked
      (ii)   the labour hours actually worked
      (iii)   the budgeted hours per tonne of fertiliser
      (iv)   the actual hours per tonne of fertiliser.

(b)   Calculate the following variances for the fourth quarter:

    (Note: you should base your calculations on the TOTAL amount of fixed overheads and NOT the individual elements.)

      (i)   the fixed overhead expenditure variance (sometimes known as the price variance)
      (ii)   the fixed overhead volume variance
      (iii)   the fixed overhead capacity variance
      (iv)   the fixed overhead efficiency variance (sometimes known as the usage variance).

Data

Claude Debussy is unfamiliar with standard costing, although he believes the actual fixed overheads for the year are higher than budgeted because more tonnes of fertiliser have been produced. He would like to use standard costing to control fixed overheads, but is uncertain what is meant by the fixed overhead variances you have prepared.

Task 1.2

Write a memo to Claude Debussy. Your memo should:

(a)   *briefly* comment on his explanation for the increase in fixed overheads for the year

(b)   for each of the following three variances, give ONE possible reason they might have occurred:

- the fixed overhead expenditure (or price) variance
- the fixed overhead capacity variance
- the fixed overhead efficiency (or usage) variance.

Data

On receiving your memo, Claude Debussy tells you that the annual budgeted fixed overheads have, in the past, simply been apportioned equally over the four quarters. However, the expenditure on power varies between quarters in a regular way depending on the outside temperature. The seasonal variations, based on many years' experience, are as follows:

	1st Quarter	2nd Quarter	3rd Quarter	4th Quarter
Seasonal variations for power costs	+5%	–10%	–20%	+25%

Claude Debussy believes that it would be more meaningful if the budgeted expenditure on power reflected these seasonal variations, but he is uncertain how this would affect the variances calculated in task 1.1 (b).

Task 1.3

Prepare notes for Claude Debussy. Your notes should:

(a)   use the seasonal variations to calculate the revised power budget for the four quarters of the year to 30 November 1997

(b)   *briefly* discuss whether or not the revised power budget for the fourth quarter should be used for calculating the fixed overhead expenditure (or price) and volume variances for that quarter.

UNIT 8 – SECTION 1 – DECEMBER 1998

Data

Pronto Ltd was recently established in the UK to assemble cars. All parts are sent directly to the UK in the form of a kit by Pronto's owner from its headquarters in a country called Erehwon.

The contract between Pronto and its owner is a fixed price contract per kit and the contract specifies zero faults in all of the parts. This fixed price was used to establish the standard cost per kit. Despite this, the managing director of Pronto, Richard Jones, is concerned to receive the following statement from the management accounting department where you are employed as an accounting technician.

	September 1998	October 1998	November 1998
Kits delivered	2,000	2,100	2,050
Actual cost invoiced	£12,059,535	£11,385,495	£10,848,600
Unit cost per kit to nearest £	£6,030	£5,422	£5,292

Richard Jones cannot understand why, with a fixed price contract and guaranteed quality, the unit cost should vary over the three months. He provides you with the following information:

- the contract's cost was fixed in Erehwon dollars of $54,243 per kit
- there has been no change in the agreed cost of the parts and no other costs incurred.

On further investigation you discover that the exchange rate between the UK pound and the Erehwon dollar was as follows:

At time Of contract $9.80	September 1998 $9.00	October 1998 $10.00	November 1998 $10.25

Task 1.1

Prepare a memo to Richard Jones. Your memo should include:

(a)   a calculation of:

   (i)   the UK cost per kit at the time the contract was agreed

   (ii)   the UK cost of the kits delivered using the exchange rates given for each of the three months

   (iii)   the price variance due to exchange rate differences for each of the three months

   (iv)   any usage variance in each of the three months, assuming no other reason for the price variance

(b)   *briefly* discuss whether price variances due to exchange rate differences should be excluded form any standard costing report prepared for the production manager of Pronto Ltd.

Data

Pronto uses a highly mechanised and computerised moving assembly line known as a track to build the cars. Although individual employees are assigned to particular parts of the track, they work in teams. If the production of cars slows below the speed of the track, teams help each other to maintain the speed of the track and the production of cars. Because of this approach:

- labour is viewed as a fixed cost
- machine hours (the hours that the track is in use) are used to charge overheads to production.

For the week ended 28 November 1998, the management accounting department has prepared a statement of budgeted and actual fixed overhead for Richard Jones. This is reproduced below.

Pronto Ltd: Budgeted and actual fixed overheads – week ended 28 November 1998		
	Budget	*Actual*
Car production	560	500
Machine (or track) hours of production	140	126
Fixed overheads:	£	£
Rent and rates	16,000	16,000
Maintenance and depreciation	10,000	13,000
Power	75,000	71,000
Labour	739,000	742,000
Total	840,000	842,000

Task 1.2

Richard Jones finds that the statement is not particularly helpful as it does not give him sufficient information to manage the company. He asks for your help.

In preparation for a meeting with Richard Jones:

(a)   Calculate the:

   (i)   budgeted overheads per machine (or track) hour
   (ii)   budgeted number of cars produced per machine (or track) hour
   (iii)   standard hours of actual production.

(b)   Calculate the following variances using the information identified in (a):

   (i)   fixed overhead expenditure variance
   (ii)   fixed overhead volume variance
   (iii)   fixed overhead efficiency variance
   (iv)   fixed overhead capacity variance.

(c)   Prepare a statement for the week ended 28 November 1998 reconciling the fixed overheads incurred to the fixed overheads absorbed in production.

UNIT 8 – SECTION 1 – JUNE 1999

Data

You are the management accountant at Brighter Chemicals Ltd. Brighter Chemicals makes a single product, Zed, which is sold in 5–litre tins.

One of your responsibilities is to prepare a report each month for the management team comparing the actual cost of Zed production with its standard cost of production. This involves taking data from a computer printout, preparing standard cost variances and reconciling the standard cost of actual production to the actual cost of actual production. After the data is analysed, you attend a management meeting where the performance of the company is discussed. The printout for May 1999 is reproduced below.

Brighter Chemicals Ltd – Production report for May 1999						
		Budgeted production			**Actual production**	
Number of tins of Zed		1,750			1,700	
Inputs	*Units of input*	*Standard cost per unit of input*	*Standard cost per tin of Zed*	*Standard of budgeted production*	*Actual cost per unit of input*	*Actual cost of actual production*
Material	5 litres	£40.00	£200,000	£350,000	£40.20	£338,283
Labour	10 hours	£6.00	£60,000	£105,000	£5.90	£110,330
Fixed overheads	10 hours	£24.00	£240,000	£420,000		£410,000
			£500,000	£875,000		£858,613

Task 1.1

In preparation for the management meeting:

(a)   Calculate the:

  (i)   actual litres of material used in producing the 1,700 tins of Zed
  (ii)   actual hours worked in May
  (iii)   standard litres of material which should have been used to produce 1,700 tins of Zed
  (iv)   standard number of labour hours that should have been incurred in producing 1,700 tins of Zed
  (v)   standard hours of fixed overheads charged to the *budgeted* production of 1,750 tins
  (vi)   standard hours of fixed overheads charged to the *actual* production of 1,700 tins.

(b)   Calculate the following variances, making use of the answers in task 1.1 (a):

  (i)   material price variance
  (ii)   material usage variance
  (iii)   labour rate variance
  (iv)   labour efficiency variance
  (v)   fixed overhead expenditure variance
  (vi)   fixed overhead volume variance
  (vii)   fixed overhead capacity variance
  (viii) fixed overhead efficiency variance.

(c)   Prepare a report reconciling the standard cost of *actual* production to the actual cost of *actual* production.

◆ FOULKS*lynch*

Data

On receiving your report, the production director makes the following comments:

- The material used in Zed production is purchased in drums. A notice on each drum states that the *minimum* content per drum is 50 litres.

- Finished production of Zed is automatically poured into tins by a machine which also measures the contents. An error of 0.5% either way in the accuracy of measurement is acceptable.

- The reported material price variance does not truly reflect the efficiency of the purchasing department. An index of raw material prices stood at 124.00 when the standard price was set but stood at 125.86 in May.

- It seems unnecessary to investigate favourable variances. Favourable variances improve profitability and should be encouraged. Only adverse variances should be investigated.

Task 1.2

Write a *short* memo to the production director. Your memo should:

(a)   subdivide the material price variance calculated in task 1.1 into that part caused by the change in the standard cost as measured by the material price index and that part caused by the efficiency or inefficiency of the purchasing department

(b)   give THREE separate reasons why Zed production might result in a favourable material usage variance

(c)   *briefly* discuss whether or not a favourable material usage variance should be investigated.

UNIT 8 – SECTION 1 – DECEMBER 1999

Data

You are the assistant management accountant at the Bare Foot Hotel complex on the tropical island of St Nicolas. The hotel complex is a luxury development. All meals and entertainment are included in the price of the holidays and guests only have to pay for drinks.

The Bare Foot complex aims to create a relaxing atmosphere. Because of this, meals are available throughout the day and guests can eat as many times as they wish.

The draft performance report for the hotel for the seven days ended 27 November 1999 is reproduced below.

Bare Foot Hotel Complex
Draft performance report for seven days ended 27 November 1999

Guests	Notes		Budget (540)		Actual (648)
		$	$	$	$
Variable costs					
Meal costs	1		34,020		49,896
Catering staff costs	2,3		3,780		5,280
Total variable costs			37,800		55,176
Fixed overhead costs					
Salaries of other staff		5,840		6,000	
Local taxes		4,500		4,200	
Light, heat and power		2,500		2,600	
Depreciation of buildings and equipment		5,000		4,000	
Entertainment		20,500		21,000	
Total fixed overheads			38,340		37,800
Total cost of providing for guests			76,140		92,976

Notes

(1)   Budgeted cost of meals: number of guests × 3 meals per day × 7 days × $3 per meal.

(2)   Budgeted cost of catering staff: each member of the catering staff is to prepare and serve 12 meals per hour. Cost = (number of guests × 3 meals per day × 7 days ÷ 12 meals per hour) × $4 per hour.

(3)   Actual hours worked by catering staff = 1,200 hours.

Other notes

The amount of food per meal has been kept under strict portion control. Since preparing the draft performance report, however, it has been discovered that guests have eaten, on average, four meals per day.

You report to Alice Groves, the general manager of the hotel, who feels that the format of the draft performance report could be improved to provide her with more meaningful management information. She suggests that the budgeted and actual data given in the existing draft performance report is rearranged in the form of a standard costing report.

Task 1.1

(a) Use the budget data, the actual data and the notes to the performance report to calculate the following for the seven days ended 27 November 1999:

(i)   the actual number of meals served

(ii)   the standard number of meals which should have been served for the actual number of guests

(iii) the actual hourly rate paid to catering staff

(iv) the standard hours allowed for catering staff to serve three meals per day for the actual number of guests

(v)   the standard fixed overhead per guest

(vi) the total standard cost for the actual number of guests.

(b) Use the data given in the task and your answers to part (a) to calculate the following variances for the seven days ended 27 November 1999:

(i)   the material price variance for meals served

(ii)   the material usage variance for meals service

(iii) the labour rate variance for catering staff

(iv) the labour efficiency variance for catering staff, based on a standard of 3 meals served per guest per day

(v)   the fixed overhead expenditure variance

(vi) the fixed overhead volume variance on the assumption that the fixed overhead absorption rate is based on the budgeted numbered of guests per seven days.

(c) Prepare a statement reconciling the standard cost for the actual number of guests to the actual cost for the actual number of guests for the seven days ended 27 November 1999.

Data

On receiving your reconciliation statement, Alice Groves asks the following questions:

- How much of the labour efficiency variance is due to the guests taking, on average, four meals per day rather than the three provided for in the budget and how much is due to other reasons?

- Would it be feasible to subdivide the fixed overhead volume variance into a capacity and efficiency variance?

Task 1.2

Write a memo to Alice Groves. Your memo should:

(a) divide the labour efficiency variance into that part due to guests taking more meals than planned and that part due to other efficiency reasons

(b) explain the meaning of the fixed overhead capacity and efficiency variances

(c) *briefly* discuss whether or not it is feasible to calculate the fixed overhead capacity and efficiency variances for the Bare Foot Hotel Complex.

UNIT 8 – SECTION 1 – JUNE 2000

Data

NGJ Ltd is a furniture manufacturer. It makes 3 products, the *Basic*, the *Grand* and the *Super*. You are the management accountant reporting to the product line manager for the *Basic*. Reproduced below is NGJ's unit standard material and labour cost data and budgeted production for the year to 31 May 2000 together with details of the budgeted and actual factory fixed overheads for the year.

Unit standard material and labour cost data by product for the year to 31 May 2000			
Product	*Basic*	*Grand*	*Super*
Material at £12 per metre	6 metres	8 metres	10 metres
Labour at £5.00 per hour	6 hours	1 hour	1 hour
Budgeted production	10,000 units	70,000 units	70,000 units

Functional analysis of factory fixed overheads for the year to 31 May 2000		
	Budgeted £	*Actual* £
Rent and rates	100,000	100,000
Depreciation	200,000	200,000
Light, heat and power	60,000	70,000
Indirect labour	240,000	260,000
Total factory fixed overheads	£600,000	£630,000

Apportionment policy:

As all products are made in the same factory, budgeted and actual total factory fixed overheads are apportioned to each product on the basis of budgeted total labour hours per product.

During the year 11,500 *Basics* were made. The actual amount of material used, labour hours worked and costs incurred were as follows:

Actual material and labour cost of producing 11,500 *Basics* for the year to 31 May 2000		
	Units	*Total cost*
Material	69,230 metres	£872,298
Labour	70,150 hours	£343,735

Task 1.1

(a)   Calculate the following information:

(i)   the total budgeted labour hours of production for NGJ Ltd
(ii)   the standard factory fixed overhead rate per labour hour
(iii)   the budgeted and actual factory fixed overhead apportioned to *Basic* production
(iv)   the actual cost of material per metre and the actual labour hourly rate for *Basic* production
(v)   the total standard absorption cost of actual *Basic* production
(v)   the actual absorption cost of actual *Basic* production.

(b)   Calculate the following variances for *Basic* production:

      (i)   the material price variance
      (ii)   the material usage variance
      (iii)   the labour rate variance
      (iv)   the labour efficiency variance
      (v)   the fixed overhead expenditure variance
      (vi)   the fixed overhead volume variance
      (vii)   the fixed overhead capacity variance
      (viii) the fixed overhead efficiency variance.

(c)   Prepare a statement reconciling the actual absorption cost of actual *Basic* production with the standard absorption cost of actual *Basic* production.

Data

The product line manager for the *Basic* is of the opinion that the standard costs and variances do not fairly reflect the effort put in by staff. The manager made the following points:

- Because of a shortage of materials for the *Basic*, the purchasing manager had entered into a contract for the year with a single supplier in order to guarantee supplies.

- The actual price paid for the material per metre was 10% less than the market price throughout the year.

- The *Basic* is a hand–made product made in a small, separate part of the factory and uses none of the expensive machines shared by the *Grand* and the *Super*.

- *Grand* and *Super* production uses the same highly mechanised manufacturing facilities and only one of those products can be made at any one time. A change in production from one product to another involves halting production in order to set up the necessary tools and production line.

In response to a request from the *Basic* product line manager, a colleague has re–analysed the budgeted and actual factory fixed overheads by function. The revised analysis is reproduced below:

Functional analysis of factory fixed overheads for the year to 31 May 2000		
	Budgeted	*Actual*
	£	£
Setting up of tools and production lines	202,000	228,000
Depreciation attributable to production	170,000	170,000
Stores	60,000	59,000
Maintenance	40,000	48,000
Light, heat and power directly attributable to production	48,000	45,000
Rent and rates directly attributable to production	80,000	80,000
Total factory fixed overheads	£600,000	£630,000

Task 1.2

Write a memo to the *Basic* product line manager. Your memo should:

(a)   identify the market price of the material used in the *Basic*

(b)   subdivide the material price variance into that part due to the contracted price being different from the market price and that due to other reasons

(c)   identify ONE benefit to NGJ Ltd, which is not reflected in the variances, arising from the purchasing manager's decision to enter into a contract for the supply of materials

(d)   *briefly* explain what is meant by activity–based costing

(e)   refer to the task data, where appropriate, to *briefly* discuss whether or not activity–based costing would have reduced the budgeted and actual fixed overheads of *Basic* production.

◇ FOULKS*lynch*

UNIT 8 – SECTION 1 – DECEMBER 2000

Data

You are employed as a management accountant in the head office of Travel Holdings plc. Travel Holdings owns a number of transport businesses. One of them is Travel Ferries Ltd. Travel Ferries operates ferries which carry passengers and vehicles across a large river. Each year, standard costs are used to develop the budget for Travel Ferries Ltd. The latest budgeted and actual operating results are reproduced below.

Travel Ferries Ltd
Budgeted and actual operating results for the year to 30 November 2000

Operating data:		*Budget*		*Actual*
Number of ferry crossings		6,480		5,760
Operating hours of ferries		7,776		7,488
Cost data:		£		£
Fuel	1,244,160 litres	497,664	1,232,800 litres	567,088
Labour	93,312 hours	466,560	89,856 hours	471,744
Fixed overheads		466,560		472,440
Cost of operations		1,430,784		1,511,272

Other accounting information:

- Fuel and labour are variable costs.
- Fixed overheads are absorbed on the basis of budgeted **operating hours**.

One of your duties is to prepare costing information and a standard costing reconciliation statement for the Chief Executive of Travel Holdings.

Task 1.1

(a)   Calculate the following information:

    (i)   the standard price of fuel per litre
    (ii)   the standard litres of fuel for 5,760 ferry crossings
    (iii)   the standard labour rate per hour
    (iv)   the standard labour hours for 5,760 ferry crossings
    (v)   the standard fixed overhead cost per budgeted operating hour
    (vi)   the standard operating hours for 5,760 crossings
    (vii)   the standard fixed overhead cost absorbed by the actual 5,760 ferry crossings.

(b)   Using the data provided in the operating results and your answers to part (a), calculate the following variances:

    (i)   the material price variance for the fuel
    (ii)   the material usage variance for the fuel
    (iii)   the labour rate variance
    (iv)   the labour efficiency variance
    (v)   the fixed overhead expenditure variance
    (vi)   the fixed overhead volume variance
    (vii)   the fixed overhead capacity variance
    (viii)   the fixed overhead efficiency variance.

(c)   Prepare a statement reconciling the actual cost of operations to the standard cost of operations for the year to 30 November 2000.

Data

On receiving your reconciliation statement, the Chief Executive is concerned about the large number of adverse variances. She is particularly concerned about the excessive cost of fuel used during the year. A colleague informs you that:

- the actual market price of fuel per litre during the year was 20 per cent higher than the standard price

- fuel used directly varies with the number of operating hours

- the difference between the standard and actual operating hours for the 5,760 ferry crossings arose entirely because of weather conditions.

Task 1.2

Write a memo to the Chief Executive. Your memo should:

(a)   subdivide the material price variance into:

      (i)   that part arising from the standard price being different from the actual market price of fuel, and
      (ii)   that part due to other reasons

(b)   identify ONE variance which is not controllable and give ONE reason why the variance is not controllable

(c)   identify TWO variances which are controllable and which should be investigated. For each variance, give ONE reason why it is controllable.

UNIT 8 – SECTION 2 – JUNE 1997

Suggested time allocation: 50 minutes.

Data

The Cam Car Company is a multinational manufacturer of motor vehicles. It operates two divisions, one producing cars and the other producing vans. You are employed as a management accountant in the van division. The labour content for each type of vehicle is very similar although the material content of a car is much greater than that of a van. Both divisions apply straight–line depreciation to fixed assets.

You have been asked to prepare information to be used in the company's annual wage negotiations. Each year, the van employee representatives make comparisons with the car division and one of your tasks is to calculate performance indicators for your division. Financial and other information relating to both divisions is reproduced below along with some of the relevant performance indicators for the car division.

Balance sheet extracts at 31 May 1997

	Van division			Car division		
	Cost	Depreciation to date	Net	Cost	Depreciation to date	Net
	£m	£m	£m	£m	£m	£m
Buildings at cost	500	400	100	1,200	240	960
Plant and machinery at cost	400	320	80	800	240	560
	900	720	180	2,000	480	1,520
Stock		60			210	
Trade debtors		210			285	
Cash		(140)			150	
Trade creditors		(30)			(265)	
			100			380
Net assets			280			1,900

Profit and loss accounts
For year to 31 May 1997

	Van division		Car division	
	£m	£m	£m	£m
Turnover		420		1,140
Materials and bought–in components	95		790	
Production labour	110		138	
Other production expenses	26		32	
Depreciation – buildings	10		24	
Depreciation – plant and machinery	40		80	
Administrative expenses	27		28	
		308		1,092
Profit		112		48

Other information

	Van division	Car division
Vehicles produced	50,000	84,000
Number of production employees	10,000	12,000

Yearly performance indicators for the car division

Return on capital employed	2.53%	Profit margin	4.21%
Asset turnover	0.6 times	Profit per employee	£4,000
Wages per employee	£11,500	Output per employee	7 vehicles
Production labour cost per unit	£1,643	Added value per employee	£29,167

Task 2.1

You have been asked to calculate the yearly performance indicators for the van division and to present them in a table with the comparable figures for the car division.

Data

Shortly after preparing the performance indicators, you receive a telephone call from Peter Ross, a member of the management team. Peter explains that the employee representatives of the van division wish to negotiate an increase in wages. The representatives are arguing that employees in the van division are paid less than the equivalent staff in the car division despite the van division being more profitable. In addition, the representatives state that their productivity is higher than in the car division. Peter explains that he is not an accountant. He is not clear how productivity is measured or what is meant by added value.

Task 2.2

You are asked to write a memo to Peter Ross. The memo should:

(a)   briefly explain what is meant by:

      (i)   productivity
      (ii)   added value

(b)   identify those performance indicators that could be used by the employees of the van division to justify their claims in terms of

      (i)   profitability
      (ii)   productivity

(c)   give ONE example from the performance indicators that could be used to counter those claims and use the financial data given in task 2.1 to identify one possible limitation to the indicator

(d)   use BOTH the return on capital employed AND the added value per employee to show why the indicators calculated in task 2.1 might be overstated.

UNIT 8 – SECTION 2 – DECEMBER 1997

Suggested time allocation: 50 minutes.

Data

The Grand Hotel is a privately–owned hotel and restaurant located in a major business and tourist centre. Because of this, demand for accommodation is spread evenly throughout the year. However, in order to increase overall demand, the Grand Hotel has recently joined World Rest, an association of similar hotels. World Rest publicises member hotels throughout the world and provides advice and control to ensure common standards amongst its members. In addition, it provides overall performance indicators by location and category of hotel, allowing members to compare their own performance.

You are employed by Green and Co, the Grand Hotel's auditors, and your firm has been asked to calculate the hotel's performance statistics required by World Rest. A colleague informs you that the Grand Hotel:

- operates for 365 days of the year
- has 80 double or twin bedrooms
- charges £80 per night for each bedroom
- charges guests separately for any meals taken.

Your colleague also gives you a copy of World Rest's performance indicators' manual. The manual details the performance indicators required and gives guidance on their calculation. The relevant performance indicators and a summary of Grand Hotel's latest set of accounts are reproduced below.

Extract from World Rest's performance indicators' manual

Indicator	Definitions
Maximum occupancy	Number of days in year × number of bedrooms
Occupancy rate	Annual total of rooms let per night as percentage of maximum occupancy
Gross margin: accommodation	Contribution from accommodation ÷ accommodation turnover
Gross margin: restaurant	Contribution from restaurant ÷ restaurant turnover
Operating profit: hotel	Profit before interest but after all other expenses
Sales margin: hotel	Operating profit ÷ total turnover
Return on capital employed: hotel	Operating profit ÷ net assets
Asset turnover: hotel	Standard definition

GRAND HOTEL

Profit and loss account – 12 months ended 30 November 1997

	Accommodation £	Restaurant £	Total £
Turnover	1,635,200	630,720	2,265,920
Variable costs	1,308,160	473,040	1,781,200
Contribution	327,040	157,680	484,720
Fixed costs			
Depreciation – land and buildings			24,000
Depreciation – fixtures and fittings			29,000
Administration			160,224
Rates and insurance			158,200
Debenture interest			80,000
Profit for the year			33,296

Extract from the balance sheet at 30 November 1997

Fixed assets	Land and buildings £	Fixtures and fittings £	Total £
Net book value	1,200,000	145,000	1,345,000
Net current assets			
Debtors		594,325	
Cash		88,125	
Creditors		(611,250)	
			71,200
Net assets			1,416,200

Task 2.1

Your colleague asks you to calculate the performance indicators list in the Data above for the Grand Hotel using the definitions laid down by World Rest.

Data

A few days later you receive a letter from Claire Hill, the manager of the Grand Hotel. She enclosed a summary sent to her by the World Rest organisation showing the average performance indicators for hotels in similar categories and locations. This is reproduced below.

World Rest Hotel Association Performance Summary	
Location Code B	**Category Code** 4
Occupancy rate	80%
Gross margin: accommodation	22%
Gross margin: restaurant	20%
Sales margin: hotel	10%
Return on capital employed: hotel	20%
Asset turnover: hotel	2 times

In her letter to you, Claire Hill expresses her concern about the performance of the Grand Hotel and provides you with the following information:

- The restaurant is currently working at maximum capacity. Any volume improvement must, therefore, come from the accommodation side of the hotel's activities.

- It is not possible to change the level of the fixed assets nor the net current assets without adversely affecting the business.

Claire Hill proposes increasing the return on capital employed to 20% by:

- increasing the occupancy rate to 80% of capacity while maintaining current prices, and

- increasing restaurant prices by 5% while decreasing the restaurant's variable costs by 5% without any change in demand.

Task 2.2

Write a letter to Claire Hill. Your letter should:

(a)   calculate the operating profit required on the existing capital employed to give a 20% return

(b)   show the revised profit of the Grand Hotel if she achieves *both* her proposed occupancy rate and her proposed changes to the restaurant's pricing and costing structure

(c)   list the following revised performance indicators assuming her proposals are achieved without changing the amount of the capital employed:

- return on capital employed
- asset turnover, and
- sales margin

(d)   use the performance indicators calculated in (c) to suggest:

(i)   what proportion of the planned increase in profits is due to the increased occupancy rates and what proportion is due to the change in the restaurant's pricing and costing structure

(ii)   ONE possible area of investigation if profits are to be further increased.

UNIT 8 – SECTION 2 – DECEMBER 1998

Data

You are employed by Micro Circuits Ltd as a financial analyst reporting to Angela Frear, the Director of Corporate Strategy. One of your responsibilities is to monitor the performance of subsidiaries within the group. Financial and other data relating to subsidiary A is reproduced below.

SUBSIDIARY A

Profit and loss account year to 30 November 1998	£'000	£'000
Sales		4,000
Less returns		100
		———
Turnover[1]		3,900
Material	230	
Labour	400	
Production overheads[2]	300	
	———	
Cost of production	930	
Opening finished stock	50	
Closing finished stock	(140)	
Cost of sales		840
	———	
Gross profit		3,060
Marketing	500	
Customer support	400	
Research and development	750	
Training	140	
Administration	295	2,085
	———	———
Operating profit		975

Extract from balance sheet at 30 November 1998

	Land and Buildings £'000	Plant and Machinery £'000	Total £'000
Fixed Assets			
Cost	2,000	2,500	4,500
Additions	–	1,800	1,800
	———	———	———
	2,000	4,300	6,300
Accumulated depreciation	160	1,700	1,860
	———	———	———
	1,840	2,600	4,440

	£'000	£'000
Raw material stock	15	
Finished goods stock	140	
	———	
	155	
Debtors	325	
Cash & Bank	40	
Creditors	(85)	
		435
	———	———
Net assets		4,875
		———

Other information

Notes

1. *Analysis of turnover*

	£'000		£'000
Regular customers	3,120	New product	1,560
New customers	780	Existing products	2,340
	———		———
	3,900		3,900

2. *Production overheads include £37,200 of reworked faulty production.*

3. *Orders received in the year totalled £4,550,000.*

Task 2.1

Angela Frear asks you to calculate the following performance indicators in preparation for a board meeting:

(a)   the return on capital employed
(b)   the asset turnover
(c)   the sales (or operating profit) margin
(d)   the average age of debtors in months
(e)   the average age of finished stock in months.

◆ FOULKS*lynch*

Data

One of the issues to be discussed at the board meeting is the usefulness of performance indicators. Angela Frear has recently attended a conference on creating and enhancing value.

Three criticisms were made of financial performance indicators:

- they could give misleading signals
- they could be manipulated
- they focus on the short term and do not take account of other key, non–financial performance indicators.

At the conference, Angela was introduced to the idea of the balanced scorecard. The balanced scorecard looks at performance measurement from four perspectives:

The financial perspective
This is concerned with satisfying shareholders. Examples include the return on capital employed and sales margin.

The customer perspective
This asks how customers view the business and is concerned with measures of customer satisfaction. Examples include speed of delivery and customer loyalty.

The internal perspective
This looks at the quality of the company's output in terms of technical excellence and customer needs. Examples would be striving towards total quality management and flexible production as well as unit cost.

The innovation and learning perspective
This is concerned with the continual improvement of existing products and the ability to develop new products as customers' needs change. An example would be the percentage of turnover attributable to new products.

Task 2.2

Angela Frear asks you to prepare briefing notes for the board meeting. Using the data from task 2.1 where necessary, your notes should:

(a)   suggest ONE reason why the return on capital employed calculated in task 2.1 might be misleading

(b)   identify ONE way of manipulating the sales (or operating profit) margin

(c)   calculate the average delay in fulfilling orders

(d)   identify ONE other possible measure of customer satisfaction other than the delay in fulfilling orders

(e)   calculate TWO indicators which may help to measure performance from an internal perspective

(f)   calculate ONE performance indicator which would help to measure the innovation and learning perspective.

UNIT 8 – SECTION 2 – JUNE 1999

Data

You are employed by ALV Ltd as an accounting technician. Two companies owned by ALV Ltd are ALV (East) Ltd and ALV (West) Ltd.   These two companies are located in the same town and make an identical electrical product which sells for £84.

Financial data relating to the two companies is reproduced below and on the following page. In addition, performance indicators for ALV (East) Ltd are also enclosed. Both companies use the same straight–line depreciation policy and assume no residual value.

ALV (East) Ltd					
Extract from balance sheet at 31 May 1999				**Income statement – year to 31 May 1999**	
	Cost £'000	*Accumulated depreciation* £'000	*Net book value* £'000		£'000
Fixed assets					
Buildings	1,000	700	300	Turnover	840
Plant and machinery	300	240	60		
	——	——	——	Material and bought–in services	340
	1,300	940	360	Production labour	180
	——	——		Other production expenses	52
Net current assets				Depreciation – buildings	20
Stock		45		Depreciation – plant and machinery	30
Debtors		30		Administration and other expenses	50
Cash		5			——
Creditors		(40)	40	Operating profit	168
		——	——		——
			400		
			——		
Other data					
Number of employees		18		Units produced	10,000
Performance indicators for ALV (East) Ltd					
Asset turnover		2.1 times		Production labour cost per unit	£18.00
Net profit margin		20.00%		Output per employee	556
Return on capital employed		42.00%		Added value per employee	£27,778
Wages per employee		£10,000		Profit per employee	£9,333

ALV (West) Ltd

Extract from balance sheet at 31 May 1999				Income statement – year to 31 May 1999	
	Cost £'000	*Accumulated depreciation* £'000	*Net book value* £'000		£'000
Fixed assets					
Buildings	1,500	120	1,380	Turnover	2,520
Plant and machinery	900	180	720		
	2,400	300	2,100	Material and bought–in services	1,020
				Production labour	260
				Other production expenses	630
Net current assets				Depreciation – buildings	30
Stock		20		Depreciation – plant and machinery	90
Debtors		30		Administration and other expenses	112
Cash		5			
Creditors		(55)	nil	Operating profit	378
			2,100		
Other data					
Number of employees		20		Units produced	30,000

ALV Ltd is considering closing one of the companies over the next two years. As a first step, the board of directors wish to hold a meeting to consider which is the more efficient and productive company.

Task 2.1

In preparation for the board meeting, calculate the following performance indicators for ALV (West) Ltd:

(a)   asset turnover
(b)   net profit margin
(c)   return on capital employed
(d)   wages per employee
(e)   production labour cost per unit
(f)   output per employee
(g)   added value per employee
(h)   profit per employee.

Data

Shortly after preparing the performance indicators for ALV (West) Ltd, the chief executive of ALV Ltd, Jill Morgan, issued a statement to a local newspaper. In that statement, she said that the workforce at ALV (East) was far less productive than at the other company despite both companies making an identical product. She concluded that it was up to the workforce to improve productivity. In response, the employees stated that the normal way of measuring efficiency is profit and, therefore, ALV (East) was more efficient than ALV (West).

Jill Morgan asks you to prepare a report for the next board meeting to explain the issues involved so that all board members can be properly briefed.

Task 2.2

Write a report to Jill Morgan for distribution to the board of directors. Your report should:

(a)   explain what is meant by:

      (i)   productivity
      (ii)   efficiency

(b)   identify the best TWO performance indicators used by ALV to measure efficiency and use those indicators to identify which of the two companies is the more efficient

(c)   identify the best TWO performance measures used by ALV to measure productivity and use those indicators to identify which of the two companies has the higher productivity

(d)   use the NET FIXED ASSETS to derive a different measure of productivity for both companies

(e)   use the data in task 2.1 and your answer to task 2.2(d) to explain ONE reason why the productivity and efficiency measures might give different rankings.

UNIT 8 – SECTION 2 – DECEMBER 1999

Data

You are employed as a financial analyst with Denton Management Consultants and report to James Alexander, a local partner. Denton Management Consultants has recently been awarded the contract to implement accrual accounting in the St Nicolas Police Force and will shortly have to make a presentation to the Head of the Police Force. The presentation is concerned with showing how performance indicators are developed in 'for profit' organisations and how these can be adapted to help 'not for profit' organisations.

James Alexander has asked for your help in preparing a draft of the presentation that Denton Management Consultants will make to the Head of the Police Force. He suggests that a useful framework would be the balanced scorecard and examples of how this is used by private sector organisations.

The balanced scorecard views performance measurement in a 'for profit' organisation from four perspectives.

The financial perspective
This is concerned with satisfying shareholders and measures used include the return on capital employed and the sales margin.

The customer perspective
This attempts to measure how customers view the organisation and how they measure customer satisfaction. Examples include the speed of delivery and customer loyalty.

The internal perspective
This attempts to measure the quality of the organisation's output in terms of technical excellence and consumer needs. Examples include unit cost and total quality measurement.

The innovation and learning perspective
This emphasises the need for continual improvement of existing products and the ability to develop new products to meet customers' changing needs. In a 'for profit' organisation, this might be measured by the percentage of turnover attributable to new products.

To help you demonstrate how performance indicators are developed in 'for profit' organisations, he gives you the following financial data relating to a manufacturing client of Denton Management Consultants:

Profit and loss account – 12 months ended 30 November 1999

	£'000	£'000
Turnover		240.0
Material	18.0	
Labour	26.0	
Production overheads	9.0	
	———	
Cost of production	53.0	
Opening finished stock	12.0	
Closing finished stock	(13.0)	
	———	
Cost of sales		52.0
		———
Gross profit		188.0
Research and development	15.9	
Training	5.2	
Administration	118.9	
	———	
		140.0
		———
Net profit		48.0
		———

Extract from Balance sheet at 30 November 1999

Fixed assets	£'000 Opening balance	£'000 Additions	£'000 Deletions	£'000 Closing balance
Cost	200.0	40.0	10.0	230.0
Depreciation	80.0	8.0	8.0	80.0
				———
Net book value				150.0

Net Current assets		
Stock of finished goods		13.0
Debtors		40.0
Cash		6.0
Creditors		(9.0)
		———
		50.0
Net assets		200.0
		———

Task 2.1

James Alexander asks you to calculate the following performance indicators and, for each indicator, to identify ONE balanced scorecard perspective being measured:

(a)   the return on capital employed
(b)   the sales margin (or net profit) percentage
(c)   the asset turnover
(d)   research and development as a percentage of production
(e)   training as a percentage of labour cost
(f)   average age of finished stock in months.

Data

On receiving your calculations, James Alexander tells you that he has recently received details of the current performance measures used by the St Nicolas Police Force. Four indicators are used:

*   the percentage of cash expenditure to allocated funds for the year
*   the average police–hours spent per crime investigated
*   the average police–hours spent per crime solved
*   the clear–up rate (defined as number of crimes solved ÷ number of crimes investigated.)

He also provides you with data for the current year used in developing the current indicators, as follows:

* funds allocated for the year:	$3,000,000
* cash expenditure during the year	$2,910,000
* number of reported crimes in the last year	8,000 crimes
* number of crimes investigated in the year	5,000 crimes
* number of crimes solved in the year	2,000 crimes
* number of police–hours spent on investigating and solving crimes	40,000 hours
* number of police hours spent on crime prevention	500 hours

Task 2.2

James Alexander asks you to prepare short notes for him. Your notes should:

(a)   calculate the four indicators currently used by the St Nicolas Police Force

(b)   identify ONE limitation in the calculation of the clear–up rate

(c)   briefly suggest:

   (i)   ONE reason why the percentage of cash expenditure to allocated funds may be an inadequate measure of the financial perspective

   (ii)   ONE reason why the clear–up rate might be an inadequate measure of the customer perspective other than because of the limitation identified in part (b)

   (iii)   ONE reason why the hours spent per crime investigated might be an inadequate measure of the internal perspective

   (iv)   ONE measure which might focus on the innovation and learning perspective.

◈ FOULKS*lynch*

UNIT 8 – SECTION 2 – JUNE 2000

Data

LandAir and SeaAir are two small airlines operating flights to Waltonville. LandAir operates from an airport based at a town on the same island as Waltonville but SeaAir operates from an airport based on another island. In both cases, the flight to Waltonville is 150 air–miles. Each airline owns a single aircraft, an 80–seat commuter jet, and both airlines operate flights for 360 days per year.

You are employed as the management accountant at SeaAir and report to Carol Jones, SeaAir's chief executive. Recently, both airlines agreed to share each other's financial and operating data as a way of improving efficiency. The data for the year to 31 May 2000 for both airlines is reproduced below. The performance indicators for LandAir are also reproduced below.

Operating statement year ended 31 May 2000	LandAir $'000	SeaAir £'000
Revenue	51,840	29,700
Fuel and aircraft maintenance	29,160	14,580
Take–off and landing fees at Waltonville	4,320	2,160
Aircraft parking at Waltonville	720	2,880
Depreciation of aircraft	500	400
Salaries of flight crew	380	380
Home airport costs	15,464	8,112
Net profit	1,296	1,188

Extract from balance sheet at 31 May 2000	LandAir $'000	SeaAir £'000
Fixed assets		
Aircraft	10,000	10,000
Accumulated depreciation	2,500	4,000
Net book value	7,500	6,000
Net current assets	3,300	5,880
	10,800	11,880

Other operating data		
Number of seats on aircraft	80	80
Return flights per day	12	6
Return fare	$200	$275
Air–miles per return flight	300	300

Performance indicators	Landair
Return on capital employed	12.00%
Asset turnover per year	4.80
Sales (or net profit) margin	2.50%
Actual number of return flights per year	4,320
Actual number of return passengers per year	259,200
Average seat occupancy [1]	75.00%
Actual number of passenger–miles [2]	77,760,000
Cost per passenger mile	$0.65

Notes

(1)   Actual number of return passengers ÷ maximum possible number of return passengers from existing flights.

(2)   Actual number of passengers carried × number of miles flown.

◇ FOULKS*lynch*

Task 2.1

Carol Jones asks you to prepare the following performance indicators for SeaAir:

(a)   return on capital employed
(b)   asset turnover
(c)   sales (or net profit) margin
(d)   actual number of return flights per year
(e)   actual number of return passengers per year
(f)   average seat occupancy
(g)   actual number of passenger–miles
(h)   cost per passenger mile.

Data

Carol Jones is concerned that the overall performance of SeaAir is below that of LandAir, despite both airlines operating to the same destination and over a similar distance. She finds it all the more difficult to understand as LandAir has to compete with road and rail transport. Carol Jones has recently attended a seminar on maintaining competitive advantage and is eager to apply the concepts to SeaAir. She explains that there are two ways to gain a competitive advantage:

* by being the lowest cost business, or
* by having a unique aspect to the product or service, allowing a higher price to be charged.

This involves managers attempting to eliminate costs which do not enhance value, that is costs for which customers are not prepared to pay either in the form of a higher price or increased demand.

She makes the following proposals for next year, the year ending 31 May 2001:

* the number of return flights is increased to 9 per day
* the estimated average seat occupancy will change to 55%
* the price of a return fare will remain the same.

As a result of the proposals, there will be some changes in operating costs:

* fuel and aircraft maintenance, and take–off and landing fees at Waltonville airport, will increase in proportion with the increase in flights

* aircraft parking at Waltonville will be halved

* aircraft depreciation will increase to $600,000 for the forthcoming year

* additional flight crew will cost an extra $58,000

* there will be no other changes in costs.

Task 2.2

Carol Jones is interested in forecasting the performance of SeaAir for next year, the year to 31 May 2001. Write a memo to Carol Jones. In your memo you should:

(a)   calculate the forecast number of passengers next year for SeaAir

(b)   calculate SeaAir's forecast net profit for next year

(c)   show SeaAir's forecast return on capital employed for next year assuming no change in its net assets other than any additional depreciation

(d)   identify ONE competitive advantage SeaAir has over LandAir

(e)   identify ONE expense in SeaAir's operating statement which does not add value.

◆ FOULKS*lynch*

UNIT 8 – SECTION 2 – DECEMBER 2000

Data

Travel Bus Ltd is another company owned by Travel Holdings plc. It operates in the town of Camford. Camford is an old town with few parking facilities for motorists. Several years ago, the Town Council built a car park on the edge of the town and awarded Travel Bus the contract to carry motorists and their passengers between the car park and the centre of the town.

Originally, the Council charged motorists £4.00 per day for the use of the car park but, to encourage motorists not to take their cars into the town centre, parking has been free since 1 December 1999.

The journey between the car park and the town centre is the only service operated by Travel Bus Ltd in Camford. A summary of the results for the first two years of operations, together with the net assets associated with the route and other operating data, is reproduced below.

Operating statement year ended 30 November

	1999 £	2000 £
Turnover	432,000	633,600
Fuel	129,600	185,328
Wages	112,000	142,000
Other variable costs	86,720	84,512
Gross profit	103,680	221,760
Bus road tax and insurance	22,000	24,000
Depreciation of buses	12,000	12,000
Maintenance of buses	32,400	28,512
Fixed garaging costs	29,840	32,140
Administration	42,000	49,076
Net profit/(loss)	(34,560)	76,032

Extract from Balance sheet at 30 November

	1999 £	2000 £
Buses	240,000	240,000
Accumulated depreciation	168,000	180,000
Net book value	72,000	60,000
Net current assets	14,400	35,040
	86,400	95,040

Other operating data	1999	2000
Fare per passenger per journey	£0.80	£1.00
Miles per year	324,000	356,400
Miles per journey	18.0	18.0
Days per year	360	360
Wages per driver	£14,000	£14,200

Throughout the two years, the drivers were paid a basic wage per week, no bonuses were paid and no overtime was incurred.

In two weeks there will be a meeting between officials of the Town Council and the Chief Executive of Travel Holdings to discuss the performance of Travel Bus for the year to 30 November 2000. The previous year's performance indicators were as follows:

Gross profit margin	24%
Net profit margin	–8%
Return on capital employed	–40%
Asset turnover	5 times
Number of passengers in the year	540,000
Total cost per mile	£1.44
Number of journeys per day	50
Maintenance cost per mile	£0.10
Passengers per day	1,500
Passengers per journey	30
Number of drivers	8

Task 2.1

In preparation for the meeting, you have been asked to calculate the following performance indicators for the year to 30 November 2000:

(a)   gross profit margin
(b)   net profit margin
(c)   return on capital employed
(d)   asset turnover
(e)   number of passengers in the year
(f)   total cost per mile
(g)   number of journeys per day
(h)   maintenance cost per mile
(i)   passengers per day
(j)   passengers per journey
(k)   number of drivers.

Data

On receiving your performance indicators, the Chief Executive of Travel Holdings raises the following issues with you:

- the drivers are claiming that the improved profitability of Travel Bus reflects their increased productivity

- the managers believe that the change in performance is due to improved motivation arising from the introduction of performance related pay for managers during the year to 30 November 2000

- the officials from the Town Council are concerned that Travel Bus is paying insufficient attention to satisfying passenger needs and safety.

The Chief Executive asks for your advice.

Task 2.2

Write a memo to the Chief Executive of Travel Holdings plc. Where relevant, you should make use of the data and answers to Task 2.1 to:

(a)   *briefly* discuss whether or not increased productivity always leads to increased profitability

(b)   develop ONE possible measure of driver productivity and suggest whether or not the drivers' claim is valid

(c)   suggest ONE reason, other than improved motivation, why the profitability of Travel Bus might have improved

(d)   suggest:

  (i)   ONE *existing* performance indicator which might measure the satisfaction of passenger needs, and

  (ii)   ONE other possible performance indicator of passenger needs which cannot be measured from the existing performance data collected by Travel Bus

(e)   suggest:

  (i)   ONE existing performance indicator which might measure the safety aspect of Travel Bus's operations, and

  (ii)   ONE other possible safety performance indicator which cannot be measured from the existing performance data collected by Travel Bus.

UNIT 9 – SECTION 1 – JUNE 1997

SECTION 1 (Suggested time allocation: 70 minutes)

Data

The Viking Smelting Company established a division, called the reclamation division, in April 1995, to extract silver from jewellers' waste materials. The waste materials are processed in a furnace, enabling silver to be recovered. The silver is then further processed into finished products by three other divisions within the company.

A performance report is prepared each month for the reclamation division which is then discussed by the management team. Sharon Houghton, the newly appointed financial controller of the reclamation division, has recently prepared her first report for the four weeks to 31 May 1997. This is shown below.

Performance Report – Reclamation Division – 4 weeks to 31 May 1997					
	Actual	*Budget*	*Variance*		*Comments*
Production (tonnes)	200	250	50	(F)	
	£	£	£		
Wages and social security costs	46,133	45,586	547	(A)	Overspend
Fuel	15,500	18,750	3,250	(F)	
Consumables	2,100	2,500	400	(F)	
Power	1,590	1,750	160	(F)	
Divisional overheads	21,000	20,000	1,000	(A)	Overspend
Plant maintenance	6,900	5,950	950	(A)	Overspend
Central services	7,300	6,850	450	(A)	Overspend
Total	100,523	101,386	863	(F)	

(A) = adverse, (F) = favourable

In preparing the budgeted figures, the following assumptions were made for May:

- the reclamation division was to employ four teams of six production employees

- each employee was to work a basic 42 hour week and be paid £7.50 per hour for the four weeks of May

- social security and other employment costs were estimated at 40% of basic wages

- a bonus, shared amongst the production employees, was payable if production exceeded 150 tonnes. This varied depending on the output achieved:

  - if output was between 150 and 199 tonnes, the bonus was £3 per tonne produced
  - if output was between 200 and 249 tonnes, the bonus was £8 per tonne produced
  - if output exceeded 249 tonnes the bonus was £13 per tonne produced

- the cost of fuel was £75 per tonne

- consumables were £10 per tonne

- power comprised a fixed charge of £500 per four weeks plus £5 per tonne for every tonne produced

- overheads directly attributable to the division were £20,000

- plant maintenance was to be apportioned to divisions on the basis of the capital values of each division

◇ **FOULKS**lynch

- the cost of Viking's central services was to be shared equally by all four divisions.

You are the deputy financial controller of the reclamation division. After attending her first monthly meeting with the board of the reclamation division, Sharon Houghton arranges a meeting with you. She is concerned about a number of issues, one of them being that the current report does not clearly identify those expenses and variances which are the direct responsibility of the reclamation division.

Task 1.1

Sharon Houghton asks you to prepare a flexible budget report for the reclamation division for May 1997 in a form consistent with responsibility accounting.

Data

On receiving your revised report, Sharon tells you about the other questions raised at the management meeting when the original report was presented. These are summarised below:

(i)   Why are the budget figures based on 2–year–old data taken from the proposal recommending the establishment of the reclamation division?

(ii)   Should the budget data be based on what we were proposing to do or what we actually did do?

(iii)   Is it true that the less we produce the more favourable our variances will be?

(iv)   Why is there so much maintenance in a new division with modern equipment and why should we be charged with the actual costs of the maintenance department even when they overspend?

(v)   Could the comments, explaining the variances, be improved?

(vi)   Should all the variances be investigated?

(vii)   Does showing the cost of central services on the divisional performance report help control these costs and motivate the Divisional managers?

Task 1.2

Prepare a memo for the management of the reclamation division. Your memo should:

(a)   answer their queries and justify your comments

(b)   highlight the main objective of your revised performance report developed in task 1.1 and give two advantages of it over the original report.

UNIT 9 – SECTION 1 – DECEMBER 1997

SECTION 1   (Suggested time allocation: 70 minutes)

Data

Eskafeld Industrial Museum opened ten years ago and soon became a market leader with many working exhibits. In the early years there was a rapid growth in the number of visitors. However, with no further investment in new exhibits, this growth has not been maintained in recent years.

Two years ago, John Derbyshire was appointed as the museum's chief executive. His initial task was to increase the number of visitors to the museum and, following his appointment, he has made several improvements to make the museum more successful.

Another of John's tasks is to provide effective financial management. This year, the museum's Board of Management has asked him to take full responsibility for producing the 1998 budget. One of his first tasks is to prepare estimates of the number of visitors next year. John had previously played only a limited role in budget preparation and so he turns to you, an accounting technician, for advice.

He provides you with the following information:

(Suggested time allocation: 70 minutes)

- previous budgets had assumed a 10% growth in attendance but this has been inaccurate
- very little is known about the visitors to the museum
- the museum keeps details of the number of visitors by quarter but this has never been analysed
- the number of visitors per quarter for the last two years is as follows:

Year	Quarter	Number of Visitors
1996	1	5,800
	2	9,000
	3	6,000
	4	14,400
1997	1	6,600
	2	9,800
	3	6,800
	4 (Estimate)	15,200

Task 1.1

(a)   Calculate the *Centred Four–Point Moving Average Trend* figures and the seasonal variations.

(b)   Construct a graph showing the trend line and actual number of visitors, by quarter, for presentation to the Board of Management.

(c)   Estimate the forecast number of visitors for each quarter of 1998, assuming that there is the same trend and seasonal variations for 1998.

(d)   Prepare notes on forecasting for John Derbyshire. Your notes should:

(i)   identify TWO ways to improve the forecasting of visitor numbers and highlight any limitations to your proposals

(ii)   explain why telephone sampling might be preferable to using postal questionnaires

(iii)   explain how the concept of the product life cycle could be applied to the museum.

◆ FOULKS*lynch*

Data

Shortly after receiving your notes, John Derbyshire contacts you. He explains that he had prepared a draft budget for the Board of Management based on the estimated numbers for 1998. This had been prepared on the basis that:

- most of the museum's expenses such as salaries and rates are fixed costs
- the museum has always budgeted for a deficit
- the 1998 deficit will be £35,000.

At the meeting with the Board of Management, John was congratulated on bringing the deficit down from £41,000 in 1996 to £37,000 (latest estimate) in 1997. However the Board of Management raised two issues:

- they felt that the planned deficit of £35,000 should be reduced to £29,000 as this would represent a greater commitment

- they also queried why the budget had been prepared without any consultation with the museum staff, ie, a top down approach.

Task 1.2

Draft a memo to John Derbyshire. Your memo should:

(a)   discuss the motivational implications of imposing the budget reduction from £35,000 to £29,000
(b)   consider the arguments for and against using a top–down budgeting approach for the museum.

UNIT 9 – SECTION 1 – DECEMBER 1998

Data

Amber Ltd is a subsidiary of Colour plc and makes a single product, the Delta. Budgets are prepared by dividing the accounting year into 13 periods, each of four weeks. Amber's policy is to avoid overtime payments wherever possible and this was one of the assumptions built into the preparation of Amber's budget for this year. However, some overtime payments have been necessary.

Helen Roy, Amber's finance director, has recently carried out an investigation and discovered why overtime has been paid. She found that the labour hours available over each four–week period were more than sufficient to meet the four–weekly production targets. However, *within* any four–week period, production levels could vary considerably. As a result, in some weeks, overtime had to be paid.

You are employed in the management accounting section of Colour plc as an assistant to Helen Roy. Although Helen did not have the next period's *production* volume analysed by individual week, she was able to explain the problem by showing you the forecast *sales* of Deltas over each of the next four weeks. These are reproduced below.

Week	1	2	3	4
Forecast *sales* of Deltas (units)	23,520	27,440	28,420	32,340

Helen Roy also gives the following information.

- Amber's maximum production capacity per week before overtime and rejections is 30,400 Deltas.

- For technical reasons, production has to take place at least one week before it is sold.

- At present, all production takes place exactly one week before it is sold.

- Sales cannot be delayed to a subsequent week.

- The weekly fixed cost of wages before overtime is £21,280.

- Overtime is equivalent to £2 per unit produced in excess of 30,400 Deltas.

- The cost of material per Delta is £5.

- There is a 2% rejection rate in the manufacture of Deltas. Rejected Deltas are only discovered on completion and have no monetary value.

- Budgeted fixed production overheads for the year are estimated to be £3,792,825. These are absorbed on the basis of an estimated annual production before rejections of 1,685,700 Deltas.

Task 1.1

Helen Roy asks you to prepare Amber's WEEKLY production budgets for weeks 1 to 3 on the current basis that all production takes place exactly one week before it is sold. The budget should identify:

(a)   the number of Deltas to be produced in each of the three weeks
(b)   the cost of any overtime paid
(c)   the cost of production for each of the three weeks, including fixed production overheads.

Data

You give Helen Roy Amber's production budget for the next three weeks. She now tells you that it may be possible to save at least some of the overtime payments by manufacturing some Deltas in advance of the normal production schedule. However, any Deltas made earlier than one week before being sold will incur financing costs of 20p per Delta per week.

Task 1.2

Helen Roy asks you to calculate:

(a)   the number of Deltas to be produced in each of the three weeks if the overall costs are to be minimised

(b)   the net savings if your revised production plan in (a) is accepted.

UNIT 9 – SECTION 1 – JUNE 1999

Data

Wilmslow Ltd makes two products, the Alpha and the Beta. Both products use the same material and labour but in different amounts. The company divides its year into four quarters, each of twelve weeks. Each week consists of five days and each day comprises 7 hours.

You are employed as the management accountant to Wilmslow Ltd and you originally prepared a budget for quarter 3, the twelve weeks to 17 September 1999. The basic data for that budget is reproduced below.

Original budgetary data: quarter 3 12 weeks to 17 September 1999		
Product	**Alpha**	**Beta**
Estimated demand	1,800 units	2,100 units
Material per unit	8 kilograms	12 kilograms
Labour per unit	3 hours	6 hours

Since the budget was prepared, three developments have taken place.

1   The company has begun to use linear regression and seasonal variations to forecast sales demand. Because of this, the estimated demand for quarter 3 has been revised to 2,000 Alphas and 2,400 Betas.

2   As a result of the revised sales forecasting, you have developed more precise estimates of sales and closing stock levels.

- The sales volume of both the Alpha and Beta in quarter 4 (the twelve weeks ending 10 December 1999) will be 20% more than in the revised budget for quarter 3 as a result of seasonal variations.

- The closing stock of finished Alphas at the end of quarter 3 should represent **5 days sales** for quarter 4.

- The closing stock of finished Betas at the end of quarter 3 should represent **10 days sales** for quarter 4.

- Production in quarter 4 of both Alpha and Beta is planned to be 20% more than in the revised budget for quarter 3. The closing stock of materials at the end of quarter 3 should be sufficient for **20 days production** in quarter 4.

3   New equipment has been installed. The workforce is not familiar with the equipment. Because of this, for quarter 3, they will only be working at 80% of the efficiency assumed in the original budgetary data.

Other data from your original budget which has not changed is reproduced below:

- 50 production employees work a 35 hour week and are each paid £210 per week

- overtime is paid for at £9 per hour

- the cost of material is £10 per kilogram

- opening stocks at the beginning of quarter 3 are as follows:

  - finished Alphas   500 units

  - finished Betas   600 units

  - material   12,000 kilograms

◆ FOULKS*lynch*

- there will not be any work in progress at any time.

Task 1.1

The production director of Wilmslow Ltd wants to schedule production for quarter 3 (the twelve weeks ending 17 September 1999) and asks you to use the revised information to prepare the following:

(a)   the revised production budget for Alphas and Betas
(b)   the material purchases budget in kilograms
(c)   a statement showing the cost of the material purchases
(d)   the labour budget in hours
(e)   a statement showing the cost of labour.

Data

Margaret Brown is the financial director of Wilmslow Ltd. She is not convinced that the use of linear regression, even when adjusted for seasonal variations, is the best way of forecasting sales volumes for Wilmslow Ltd.

The quality of sales forecasting is an agenda item for the next meeting of the Board of Directors and she asks for your advice.

Task 1.2

Write a *brief* memo to Margaret Brown. Your memo should:

(a)   identify TWO limitations of the use of linear regression as a forecasting technique
(b)   suggest TWO other ways of sales forecasting.

UNIT 9 – SECTION 1 – DECEMBER 1999

Data

You have recently been promoted to the post of management accountant with Northern Products Ltd, a company formed four years ago. The company has always used budgets to help plan its production of two products, the Exe and Wye. Both products use the same material and labour but in different proportions.

You have been asked to prepare the budget for quarter 1, the twelve weeks ending 24 March 2000. In previous budgets, the closing stocks of both raw materials and finished products were the same as opening stocks. You questioned whether or not this was the most efficient policy for the company.

As a result, you have carried out an investigation into the stock levels required to meet the maximum likely sales demand for finished goods and production demand for raw materials. You conclude that closing stocks of finished goods should be expressed in terms of days sales for the next quarter and closing stocks of raw materials in terms of days production for the next quarter.

Your findings are included in the data below, which also shows data provided by the sales and production directors of Northern Products Ltd.

Product data	Exe	Wye
• Budgeted sales in units, quarter 1	930 units	1,320 units
• Budgeted sales in units, quarter 2	930 units	1,320 units
• Budgeted material per unit (litres)	6 litres	9 litres
• Budgeted labour hours per unit	12 hours	7 hours
• Opening units of finished stock	172 units	257 units
• Closing units of finished stocks (days sales next quarter)	8 days	9 days
• Failure rate of finished production*	2%	3%
• Finance and other costs of keeping a unit in stock per quarter	£4.00	£5.00

     * Failed products are only discovered on completion of production and have no residual value.

Other accounting data

• Weeks in accounting period	12 weeks
• Days per week for production and sales	5 days
• Hours per week	35 hours
• Number of employees	46 employees
• Budgeted labour rate per hour	£6.00
• Overtime premium for hours worked in excess of 35 hours per week	30%
• Budgeted cost of material per litre	£15.00
• Opening raw material stocks (litres)	1,878 litres
• Closing raw material stocks (days production next quarter)	5 days
• Financing and other costs of keeping a litre of raw material in stock per quarter	£1.00

Task 1.1

(a) Calculate the following information for quarter 1, the twelve weeks ending 24 March 2000:

     (i)   the number of production days
     (ii)   the closing finished stock for Exe and Wye in units
     (iii)   the labour hours available before overtime has to be paid.

(b) Prepare the following budgets for quarter 1, the twelve weeks ending 24 March 2000:

     (i)   the production budget in units for Exe and Wye, including any faulty production
     (ii)   the material purchases budget in litres and value
     (iii)   the production labour budget in hours and value, including any overtime payments.

(c)   Calculate the savings arising from the change in the required stock levels for the twelve weeks ending 24 March 2000.

Data

On completing the budget for quarter 1, the production director of Northern Products Ltd tells you that the company is likely to introduce a third product, the Zed, in the near future. Because of this, he suggests that future budgets should be prepared using a spreadsheet. He explains that the use of spreadsheets to prepare budgets not only saves time but also provides flexibility by allowing the results of changes in the budget to be readily shown. The sales director is not convinced.

The production director suggests you demonstrate the advantages of budgets prepared on spreadsheets by using a template of a spreadsheet and sales data for the planned third product.

He gives you the following sales data he has received from the sales director:

- estimated annual volume for Zed: 20,000 units
- planned unit selling price: £90.00
- seasonal variations:

Quarter	Seasonal variation percentage change
1	+20%
2	+30%
3	-10%
4	-40%

Task 1.2

(a)   Calculate the budgeted volume of Zed for each quarter.

(b)   Using the information provided by the sales director and a copy of the suggested spreadsheet template reproduced below, express the data provided by the sales director as formulae which would enable revised sales budgets to be calculated with the minimum of effort if sales price and annual volume were to change. (You may amend the template if desired to suit any spreadsheet with which you are familiar.)

A	B	C	D	E	F
1	Unit selling price	£90			
2	Annual volume	20,000			
3	Seasonal variations	20%	30%	-10%	-40%
4		Quarter 1	Quarter 2	Quarter 3	Quarter 4
5	Seasonal variations (units)				
6	Quarterly volume				
7	Quarterly turnover				

UNIT 9 – SECTION 1 – JUNE 2000

Data

You are employed as a management accountant in the head office of Alton Products plc. One of your tasks involves helping to prepare quarterly budgets for the divisional companies of Alton Products. Each quarter consists of 12 five–day weeks for both production and sales purposes.

One division, Safety Care, makes two chemicals, *Delta and Omega*. These are sold in standard boxes. Both products use the same material and labour but in different proportions. You have been provided with the following information relating to the two products for quarter 3, the 12 weeks ending 29 September 2000.

		Delta	*Omega*
•	**Budgeted sales**		
	Quarter 3: 12 weeks to 29 September 2000	3,000 boxes	2,400 boxes
	Quarter 4: 12 weeks to 22 December 2000	3,300 boxes	2,640 boxes
•	**Finished stocks for quarter 3**	*Delta*	*Omega*
	Opening stock	630 boxes	502 boxes
	Closing stock (days sales in quarter 4)	6 days	8 days
•	**Production inputs**	*Delta*	*Omega*
	Material per box	12 kilograms	15 kilograms
	Labour per box	3 hours	6 hours
•	**Material stocks and costs for quarter 3**		
	Opening stock (kilograms)	13,560	
	Closing stock (kilograms)	21,340	
	Budgeted purchase price per kilogram	£7.00	

• **Labour costs for quarter 3**
   52 production employees work a 36–hour week and are each paid £180 per week.
   Any overtime is payable at £7.50 per hour.

• **Faulty production**
   10% of production is found to be faulty on completion. Faulty production has to be scrapped and has no scrap value.

Task 1.1

The production director of Safety Care asks you to prepare the following for quarter 3:

(a)   the number of boxes of *Delta* and *Omega* planned to be in closing stock
(b)   the number of labour hours available for production before incurring overtime
(c)   the production budget for *Deltas* and *Omegas* required to meet the budgeted sales
(d)   the material purchases budget in kilograms and cost
(e)   the labour budget in hours and cost.

Data

Garden Care is another division of Alton Products plc. The sales director of Garden Care, Hazel Brown, has noticed a distinct trend and pattern of seasonal variations for one of Garden Care's products since the product was introduced in the third quarter of 1997. She provides you with the following sales volumes for the product.

UNITS SOLD BY QUARTER				
Year	Quarter 1	Quarter 2	Quarter 3	Quarter 4
1997			142	142
1998	150	150	142	158
1999	150	166	142	174
2000	150	182*		
				* estimate

Task 1.2

Hazel Brown asks you to:

(a)   calculate the *Centred Four–Point Moving Average Trend* figures

(b)   calculate the seasonal variations on the assumption that the seasonal variations are additive

(c)   use your results in (a) and (b) to forecast the sales volume for quarter 2 of year 2000

(d)   suggest TWO reasons why there might be a difference between the forecast figure calculated in (c) and the result given in the data.

UNIT 9 – SECTION 1 – DECEMBER 2000

Data

You are a management accountant employed by Aspen Ltd and you report to Adrian Jones, the managing director. One of your responsibilities is the production of budgets. Aspen Ltd only has one customer, Advanced Industries plc, for whom it makes the Omega, a specialist product. Advanced Industries demands that Aspen keeps a minimum closing stock of Omegas in case there is an error in the forecast requirements. There is no work–in–progress at any time.

- Both companies divide the year into four–week periods. Each week consists of five days and each day comprises eight hours.

- Advanced Industries plc has recently informed Aspen Ltd of its Omega requirements for the five periods ending Friday 25 May 2001. The details are reproduced below.

Forecast demand for Omegas

Four weeks ending:	2 February	2 March	30 March	27 April	25 May
	Period 1	Period 2	Period 3	Period 4	Period 5
Number of Omegas required	5,700	5,700	6,840	6,460	6,080

Closing stocks of Omegas
Closing stocks are to equal 3 days of the next period's demand for Omegas.

The production director gives you the following information:

- The actual opening stocks for period 1, the four weeks ending 2 February, will be 1,330 Omegas

- Each Omega requires 6 litres of material

- The material is currently supplied under a long–term contract at a cost of £8.00 per litre and is made exclusively for Aspen by Contrax plc

- Contrax only has sufficient production capacity to make a maximum of 34,000 litres in any four–week period. Aspen normally purchases the material in the same four–week period it is used

- Should Aspen require more than 34,000 litres in a four–week period, Contrax would be willing to supply additional material in the preceding period, providing it had spare capacity

- There is a readily available source for the material but the cost is £12.00 per litre

- Before buying from the alternative source, any shortage of material in a period should be overcome, where possible, by first purchasing extra material from Contrax in the **immediately preceding** period

- There are 78 production employees who are paid a guaranteed basic wage of £160 per 40–hour week

- Each Omega should take 2 labour–hours to make but, due to temporary technical difficulties, the workforce is only able to operate at 95 per cent efficiency in periods 1 to 4

- Any overtime incurred is payable at a rate of £6.00 per hour.

Task 1.1

Adrian Jones asks you to prepare the following budgets for each of the periods 1 to 4:

(a)   the production budget in Omegas, using the stock levels given in the data
(b)   the material purchases budget in litres
(c)   the cost of the material purchases
(d)   the labour budget in hours, including any overtime hours
(e)   the cost of the labour budget, including the cost of any overtime.

◆ FOULKS*lynch*

Data

On receiving your budgets, Adrian Jones, the managing director, tells you that:

- he is concerned about the cost of the planned overtime and the extra cost of purchasing materials from the alternative supplier

- the minimum demand in any four–week period is forecast to be 5,700 Omegas

- it is not possible to reduce costs by Advanced Industries plc improving its current method of forecasting.

However, he believes that some immediately and long–term cost savings are possible.

Task 1.2

Write a memo to Adrian Jones. In your memo, you should:

(a)   use the budget information prepared in Task 1.1 to identify ONE immediate possible cost saving proposal other than renegotiating the conditions imposed by Advanced Industries plc

(b)   calculate the value of the cost savings in the proposal identified in part (a)

(c)   use the forecast minimum demand for Omegas to show whether or not:

   (i)   the need to obtain material supplies from the alternative source is a short–term problem, and
   (ii)   the need for overtime payments is also a short–term problem

(d)   suggest TWO cost savings which may be possible in the longer term.

UNIT 9 – SECTION 2 – JUNE 1997

You are advised to spend approximately 50 minutes on Section 2. All essential workings should be included within your answers, where appropriate.

Data

The Pickerings Canning Company produces a range of canned savoury and sweet products. The company prepares its budgets annually. The cost accountant has recently left and you, as the assistant cost accountant, have been requested to take over the responsibility of budget preparation. The managers of the company need the information quickly but they realise that the full budget will take too long to prepare. Because of this, a short–term budget for the month of September is requested. Before leaving, the cost accountant provided you with the following information:

- the only product which will be produced during the month is Apple Pie Filling and 80,000 cans per month are required by customers

- the apples are purchased whole and there is approximately 50% waste in production

- the net amount of apple in 1,000 cans is 100kg

- at the final stage of the production process 5% of the cans are damaged and they are sold to employees

- the labour required to produce 1,000 cans is 6 hours

- each employee works 38 hours per week

- the employees are currently in dispute with the company and there is 10% absenteeism. This problem is likely to continue for the foreseeable future

- the employees are paid £4 per hour

- the buyer at the company has provided prices for the apples but these are estimates mainly based on the actual figures for last year

    – the basic price of apples is budgeted at £200 per tonne for August

    – an internal index of apple prices for last year for the same period was:

    1996
    August   120
    September   125

Task 2.1

For the month of September 1997:

(a)   prepare a materials purchases budget (at basic price):

(b)   prepare a labour budget in terms of numbers of employees

(c)   assuming the rate of price increase is the same this year as last year, recalculate the cost of materials purchased.

Data

The budget has been discussed with the production manager and he is concerned about two issues, namely:

- How useful are the materials price indices supplied by the buyer for budgeting the costs of materials?

- Given that the wages costs are significant, what information should be supplied daily, weekly and monthly to control this area?

Task 2.2

Prepare a memo for the production manager. Your memo should:

- address the issues of concern
- suggest and justify an alternative method for predicting materials prices.

UNIT 9 – SECTION 2 – DECEMBER 1997

Suggested time allocation: 50 minutes.

Data

George Phillips makes and sells two types of garden ornament, the Alpha and the Beta. George prepared his 1998 budget several months ago but since then he has discovered that there is a shortage of raw material used for making the ornaments. As a result, he will only be able to acquire 20,000 kilograms of the raw material for the first 13 weeks of 1998.

An extract from his original budget is reproduced below:

Sales budget

	Units	Selling Price	Turnover
Alpha	6,500	£36.00	£234,000
Beta	7,800	£39.00	£304,200

Extract from the production budget

	Units produced	Material per unit	Total material
Alpha	6,900	2.0 kg	13,800 kg
Beta	9,000	1.5 kg	13,500 kg
Materials issued to production			27,300 kg

Purchases budget

	Kilograms	Price per kilogram	Total cost
Materials issued to production	27,300	£5.00	£136,500
Opening stock	(6,000)	£5.00	(£30,000)
Closing stock	6,600	£5.00	£33,000
Purchases	27,900		£139,500

Labour budget

	Units Produced	Labour hours per unit	Total hours
Alpha	6,900	2.500	17,250
Beta	9,000	2.785	25,065
Labour hours			42,315
Labour cost			£169,260

◈ FOULKS*lynch*

George also provides you with additional information:

- the budget is based on a 13-week period

- employees work a 35-hour week

- the closing stocks of materials and finished products must be kept to the figures in the original budget

- the original sales budget represents the maximum demand for the Alpha and the Beta in a 13-week period.

Task 2.1

You are the recently appointed accounting trainee at the company. George Phillips asks you to revise his budget for the first 13 weeks of 1998 to take account of the shortage of the raw materials. You should prepare the budgets for:

(a)   materials purchases
(b)   materials issued to production
(c)   sales volume and turnover
(d)   labour hours and cost
(e)   the number of employees required.

Data

On reviewing the revised figures George realises that there are too many employees and he calls a meeting of the managers of the business. During the meeting the following issues are raised:

- The production manager does not wish to reduce the number of employees as he will lose key trained staff who may not wish to be re–employed later. He argues that the labour costs are fixed as the employees are not employed on a piece work basis.

- In preparing the original budget George had been advised by one of the partners at the firm's auditors that the key factor should be identified before the budget was prepared. He had assumed that sales would be a key factor and therefore the budget had been based on sales this was invalid since materials are now the limiting factor.

- George complains that the original budget took many hours to prepare and he seeks your advice on the benefits of using a relevant spreadsheet package.

Task 2.2

You have been requested to prepare a report covering the issues raised by George Phillips and his managers at the meeting.

UNIT 9 – SECTION 2 – DECEMBER 1998

Data

Colour plc has two more subsidiaries, Red Ltd and Green Ltd. Red Ltd makes only one product, a part only used by Green Ltd. Because Green is the only customer and there is no market price for the part, the part is sold to Green at cost.

Last year, Red prepared two provisional budgets because Green was not certain how many parts it would buy from Red in the current year. These two budgets are reproduced below.

Red Ltd provisional budgets 12 months to 30 November 1998		
Volume (units)	18,000	20,000
	£	£
Material	180,000	200,000
Labour	308,000	340,000
Power and maintenance	33,000	35,000
Rent, insurance and depreciation	98,000	98,000
	619,000	673,000

Shortly afterwards, Green told Red that it needed 20,000 parts over the year to 30 November 1998. Red's budget for the year was then based on that level of production.

During the financial year, Green Ltd only bought 19,500 parts. Red's performance statement for the year to 30 November 1998 is reproduced below.

Red Ltd performance statement – year to 30 November 1998			
	Budget	Actual	Variances
Volume (units)	20,000	19,500	
	£	£	£
Material	200,000	197,000	3,000 (F)
Labour	340,000	331,000	9,000 (F)
Power and maintenance	35,000	35,000	–
Rent, insurance and depreciation	98,000	97,500	500 (F)
Total cost	673,000	660,500	12,500 (F)

Key: (F) = favourable, (A) = adverse

Task 2.1

(a)   Using the data in the provisional budgets, calculate the fixed and variable cost elements within each of the expenditure headings.

(b)   Using the data in the performance statement and your solution to part (a), prepare a revised performance statement using flexible budgeting. Your statement should show both the revised budget and the variances.

Data

Colour plc is about to introduce performance–related payments for all senior managers in the three subsidiaries. The purpose is to motivate senior managers to improve performance.

For Red Ltd, the additional payments will be based on two factors:

- achieving or exceeding annual budgeted volumes of production set by the Board of Directors of Colour plc at the beginning of the year

- keeping unit costs below budget.

Tony Brown, the managing director of Red Ltd, is about to call a meeting of his senior managers to discuss the implications of the proposals. He is not certain that performance–related pay will automatically lead to improved performance in the subsidiaries. Even if it does, he is not certain that performance–related pay will help *his* subsidiary improve performance.

Task 2.2

Write a memo to Tony Brown. Your memo should identify:

(a)   THREE general conditions necessary for performance–related pay to lead to improved performance

(b)   TWO reasons why the particular performance scheme might not be appropriate to the senior management of Red Ltd

(c)   ONE example where it would be possible for the managers of Red Ltd to misuse the proposed system by achieving performance–related pay without extra effort on their part.

UNIT 9 – SECTION 2 – JUNE 1999

Data

Rivermede Ltd makes a single product called the Fasta. Last year, Steven Jones, the managing director of Rivermede Ltd, attended a course on budgetary control. As a result, he agreed to revise the way budgets were prepared in the company. Rather than imposing targets for managers, he encouraged participation by senior managers in the preparation of budgets.

An initial budget was prepared but Mike Fisher, the sales director, felt that the budgeted sales volume was set too high. He explained that setting too high a budgeted sales volume would mean his sales staff would be demotivated because they would not be able to achieve that sales volume. Steven Jones agreed to use the revised sales volume suggested by Mike Fisher.

Both the initial and revised budgets are reproduced below complete with the actual results for the year ended 31 May 1999.

Rivermede Ltd – budgeted and actual costs for the year ended 31 May 1999

	Original budget	Revised budget	Actual results	Variances from revised budget
Fasta production and sales (units)	24,000	20,000	22,000	2,000 (F)
	£	£	£	£
Variable costs				
Material	216,000	180,000	206,800	26,800 (A)
Labour	288,000	240,000	255,200	15,200 (A)
Semi–variable costs				
Heat, light and power	31,000	27,000	33,400	6,400 (A)
Fixed costs				
Rent, rates and depreciation	40,000	40,000	38,000	2,000 (F)
	575,000	487,000	533,400	46,400 (A)

Assumptions in the two budgets

– No change in input prices
– No change in the quantity of variable inputs per Fasta

As the management accountant at Rivermede Ltd, one of your tasks is to check that invoices have been properly coded. On checking the actual invoices for heat, light and power for the year to 31 May 1999, you find that one invoice for £7,520 had been incorrectly coded. The invoice should have been coded to materials.

Task 2.1

(a)   Using the information in the original and revised budgets, identify:

- the variable cost of material and labour per Fasta
- the fixed and unit variable cost within heat, light and power.

(b)   Prepare a flexible budget, including variances, for Rivermede Ltd after correcting for the miscoding of the invoice.

Data

On receiving your flexible budget statement, Steven Jones states that the total adverse variance is much less than the £46,400 shown in the original statement. He also draws your attention to the actual sales volume being greater than in the revised budget. He believes these results show that a participative approach to budgeting is better for the company and wants to discuss this belief at the next board meeting. Before doing so, Steven Jones asks for your comments.

Task 2.2

Write a memo to Steven Jones. Your memo should:

(a)   *briefly* explain why the flexible budgeting variances differ from those in the original statement given in the data to task 2.1

(b)   give TWO reasons why a favourable cost variance may have arisen other than through the introduction of participative budgeting

(c)   give TWO reasons why the actual sales volume compared with the revised budget's sales volume may not be a measure of improved motivation following the introduction of participative budgeting.

UNIT 9 – SECTION 2 – DECEMBER 1999

Data

HFD plc opened a new division on 1 December 1998. The division, HFD Processes Ltd, produces a special paint finish. Because of the technology, there can never be any work in progress. The original budget was developed on the assumption that there would be a loss in the initial year of operation and that there would be no closing stock of finished goods.

One year later, HFD Processes Ltd prepared its results for its first year of operations. The chief executive of HFD plc was pleased to see that, despite budgeting for an initial loss, the division had actually returned a profit of £74,400. As a result, the directors of HFD Processes were entitled to a substantial bonus. Details of the budget and actual results are reproduced below.

HFD Processes Ltd Operating results – year ended 30 November 1999

	Budget		Actual	
Volume (units)		20,000		22,000
	£	£	£	£
Turnover		960,000		1,012,000
Direct costs				
Material	240,000		261,800	
Production labour	260,000		240,240	
Light, heat and power	68,000		65,560	
	568,000		567,600	
Fixed overheads	400,000		370,000	
Cost of sales		968,000		937,600
Operating profit/(loss)		(8,000)		74,400

You are employed as a management accountant in the head office of HFD plc and have been asked to comment on the performance of HFD Processes Ltd. Attached to the budgeted and actual results were the relevant working papers. A summary of the contents of the working papers is reproduced below.

- The budget assumed no closing finished stocks. Actual production was 25,000 units and actual sales 22,000 units.

- Because of the technology involved, production employees are paid per week, irrespective of production levels. The employees assumed in the budget are capable of producing up to 26,000 units.

- The cost of material varies directly with production.

- The cost of light, heat and power includes a fixed standing charge. In the budget this fixed charge was calculated to be £20,000 per year. However, competition resulted in the supplier reducing the actual charge to £12,000 for the year.

- During the year, HFD Processes Ltd produced 25,000 units. The 3,000 units of closing finished stock were valued on the basis of direct cost plus 'normal' fixed overheads:

  - the number of units was used to apportion direct costs between the cost of sales and closing finished stock

  - the budgeted fixed overhead of £20 per unit was used to calculate the fixed overheads in closing finished stocks

◇ FOULKS*lynch*

- The detailed composition of the cost of sales and closing stocks using these policies was:

	Closing finished stocks	Cost of sales	Cost of production
Units	3,000	22,000	25,000
	£	£	£
Material	35,700	261,800	297,500
Production Labour	32,760	240,240	273,000
Light, heat and power	8,940	65,560	74,500
Fixed overheads	60,000	370,000	430,000
	137,400	937,600	1,075,000

Task 2.1

(a)   Calculate the following:

(i)   the budgeted unit selling price
(ii)   the budgeted material cost per unit
(iii)   the budgeted marginal cost of light, heat and power per unit
(iv)   the actual marginal cost of light, heat and power per unit.

(b)   Prepare a flexible budget statement for the operating results of HFD Processes Ltd using a *marginal costing* approach, identifying fixed costs for the year and showing any variances.

Data

You present your flexible budget statement to the chief executive of HFD plc who is concerned that your findings appear different to those in the original operating results.

Task 2.2

You are asked to write a *brief* memo to the chief executive. In your memo, you should:

- give TWO reasons why the flexible budget operating statement shows different results from the original operating results
- give ONE reason why the flexible budget operating statement might be a better measure of management performance than the original operating results.

◆ FOULKS*lynch*

UNIT 9 – SECTION 2 – JUNE 2000

Data

Visiguard Ltd is another division of Alton Products plc. It makes a single product, the Raider. Just over a year ago, the chief executive of Alton Products, Mike Green, was concerned to find that Visiguard was budgeting to make only £20,000 profit in the year to 31 May 2000. As a result, he imposed his own budget on the division. His revised budget assumed:

- increased sales volume of the Raider
- increased selling prices, and
- that suppliers would agree to reduce the cost of the material used in the Raider by 10%.

The only other changes to the original budget arose solely as a result of the increased volume in the revised budget.

The original budget and the revised budget imposed by Mike Green are reproduced below, together with the actual results for the year to 31 May 2000.

Visiguard Limited: Budgeted and actual operating statements for one year ended 31 May 2000

	Original budget	Revised budget	Actual results
Sales and production volume	10,000	11,000	11,600
	£	£	£
Turnover	1,400,000	1,760,000	1,844,400
Variable materials	400,000	396,000	440,800
Production and administrative labour	580,000	630,000	677,600
Light, heat and power	160,000	164,000	136,400
Fixed overheads	240,000	240,000	259,600
Budgeted profit	20,000	330,000	330,000

Task 2.1

Using the information provided in the two budgets, calculate the following:

(a)   the unit selling price of the Raider in the revised budget
(b)   the material cost per Raider in the revised budget
(c)   the variable cost of production and administrative labour per Raider
(d)   the fixed cost of production and administrative labour
(e)   the variable cost of light, heat and power per Raider
(f)   the fixed cost of light, heat and power.

Data

On receiving the actual results for the year, Mike Green states that they prove that his revised budget motivated managers to produce better results.

Task 2.2

Write a memo to Mike Green . Your memo should:

(a)   use the information calculated in task 2.1 to prepare a flexible budget statement for Visiguard including any variances

(b)   identify TWO situations where an imposed budget might be preferable to one prepared with the participation of managers

(c)   briefly discuss whether or not his requirement that material costs be reduced would have motivated the managers of Visiguard

(d)   identify TWO ways in which profit could have increased without additional effort by the managers of Visiguard.

UNIT 9 – SECTION 2 – DECEMBER 2000

Data

You have recently been appointed as the management accountant of Parkside Manufacturing Ltd. Parkside Manufacturing makes a single product, the Delta. The previous management accountant has already prepared an analysis of budgeted and actual results for the year to 30 November 2000. These are reproduced below.

Parkside Manufacturing Ltd
Operating Statement for year ended 30 November 2000

	Budget		Actual		Variance
Volume (number of Deltas)	100,000		125,000		
	£'000	£'000	£'000	£'000	£'000
Turnover		2,000		2,250	250 (F)
Material	600		800		200 (A)
Light, heat and power	200		265		65 (A)
Production labour	120		156		36 (A)
Rent, rates and depreciation	140		175		35 (A)
Administrative expenses	110		110		nil
		1,170		1,506	
Profit		830		744	86 (A)

Key: (F) = favourable
     (A) = adverse

Judith Green, the production director, tells you that the following assumptions were made when the budget was originally prepared:

- material is entirely a variable cost

- light, heat and power is a semi–variable cost. The fixed element included in the budgeted figure was £40,000

- production labour is a stepped cost. Each production employee can make up to 10,000 Deltas. Each production employee was budgeted to receive a basic wage of £12,000 per year with no overtime and no bonuses

- there are no part–time employees

- rent, rates and depreciation, and administrative expenses are fixed costs.

Task 2.1

(a)   In preparation for the next Board meeting of Parkside Manufacturing Ltd, calculate the:

    (i)   budgeted cost of material per Delta
    (ii)   budgeted variable cost per Delta of light, heat and power
    (iii)   number of production employees assumed in the budget.

(b)   Prepare a statement which compares the actual results of Parkside Manufacturing with the flexible budget, and identify any variances.

Data

On receiving your flexible budget and variances, Judith Green tells you that:

- she does not understand why there is a need for the two types of budget, the one prepared by the previous management accountant and the flexible budget prepared by yourself

- she does not know if it is necessary to investigate all variances

- she is concerned that the original budgeted sales volume was so different from the actual sales volume and is considering the use of linear regression to improve sales forecasting of Deltas.

Task 2.2

Judith Green asks you to write a brief report in preparation for the Board meeting. In your report, you should:

(a)   briefly explain the different purposes of the two types of budget, and explain which one should be used to compare with the actual results

(b)   suggest THREE general factors that need to be taken into account in deciding whether or not to investigate variances

(c)   briefly explain THREE limitations to the use of linear regression in sales forecasting.

UNIT 16 – SECTION 1 – DECEMBER 1996

Suggested time allocation: 55 minutes.

Data

York plc was formed three years ago by a group of research scientists to market a new medicine that they had invented. The technology involved in the medicine's manufacture is both complex and expensive. Because of this, the company is faced with a high level of fixed costs.

This is of particular concern to Dr Harper, the company's chief executive. She recently arranged a conference of all management staff to discuss company profitability. Dr Harper showed the managers how average unit cost fell as production volume increased and explained that this was due to the company's heavy fixed cost base. 'It is clear,' she said, 'that, as we produce closer to the plant's maximum capacity of 70,000 packs, the average cost per pack falls. Producing and selling as close to that limit as possible must be good for company profitability.' The data she used is reproduced below.

Production volume (packs)	40,000	50,000	60,000	70,000
Average cost per unit*	£430	£388	£360	£340

Current sales and production volume: 65,000 packs

Selling price per pack: £420

*Defined as the total of fixed and variable costs, divided by the production volume.

You are a member of York plc's management accounting team and shortly after the conference you are called to a meeting with Ben Cooper, the company's marketing director. He is interested in knowing how profitability changes with production.

Task 1.1

Ben Cooper asks you to calculate:

(a)   the amount of York plc's fixed costs
(b)   the profit of the company at its current sales volume of 65,000 packs
(c)   the break–even point in units
(d)   the margin of safety expressed as a percentage.

Data

Ben Cooper now tells you of a discussion he has recently had with Dr Harper. Dr Harper had once more emphasised the need to produce as close as possible to the maximum capacity of 70,000 packs. Ben Cooper has the possibility of obtaining an export order for an extra 5,000 packs but, because the competition is strong, the selling price would only be £330. Dr Harper has suggested that this order should be rejected as it is below cost and so will reduce company profitability. However, she would be prepared, on this occasion, to sell the packs on a cost basis for £340 each, provided the order was increased to 15,000 packs.

Task 1.2

Write a memo to Ben Cooper. Your memo should:

(a)   calculate the change in profits from accepting the order for 5,000 packs at £330

(b)   calculate the change in profits from accepting an order for 15,000 packs at £340

(c)   briefly explain and justify which proposal, if either, should be accepted

(d)   identify TWO non–financial factors which should be taken into account before making a final decision.

UNIT 16 – SECTION 1 – JUNE 1997

Suggested time allocation: 70 minutes.

Data

You are employed as an accounting technician by Smith, Williams and Jones, a small firm of accountants and registered auditors. One of your clients is Winter plc, a large department store. Judith Howarth, the purchasing director for Winter plc, has gained considerable knowledge about bedding and soft furnishings and is considering acquiring her own business.

She has recently written to you requesting a meeting to discuss the possible purchase of Brita Beds Limited. Brita Beds has one outlet in Mytown, a small town 100 miles from where Judith works. Enclosed with her letter was Brita Beds' latest profit and loss account. This is reproduced below.

Brita Beds Ltd

Profit and loss account – year to 31 May 1997

Sales	Units	£
Model A	1,620	336,960
Model B	2,160	758,160
Model C	1,620	1,010,880
		—————
Turnover		2,106,000

Expenses	£	
Cost of beds	1,620,000	
Commission	210,600	
Transport	216,000	
Rates and insurance	8,450	
Light, heat and power	10,000	
Assistants' salaries	40,000	
Manager's salary	40,000	2,145,050
	—————	
Loss for year		39,050
		—————

Also included in the letter was the following information:

- Brita Beds sells three types of bed, models A to C inclusive.

- Selling prices are determined by adding 30% to the cost of beds.

- Sales assistants receive a commission of 10% of the selling price for each bed sold.

- The beds are delivered in consignments of 10 beds at a cost of £400 per delivery. This expense is shown as *Transport* in the profit and loss account.

- All other expenses are annual amounts.

- The mix of models sold is likely to remain constant irrespective of overall sales volume.

Task 1.1

In preparation for your meeting with Judith Howarth, you are asked to calculate:

(a)   the minimum number of beds to be sold if Brita Beds is to avoid making a loss
(b)   the minimum turnover required if Brita Beds is to avoid making a loss.

Data

At the meeting Judith Howarth provides you with further information:

- the purchase price of the business is £300,000

- Judith has savings of £300,000 currently earning 5% interest per annum which she can use to acquire Brita Beds

- her current salary is £36,550.

To reduce costs, Judith suggests that she should take over the role of manager as the current one is about to retire. However, she does not want to take a reduction in income. Judith also tells you that she has been carrying out some market research. The results of this are as follows:

- the number of households in Mytown is currently 44,880

- Brita Beds Ltd is the only outlet selling beds in Mytown

- according to a recent survey, 10% of households change their beds every 9 years, 60% every 10 years and 30% every 11 years

- the survey also suggested that there is an average of 2.1 beds per household.

Task 1.2

Write a letter to Judith Howarth. Your letter should:

(a)   identify the profit required to compensate for the loss of salary and interest

(b)   show the number of beds to be sold to achieve that profit

(c)   calculate the likely maximum number of beds that Brita Beds would sell in a year

(d)   use your answers in (a) and (c) to justify whether or not Judith Howarth should purchase the company and become its manager

(e)   give TWO possible reasons why your estimate of the maximum annual sales volume may prove inaccurate.

Data

On receiving your letter, Judith Howarth decides she would prefer to remain as the purchasing director for Winter plc rather than acquire Brita Beds Ltd. Shortly afterwards, you receive a telephone call from her. Judith explains that Winter plc is redeveloping its premises and that she is concerned about the appropriate sales policy for Winter's bed department while the redevelopment takes place. Although she has a statement of unit profitability, this had been prepared before the start of the redevelopment and had assumed that there would be in excess of 800 square metres of storage space available to the bed department. Storage space is critical as customers demand immediate delivery and are not prepared to wait until new stock arrives.

The next day, Judith Howarth sent you a letter containing a copy of the original statement of profitability. This is reproduced below:

Model	A	B	C
Monthly demand (beds)	35	45	20
	£	£	£
Unit selling price	240.00	448.00	672.00
Unit cost per bed	130.00	310.00	550.00
Carriage inwards	20.00	20.00	20.00
Staff costs	21.60	40.32	60.48
Departmental fixed overheads	20.00	20.00	20.00
General fixed overheads	25.20	25.20	25.20
Unit profit	23.20	32.48	(3.68)
Storage required per bed (square metres)	3	4	5

In her letter, she asks for your help in preparing a marketing plan which will maximise the profitability of Winter's bed department while the redevelopment takes place. To help you, she has provided you with the following additional information:

• Currently storage space available totals 300 square metres.

• Staff costs represent the salaries of the sales staff in the bed department. Their total cost of £3,780 per month is apportioned to units on the basis of planned turnover.

• Departmental fixed overhead of £2,000 per month is directly attributable to the department and is apportioned on the number of beds planned to be sold.

• General fixed overheads of £2,520 are also apportioned on the number of beds planned to be sold. The directors of Winter plc believe this to be a fair apportionment of the store's central fixed overheads.

• The cost of carriage inwards and the cost of beds vary directly with the number of beds purchased.

Task 1.3

(a)   Prepare a recommended monthly sales schedule in units which will maximise the profitability of Winter plc's bed department.

(b)   Calculate the profit that will be reported per month if your recommendation is implemented.

◈ FOULKS*lynch*

UNIT 16 – SECTION 1 – DECEMBER 1997

Suggested time allocation: 75 minutes.

Data

Fortune plc has three divisions. One of these is the Taste division, which manufactures a flavouring ingredient used in the food industry. The ingredient is produced using a 24-hour continuous process. Because of this, total output cannot exceed 100,000 litres per year. Currently, this is not a problem as the Taste division is operating below capacity.

You are employed as the assistant management accountant in Fortune's head office. In seven days' time, the directors are meeting to consider the budgets for the forthcoming year. Reproduced below is the budgeted operating statement for the Taste division.

Taste Division
Budgeted Operating Statement for the year to 31 December 1998

	£000	£000
Turnover		16,000
Variable material	6,400	
Variable labour	3,200	
Variable overhead	1,600	
Fixed production overhead absorbed†	640	
		11,840
Gross profit		4,160
Sales commission (5% of turnover)	800	
Fixed selling expenses	600	
Fixed administration expenses	400	
Fixed production overhead unabsorbed†	160	
		1,960
Operating profit		2,200

† Fixed production overhead rates are based on maximum capacity

---

Task 1.1

In preparation for the meeting, you have been asked to provide the directors with additional information. (In providing this information, you should assume no change in unit selling price, no change in unit variable costs and no change in the cost of fixed expenses). The directors ask you to calculate the following:

(a)   Taste Division's budgeted sales volume in litres for the year to 31 December 1998
(b)   Taste Division's break–even point in litres and value
(c)   the percentage decrease in budgeted sales which will result in the division breaking even.

Data

Another division of Fortune plc is the Colouring Division. This division produces food colourings and also uses a 24–hour continuous process. Its maximum capacity – which cannot be exceeded – is 120,000 litres per year. The divisional management accountant gives you the working papers for the Colouring Division and a copy of this is shown below.

Working papers for the 1998 budget – Colouring Division	
Maximum capacity of division (litres)	120,000
Planned sales to existing customers (litres)	100,000
Marginal cost per litre	£60
Contribution per litre	£40
Divisional fixed costs	£2,400,000

He tells you that the Colouring Division has not been able to prepare its budget for 1998 as its sales manager is still considering a large special order from a new customer. He also gives you the following information:

- the special order is for a minimum of 30,000 litres

- the agreed price will be £90 per litre

- the Colouring Division is able to obtain an identical product to its own from a competitor in another country at a cost of £105 per litre inclusive of import duties and transport to the Colouring Division's premises.

Task 1.2

Write a brief memo to the sales manager of the Colouring Division. Your memo should:

(a)   identify the budgeted turnover and profitability of the Colouring Division if the special order is NOT accepted

(b)   show the change in budgeted profit of accepting the special order of 30,000 litres if:

(i)   the division is not allowed to purchase any of the product from the competitor
(ii)   the division is allowed to purchase from the competitor

(c)   identify TWO non–financial issues to be considered before making a final decision on the special order.

Data

Fortune's third division is the Packaging Division. This division blends ingredients. These are then sold to customers who then resell them to the public using their own brand names. The sales manager of the Packaging Division is considering accepting a contract and has asked for your advice. The customer has offered to pay £85,000 for the completed contract, but this is less than the estimated cost prepared by the sales manager. The estimate is reproduced below.

Proposed Contract – Estimated Costs		
Expenditure	*Quantity*	*Cost*
Material A	1,000 kilograms	£30,000
Material B	2,000 kilograms	£40,000
Labour	1,000 hours	£8,000
Divisional fixed overheads	1,000 hours	£8,000
		£86,000

A colleague of yours in the Packaging Division provides you with the following additional information:

- Material A is regularly used in the division. Its standard cost is £30 per kilogram, although the current purchase price is £28 per kilogram.

- Material B is no longer used in the business, although 500 kilograms are still in stock at its original cost of £20 per kilogram. This stock could be sold for £13,000. Its current purchase price is £28 per kilogram.

- There is a single class of labour throughout the division. Each production employee is paid a flat rate of £280 per 35–hour week, although for costing purposes this is converted to an hourly rate.

- Divisional fixed overheads are 100% of the labour rate.

- Employees working in excess of 35 hours are paid an overtime rate of £10 per hour.

- The division has a policy of no redundancies, although over the life of the contract there will be 900 spare labour hours because of a shortage of orders.

Task 1.3

Prepare notes for the sales manager. Your notes should:

(a)   recommend the minimum contract price which would avoid the Packaging Division making a loss

(b)   *briefly* explain the technique or techniques you have used to calculate the minimum contract price

(c)   explain how you used the technique or techniques to obtain the cost of the labour and the divisional fixed overheads.

UNIT 16 – SECTION 2 – DECEMBER 1996

Suggested time allocation: 65 minutes.

Data

The Portsmere Hospital operates its own laundry. Last year, the laundry processed 120,000 kilograms of washing and this year the total is forecast to grow to 132,000 kilograms. This growth in laundry processed is forecast to continue at the same percentage rate for the next seven years. Because of this, the hospital must immediately replace its existing laundry equipment. Currently, it is considering two options, the purchase of machine A or the rental of machine B. Information on both options is given below.

Machine A – purchase		Machine B – rent	
Annual capacity (kilograms)	180,000	Annual capacity (kilograms)	170,000
Material cost per kilogram	£2.00	Material cost per kilogram	£1.80
Labour cost per kilogram	£3.00	Labour cost per kilogram	£3.40
Fixed costs per annum	£20,000	Fixed costs per annum	£18,000
Life of machine	3 years	Rental per annum	£20,000
Capital cost	£60,000	Rental agreement	3 years
Depreciation per annum	£20,000	Depreciation	nil

Other information

(1)   The hospital is able to call on an outside laundry if there is either a breakdown or any other reason why the washing cannot be undertaken in–house. The charge would be £10 per kilogram of washing.

(2)   Machine A, if purchased, would have to be paid for immediately. All other cashflows can be assumed to occur at the end of each year.

(3)   Machine A will have no residual value at any time.

(4)   The existing laundry equipment could be sold for £10,000 cash.

(5)   The fixed costs are a direct cost of operating the laundry.

(6)   The hospital's discount rate for projects of this nature is 15%.

Task 2.1

You are an accounting technician employed by the Portsmere Hospital and you are asked to write a brief report to its chief executive. Your report should:

(a)   evaluate the two options for operating the laundry, using discounted cashflow techniques
(b)   recommend the preferred option and identify ONE possible non–financial benefit
(c)   justify your treatment of the £10,000 cash value of the existing equipment
(d)   explain what is meant by discounted cashflow.

Notes

Inflation can be ignored. An extract from the present value tables used by the hospital is reproduced below.

End of Year	Discounted factors 10%	15%	20%
1	0.909	0.870	0.833
2	0.826	0.756	0.694
3	0.751	0.658	0.579
4	0.683	0.572	0.482
5	0.621	0.497	0.402
6	0.564	0.432	0.335
7	0.513	0.376	0.279

UNIT 16 – SECTION 2 – JUNE 1997

Suggested time allocation: 50 minutes.

Data

Sound Equipment Ltd was formed five years ago to manufacture parts for hi–fi equipment. Most of its customers were individuals wanting to assemble their own systems. Recently, however, the company has embarked on a policy of expansion and has been approached by JBZ plc, a multinational manufacturer of consumer electronics. JBZ has offered Sound Equipment Ltd a contract to build an amplifier for its latest consumer product. If accepted, the contract will increase Sound Equipment's turnover by 20%.

JBZ's offer is a fixed price contract over three years although it is possible for Sound Equipment to apply for subsequent contracts. The contract will involve Sound Equipment purchasing a specialist machine for £150,000. Although the machine has a 10–year life, it would be written off over the 3 years of the initial contract as it can only be used in the manufacture of the amplifier for JBZ.

The production director of Sound Equipment has already prepared a financial appraisal of the proposal. This is reproduced below. With a capital cost of £150,000 and total profits of £60,300, the production director has calculated the return on capital employed as 40.2%. As this is greater than Sound Equipment's cost of capital of 18%, the production director is recommending that the board accepts the contract.

Proposal to build amplifier for JBZ plc				
	Year 1 £	Year 2 £	Year 3 £	Total £
Turnover	180,000	180,000	180,000	540,000
Materials	60,000	60,000	60,000	180,000
Labour	40,000	40,000	40,000	120,000
Depreciation	50,000	50,000	50,000	150,000
Pre–tax profit	30,000	30,000	30,000	90,000
Corporation tax at 33%	9,900	9,900	9,900	29,700
After tax profit	20,100	20,100	20,100	60,300

You are employed as the assistant accountant to Sound Equipment Ltd and report to John Green, the financial director, who asks you to carry out a full financial appraisal of the proposed contract. He feels that the production director's presentation is inappropriate. He provides you with the following additional information:

- Sound Equipment pays corporation tax at the rate of 33%

- the machine will qualify for a 25% writing down allowance on the reducing balance

- the machine will have no further use other than in manufacturing the amplifier for JBZ

- on ending the contract with JBZ, any outstanding capital allowances can be claimed as a balancing allowance

- the company's cost of capital is 18%

- the cost of materials and labour is forecast to increase by 5% per annum for years 2 and 3.

John Green reminds you that Sound Equipment operates a Just in Time stock policy and that production will be delivered immediately to JBZ who will, under the terms of the contract, immediately pay for the deliveries. He also reminds you that suppliers are paid immediately on receipt of goods and that employees are also paid immediately.

◈ FOULKS*lynch*

Task 2.1

Write a report to the financial director. Your report should:

(a)   use the net present value technique to identify whether or not the initial 3–year contract is worthwhile

(b)   explain your approach to taxation in your appraisal

(c)   identify ONE other factor to be considered before making a final decision.

Notes

For the purpose of this task, you may assume the following:

- the machine would be purchased at the beginning of the accounting year
- there is a one year delay in paying corporation tax
- all cashflows other than the purchase of the machine occur at the end of each year
- Sound Equipment has no other assets on which to claim capital allowances.

An extract from the present value tables used by Sound Equipment Ltd is reproduced below:

End of year	16%	17%	18%	19%	20%
1	0.862	0.855	0.847	0.840	0.833
2	0.743	0.731	0.718	0.706	0.694
3	0.641	0.624	0.609	0.593	0.579
4	0.552	0.534	0.516	0.499	0.482
5	0.476	0.456	0.437	0.419	0.402
6	0.410	0.390	0.370	0.352	0.335
7	0.354	0.333	0.314	0.296	0.279

UNIT 16 – SECTION 2 – DECEMBER 1997

Suggested time allocation: 45 minutes.

Data

You are an accounting technician employed in the management accounting department of Brendon Engineering Ltd and Ann Spring is the company's marketing director. Last week, she was offered a contract by a major customer. After discussing the details of the contract with Brendon Engineering's production director and the company's financial controller, she has turned to you for further advice. The contract would be for four years and Brendon Engineering would have to purchase a special machine costing £100,000. Although production would be 10,000 units in the first year, this would grow by 10% per year in each of the following three years. At the end of the fourth year, the machine would have no further use and its residual value would be negligible. Ann Spring's working papers are shown below.

Working papers	
Units to be produced and sold in the first year of the contract	10,000
Annual growth in sales volume and production	10%
Selling price per unit	£42
Material cost per unit	£20
Labour cost per year for production up to 12,000 units	£150,000
Labour cost per unit in excess of 12,000	£20
Annual rent of premises for each of the four years	£20,000
Apportionment of central overheads to contract	£1,000
Annual depreciation of machine purchased for the contract	£25,000

Ann Spring also provides you with the following information:

- a clause in the contract specifies that the customer must pay for units immediately on delivery

- Brendon Engineering pays suppliers on receipt of materials

- the company plans to carry no stocks for this contract

- employees' wages are paid in the period in which they are incurred

- Brendon Engineering's cost of capital is 30%

- if the contract is accepted, Brendon Engineering will have to rent premises as it is currently working at full capacity

- all cashflows – other than the initial outlay – can be assumed to occur at the end of each year.

Task 2.1

Ann Spring has asked you to prepare a report on the proposed contract. Your report should:

(a)   calculate the net present value of the proposed contract using Brendon Engineering's 30% cost of capital

(b)   calculate the net present value of the proposed contract using a discount rate of 70%

(c)   use the solutions to parts (a) and (b) to determine the internal rate of return for the contract

(d)   explain what is meant by the internal rate of return.

Notes

Inflation and risk can be ignored. An extract from the discounted cash flow tables used by Brendon Engineering Ltd is reproduced below.

End of year	Discount factors 30%	70%
1	0.769	0.588
2	0.592	0.346
3	0.455	0.204
4	0.350	0.120
5	0.269	0.070

PRACTICE CENTRAL ASSESSMENTS

QUESTIONS

◈ FOULKS*lynch*

TECHNICIAN STAGE

NVQ/SVQ LEVEL 4 IN ACCOUNTING

PRACTICE CENTRAL ASSESSMENT

CONTRIBUTING TO THE MANAGEMENT OF COSTS
AND THE ENHANCEMENT OF VALUE
(UNIT 8)

Time allowed – 2 hours plus 15 minutes' reading time

SECTION 1 (Suggested time allocation: 70 minutes)

Data

You are employed as an Accounting Technician by Bay Feeds Ltd, who manufacture animal foodstuffs. One of its products Pigplus uses a standard raw material P1. The average unit prices for this material in each quarter last year (20X7) and the seasonal variations based on several years' observations are:

	Q1	Q2	Q3	Q4
Average price per unit	£20	£22	£32	£38
Seasonal variation	-£2	-£4	+£2	+£4

Task 1.1

(a)   Calculate the seasonally adjusted unit price for Pigplus material P1 for each of the four quarters of last year.

(b)   Assuming a similar pattern to price movements in future years, forecast the likely purchase price per unit for the four quarters of the current year.

Data

Bay Feeds Ltd operate a standard absorption costing system across its product range. Certain product groups form profit centres. Standards are pre–determined in the budget setting mechanism and are set for each six month budget period. Each four week period a management accounting report is prepared, which reconciles the actual cost of production with the standard cost of actual production.

Standard and actual costing data for period 3 of 20X8 is given below.

Product: Calfmeal 3

Standard hours per tonne	1.3
Standard rate of pay	£6
Material usage per tonne of product	1.1 tonnes
Standard price, material per tonne	£25
Budget production, tonnes	1,200
Variable costs per 4 week period	£6,240
Fixed costs per 4 week period	£4,500

Actual costs period 3 20X8

Direct labour	1,600 hours worked
Cost	£9,680
Direct material usage	1,323 tonnes
Cost	£32,414
Actual production	1,150 tonnes
Variable costs incurred	£6,400
Fixed costs incurred	£4,700

Task 1.2

Calculate ratios for period 3 20X8, which show measures of:

(a)   Productivity
(b)   Production volume
(c)   Utilisation.

Comment briefly on your results.

Data

You are required to complete the reconciliation of actual to standard cost for the period. Your colleague has prepared some of the figures, prior to taking a couple of day's leave.

The part complete information includes:

Direct labour variance	£710 adverse
Direct material variance	£789 adverse
Direct material price variance	£661 favourable
Direct material usage variance	£1,450 adverse
Variable overhead variance	£420 adverse

Task 1.3

Calculate:

(a)   The direct labour rate variance
(b)   The direct labour efficiency variance
(c)   The fixed overhead variance
(d)   The fixed overhead expenditure variance
(e)   The fixed overhead volume variance

and prepare the reconciliation.

Data

During a meeting with your production director, he notes that there is a relationship between the efficiency and capacity ratios, in that these two factors affect production volume or activity. He asks whether it is possible to split the volume variance to show the effect of efficiency and capacity on overhead recovery.

Task 1.4

Write a memo to the production director, showing clearly this analysis and explaining the reason for the under or over–recovery of fixed overhead in period 3.

SECTION 2 (Suggested time allocation: 50 minutes)

Data

The Managing Director of Bay Feeds Ltd, Ray Staniland, is concerned that although turnover continues to rise, the profitability of the business has fallen in recent years.

An extract from the current year's financial statements shows the following:

Profit and loss account

	£m	
Turnover	3.30	
Operating costs	2.91	**
Operating profit before tax	0.39	
Tax	0.13	
Profit after tax	0.26	
Dividends	0.08	
Retained profit	0.18	

** Operating costs include:

	£m
Wages, salaries and other employee costs	0.62
Bought out items	2.16
Depreciation	0.13
	2.91

Note: Operating costs include distribution and administration costs of £0.44m.

Balance sheet

	£m	£m
Fixed assets		1.44
Current assets		
Stocks Raw materials	0.08	
Finished goods	0.22	
Debtors	0.92	
Bank	0.02	
	1.24	
Less: Current liabilities	0.85	
Net current assets		0.39
		1.83
Financed by:		
Capital and reserves		1.83

Note: One year previously, debtors amounted to £0.66m.

The latest inter–firm comparison statistics for this sector of industry are available, and show:

Agricultural and animal feeds
Sector ratios – Inter–firm comparison

(1)	Return on capital employed	26%
(2)	Asset turnover	1.79
(3)	Net profit before tax to sales	14.5%
(4)	Current ratio	1.5
(5)	Acid test	1.03
(6)	Debtors collection period	83 days
(7)	Cost of sales to finished stock	8.1
(8)	Operating costs % of sales	85%
(9)	Labour costs % of sales	18.1%
(10)	Value added per £ of employee costs	1.95
(11)	Distribution and administration cost as % of sales	13%

Task 2

Ray Staniland asks you to prepare an analysis of Bay Feeds Ltd's accounts, using the ratios shown in the sector report.

Tabulate your findings and compare the performance with the sector as a whole.

TECHNICIAN STAGE

NVQ/SVQ LEVEL 4 IN ACCOUNTING

PRACTICE CENTRAL ASSESSMENT

CONTRIBUTING TO THE PLANNING AND ALLOCATION OF RESOURCES
(UNIT 9)

Time allowed – 2 hours plus 15 minutes' reading time

◇ **FOULKS**lynch

SECTION 1 (Suggested time allocation: 50 minutes)

Data

Bay Heavy Horse Centre is a working farm using shire horses and an agricultural museum, situated in North Yorkshire.

Three years ago, John Jenkins who owns and developed the centre, appointed Jack Martin as manager of the centre. His initial task was to increase the number of visitors to the centre and in recent times he has made several improvements to make the centre more successful.

Jack is also responsible for effective financial management, and this year John has asked him to be fully responsible for producing the budget for 20X9.

One of his first tasks is to prepare estimates of the number of visitors next year. He had previously only limited experience in budget preparation and he turns to you, an accounting technician with the centre's accountants, for help.

He provides you with the following information:

- Previous budgets had assumed an 8% growth in attendance, but this had been inaccurate.

- Little is known of the visitors to the centre.

- The centre keeps records of visitor numbers per quarter, but little analysis had been done on these statistics.

- The number of visitors per quarter for the last two years were:

	Quarter	Visitors
20X7	1	6,000
	2	9,200
	3	15,000
	4	6,500
20X8	1	6,800
	2	10,000
	3	15,800
	4 (Estimate)	7,300

Task 1.1

(a) Calculate the centred four–point moving average trend figures and the seasonal variations.

(b) Construct a graph showing the trend line and actual number of visitors, by quarter, for presentation to the centre's owners.

(c) Estimate the forecast number of visitors for each quarter of 20X9, assuming there is the same trend and seasonal variation for 20X9.

(d) Prepare notes on forecasting for Jack Martin. Your notes should:

(i) identify two ways to improve the forecasting of visitor numbers and highlight any limitations to your proposals

(ii) outline two methods of selective sampling that could be used by the centre to identify visitor needs and interests.

Data

The centre uses its budgets and performance statements to motivate its manager and staff as well as for financial control. If the manager keeps expenses below budget, he is paid a bonus, and the staff also receive a bonus. Most of the centre's costs are fixed costs.

At a meeting with the centre's owners you are asked the following questions.

(a)   Do budgets motivate managers to meet objectives?

(b)   Does motivating managers lead to improved performance?

(c)   Does the current method of reporting performance motivate the manger and staff to be more efficient?

Task 1.2

Write a memo to the owners of the centre addressing their questions and justifying your response.

SECTION 2 (Suggested time allocation: 70 minutes)

Data

You work as an accounting technician for an electronics company, PED plc.

One of your subsidiary companies, PM Ltd, produces a single product and use flexible budgets to control expenditure.

The following forecasts have been prepared for the production costs to be incurred at the highest and lowest activity levels likely to be experienced in a budget period.

	Production level	
	10,000 units	30,000 units
	£	£
Direct material	50,000	150,000
Direct labour	20,000	60,000
Indirect material	16,000	36,000
Indirect labour	24,000	44,000
Machine rental	8,000	16,000
Rent, rates etc	12,000	12,000

Indirect labour costs are fixed for activity levels up to and including activity levels of 20,000 units. For all units produced in excess of 20,000 per period, a bonus payment of £2 per unit is paid, in addition to the fixed costs.

All other variable costs and the variable part of semi–variable costs follow a linear pattern.

Machine rental costs are stepped fixed costs. For activity levels up to and including 12,000 units, one machine is required at a cost of £8,000 per period. Above 12,000 units, two machines are needed.

Task 2.1

Prepare a set of flexible budgets which show the production cost allowances for the period for the following levels of activity:

10,000 units, 20,000 units, 24,000 units and 30,000 units.

Data

During the budget period ended 31 March the subsidiary operated at full capacity and the actual costs incurred were:

Production output	30,000 units

	£
Direct material	154,500
Direct labour	61,500
Indirect material	36,100
Indirect labour	43,900
Machine rental	16,000
Rent, rates etc	11,800

Task 2.2

Prepare a budgetary control statement for the period.

Comment briefly on the variances shown in the report.

TECHNICIAN STAGE

NVQ/SVQ LEVEL 4 IN ACCOUNTING

PRACTICE DEVOLVED ASSESSMENT

EVALUATING CURRENT AND PROPOSED ACTIVITIES (UNIT 16)

THE SITUATION

Your name is Pauline Musgrave and you are employed as an Accounting Technician with Cuescraft Ltd, a company which has three divisions A, B and C. Division A manufactures a range of snooker and pool cues, Division B manufactures snooker and pool tables and Division C wholesales a wide range of sportsware and equipment.

The total investment in the company is £1.2m.

Personnel involved in the simulation

Accounting Technician	–	Yourself, Pauline Musgrave
Managing Director	–	James Musgrave
Financial Director	–	Harry Dunn
Production Director	–	Ray Steriland
Sales Director	–	Barry Curran

CONTRIB RATHER THAN PROFIT

The company organisation

Cuescraft Ltd is divisionalised and each division shares the same site comprising a single manufacturing unit and a central office block containing personnel, finance and administrative functions.

The company products

Division A manufactures a range of six cues with product identification 'SD', 'AH', 'JV', 'SH', 'JP' and 'JJ'.

Division B produces a standard snooker table and a standard pool table.

Division C markets on a wholesale basis, a wide range of sportsware and equipment to small and medium size sports retailers.

In recent times the company has expanded its activities in Divisions A and C, however Division B has failed to contribute positively to the company performance and it is clear that its market share is falling significantly.

The date is late in 20X8.

TASKS TO BE COMPLETED

Note: Annexes 1 to 6 referred to below follow immediately after the tasks.

(1)   Refer to the memo from James Musgrave, Managing Director to Harry Dunn, Financial Director, reproduced in Annex 1 and Annex 2.

- Identify those costs which would be saved and those costs which would still be incurred if the activities in Division B were discontinued.

- Use your findings to identify the change in Cuescraft Ltd profit if Division B was closed.

- Prepare brief notes for Harry Dunn, stating and justifying your recommendation for the future of Division B.

- Using the data in Annex 1, identify one limitation to your proposal.

(2)   Refer to the memos from the Production Director, reproduced in Annex 3, with details of product costs for Division A and an overview of the division's budget for the quarter ended 31 March 20X9.

- Prepare the original budgeted profit statement for the quarter.

- Prepare a schedule to show the contribution per unit of output and the contribution per unit of limiting factor.

- Draft a revised production and sales schedule which will maximise the profits of Division A, for the first quarter of 20X9.

- Identify the total contribution and effect on profit from your proposal.

- Suggest at least one reason why such a revised mix might not be acceptable.

- Suggest one other option to deal with the shortfall in units to be produced.

(3)   Refer to the memo from the Managing Director reproduced in Annex 4.

- Using the budgeted operating statement that you produced in Task 2, calculate the breakeven point in sales value for the quarter.

- Calculate the breakeven point in units of output (based on total units and an average contribution per unit of output).

- Calculate the total units to be produced and sold if a profit target of £40,000 is to be achieved, assuming additional fixed costs of £5,000 are incurred and contribution per unit is reduced by £1.00.

- Calculate the revised breakeven point in sales value and units of output.

- Draw a profit volume graph to show the original and revised breakeven point in units.

(4)   Refer to the memo from Barry Curran reproduced in Annex 5.

- Determine the contribution per unit of output for products 'SH', 'JP' and 'JJ' for the year 20X0 and 20Y1, assuming the units are produced 'in-house'.

- Determine the extra contribution from this incremental business for the two years, and the additional contribution from the efficiency gains on the other production.

- Determine the total effect of the contribution on profit for the periods.

- Determine the contribution per unit of output for products 'SH', 'JP' and 'JJ' if the units are 'bought-in'.

- Determine the total contribution and effect on profit from this policy.

- Recommend which policy should be adopted on this order.

(5)   Refer to the memo from Harry Dunn reproduced in Annex 6.

- Evaluate the proposal using the pay-back period.

- Evaluate the proposal using the net present value method, basing your figures on post-tax cashflows.

- Estimate the IRR (Internal Rate of Return) of the project.

- Recommend whether or not the investment should be adopted.

Annex 1

Cuescraft Ltd
Internal Memo

To: Harry Dunn   **Date:** 18 November 20X8

From: James Musgrave

Subject: Future of Division B, snooker and pool table activities.

I note from the budgeted profit statement for next year, that yet again Division B fails to make a profit.

The Board recently acknowledged that Division B's market is contracting significantly and our aim is to increase overall the company's profitability and return on capital.

It seems to me that if we close Division B, then profits would increase by £125,000. I think that we can dispose of the plant and machinery quite easily.

Can you ask Pauline to prepare a report on a possible closure of Division B for the next Board meeting?

Annex 2

Cuescraft Ltd
Budgeted Profit Statement
for the year 20X9

Division	A £	B £	C £	Total £
Turnover	800,000	950,000	750,000	2,500,000
Less: Variable Costs				
Materials	120,000	570,000	178,000	868,000
Labour	250,000	199,000	100,000	549,000
Variable				
production overhead	96,000	120,000	–	216,000
	466,000	889,000	278,000	1,633,000
Contribution	334,000	61,000	472,000	867,000
Fixed overheads				
Rent	25,000	20,000	15,000	60,000
Rates	17,000	13,000	10,000	40,000
Heat & light	38,000	30,000	22,000	90,000
Depreciation	40,000	30,000	10,000	80,000
Plant insurance	15,000	11,000	4,000	30,000
Selling & Distribution Overheads				
Sales Commission	16,000	19,000	15,000	50,000
Selling Expenses	30,000	32,000	18,000	80,000
Central Overheads				
Personnel	8,000	9,000	8,000	25,000
Finance	10,000	10,000	10,000	30,000
Administration	10,000	12,000	10,000	32,000
	209,000	186,000	122,000	517,000
Profit/(Loss)	125,000	(125,000)	350,000	350,000

Annex 3.1

Cuescraft Ltd
Internal Memo

To: Pauline Musgrave   **Date:** 5 December 20X8

From: Ray Steriland

Subject: Division A

Further to our recent discussion, I enclose details of Division A's plans for the first quarter of 20X9. The sales targets, selling prices and product costs are those agreed at our management meeting in November and the standards have been set after discussions with my staff.

Products	'SD'	'AH'	'JV'	'SH'	'JP'	'JJ'
Selling prices (£)	40.00	37.50	36.00	32.50	32.00	30.00
Production and Sales (Units)	960	900	825	900	930	1,050
	38400	*33750*	*29700*	*29250*	*29760*	*31500*
Material usage per unit of output	1.3	1.2	1.1	1.05	1.05	1.00
	1248	*1080*	*907.5*	*945*	*976.5*	*1050*
Cost of a unit of material £4.50	*5616*	*4860*	*4083.75*	*4252.5*	*4394.25*	*4725*
Std hours per unit of output	2.5	2.25	2.1	2.0	2.0	1.9
	2400	*2025*	*1732.5*	*1800*	*1860*	*1995*
Std rate of pay per hour £6	*14400*	*12150*	*10395*	*10800*	*11160*	*11970*

(handwritten note beside Std hours row: 10%)

Variable overhead	£24,000
Fixed and other costs	£45,000

(handwritten notes at bottom of page:)

Tlover	192360
Mat	27931.50
Lab	70875
V o/h	24000
F + O	45000
	24553.50

Annex 3.2

Cuescraft Ltd
Internal Memo

To: Pauline Musgrave   **Date:** 20 December 20X8

From: Ray Steriland

Subject: Division A's budget for the quarter ended March X9

Since we agreed the plans for the first quarter, we have had a major machine breakdown.

Parts are not immediately available from the supplier and therefore I estimate that there will be a 10% reduction in capacity, ie, standard hours available during the quarter. This is the most pessimistic view of the position.

I will notify you if there are any further developments on this issue.

Annex 4

Cuescraft Ltd
Internal Memo

To: Pauline Musgrave   **Date:** 21 December 20X8

From: James Musgrave

Subject: Expansion of Division A's capacity

You are aware that with the possible closure of Division B, we are considering a significant expansion of the cue production.

At a recent management meeting it was decided that using the first quarter's budget for 20X9 we should aim for a profit target of £40,000.

This would require further investment in plant and machinery and we would incur a further £5,000 fixed costs per quarter.

Our sales manager suggests that to achieve the extra volume we would need to reduce selling prices and thus reduce the average contribution per unit of output by £1.00 to £11.50.

Could you please note these issues as I will need to discuss their effect with you later this week.

Annex 5

Cuescraft Ltd, Division A
Internal Memo

To: Pauline Musgrave   **Date:** 4 April 20X9

From: Barry Curran

Subject: Special order : Northcliffe Holiday Parks Ltd

We have had an enquiry from Northcliffe for the supply of 500 of each of 'SH', 'JP' and 'JJ' cues for the next two years 20X0 and 20X1.

You are aware that our budgeted selling prices for the current period and the next two years are £32.50, £32.00 and £30.00. Northcliffe are prepared to pay £27.50, £27.00 and £25.00 per cue.

I feel that to secure this additional business, which would suit our expansion strategy, we have two options.

Option 1

To invest in additional plant, which will add a further £4,000 to our existing fixed costs. It is likely that our production costs ie, labour, materials and variable overhead will increase by 3% per annum over the next two years. However, this new plant will aid productivity and reduce the standard labour hours per unit on these three products to 1.9, 1.9 and 1.8 (on all the production). Without this incremental business we had planned, in our three year strategy, to produce 1,100, 1,150 and 1,250 units of 'SH', 'JP' and 'JJ' in years 20Y0, 20Y1 and 20Y2.

Option 2

To 'buy in' this extra output and add our 'logo' and pack them for distribution.

We can purchase these from a supplier for £24.00, £23.50 and £21.50 per unit. It will cost us a further 60p per unit to add our 'logo' and pack them throughout the period.

I am calling a management meeting shortly to discuss this issue and would like you to give it some thought before then.

Annex 6

Cuescraft Ltd, Division A
Internal Memo

To: Pauline Musgrave   **Date:** 10 April 20X9

From: Harry Dunn

Subject: Investment in additional plant for special order and extra expansion in Cue assembly unit

I understand you have recently completed an exercise on the viability of the additional business from the Northcliffe contract. It is now likely that this contract would be for a period of at least five years.

I have discussed the contract fully with James this past two days and we have prepared the figures below for your consideration.

Initial investment in plant and machinery £24,000; life of plant estimated as 5 years; projected residual value £4,000.

Incremental cash flows from the project are:

Year	£
20Y0	11,600
1	10,700
2	10,500
3	10,350
4	10,210

We will be allowed an initial capital allowance of 40% followed by a 25% writing down allowance.

Our existing return on capital is 30% and in any capital investment appraisal we use this figure as our cost of capital.

The company pays its tax in the year following the year in which profits are earned. Assume the tax rate to be 25%.

Could you please give some thought to this paper, as I wish to discuss this with the senior management team early next week.

Note: Discount factors

Time:	30%	35%
1	0.769	0.741
2	0.591	0.549
3	0.455	0.407
4	0.355	0.301
5	0.269	0.223
6	0.207	0.165

CHAPTER ANSWERS

Chapters 1 – 2

INTRODUCTORY PRINCIPLES

1 Solution

Answer plan

(1) Define direct cost Example.
Define indirect cost Example.

(2) Types of indirect cost – material, labour, expenses.
Allocation and absorption.
Stocks at cost.
Work–in–progress – direct and indirect.

Task 1

A direct cost is expenditure which can be economically identified with and specifically measured in respect to a relevant cost object.

An example of direct costs are materials that are directly used in the manufacture of a product.

An indirect cost (or overhead) is expenditure on labour, materials or services which cannot be economically identified with a specific saleable cost unit.

An example of an indirect cost is the cost of a supervisor's wages. The supervisor may be in charge of a number of workers who are working on different products.

Task 2

(a) Indirect costs will generally include indirect materials, indirect labour and indirect expenses.

Indirect materials should be charged at their cost to the various user departments as they are used.

Indirect labour time should be recorded on labour time sheets with enough information to ascertain which user departments have benefited from the indirect labour.

Indirect expenses will generally tend to be controlled centrally and then apportioned to user departments in an equitable fashion.

All of the indirect costs, be they materials, labour or expenses, will be allocated to the user departments in an equitable manner and then absorbed into the total costs of the product or process on an appropriate basis such as time or machine usage.

(b) The cost of raw materials stocks in a manufacturing organisation should usually be ascertained from the purchase invoice.

The cost of work–in–progress will include both direct costs and a proportion of indirect costs. The direct materials costs should be available from the original invoice or the requisition details. The direct labour costs should be collected from the labour time recording system. This should give the hours worked and this will be multiplied by the hourly rate of pay. The indirect costs will be apportioned to the work–in–progress on some equitable basis.

2   Solution

REPORT

To: The managing director

From: The accounting technician

Date: X–X–20XX

Subject: Cost behaviour

Costs can be classified in many different ways. They can be classified according to their function eg selling costs or production costs. They can be classified as to whether or not they directly relate to units or output or they can be classified according to their behaviour.

For budgetary control purposes it is important to classify costs according to their behaviour as it is necessary to be aware of which costs will vary with a change in production levels and which will remain substantially the same. Also if the organisation uses marginal costing techniques then it is necessary to be able to recognise the different types of cost behaviour in order to be able to value stocks accordingly.

Some costs are said to be fixed costs. These are costs that remain constant regardless of the level of activity of the organisation. These might include building rentals, business rates and basic salaries.

A sketch graph of a fixed cost would look like this:

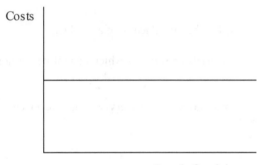

Variable costs in contrast are costs that will increase as the volume of activity of the organisation increases. Variable costs might include overtime payments, direct materials and sales commissions.

Variable costs could be illustrated as follows:

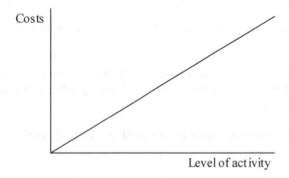

Step costs are costs that are fixed within a certain range of activity, known as the relevant range, but increase if the activity of the organisation strays outside that range. For example warehousing space may be fixed costs until production exceeds a certain amount at which point additional warehousing space must be rented.

Step costs could be represented graphically as follows:

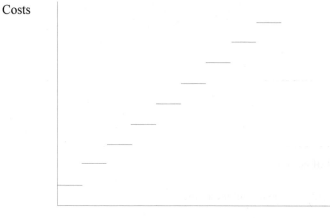

Finally some costs are known as semi–variable or semi–fixed costs. These are cost items that have both a fixed and a variable element, such as the telephone bill with its standing charge and charge for calls made.

The graph of a semi–variable cost would be as follows:

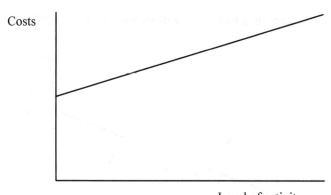

The graphs above have illustrated how the total cost of each type varies with output. If we consider the cost per unit then as volume increases the fixed costs will be absorbed by a greater number of units and therefore the cost will decrease per unit as illustrated below.

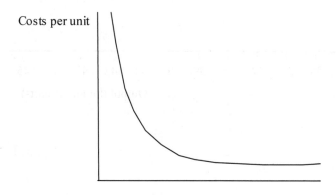

However variable costs per unit will remain constant whatever the level of output as illustrated below:

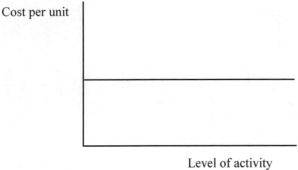

Level of activity

If you require any further information on this area please let me know.

3   Solution

Task 1

'59.8'   indicates that if zero units were output the total costs would be £5,980. This represents the monthly fixed costs of the factory.

'1.48'   means that if output increases by 100 units then total costs will increase by £148. This, therefore, indicates a variable cost of £1.48 per unit.

Task 2

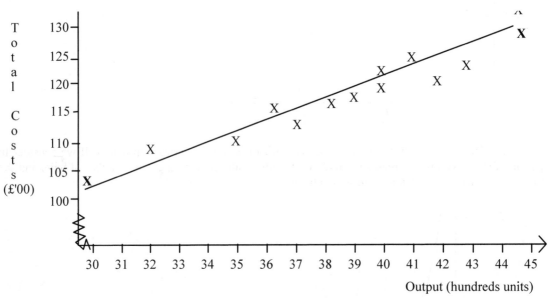

Output (hundreds units)

To plot the equation:

$$TC = 59.8 + 1.48$$

when = 30, $TC = 59.8 + 1.48 \times 30$
$TC = 104.2$

when = 45, $TC = 59.8 + 1.48 \times 45$
$TC = 126.4$

(*Note:* these points are only two of many possible different points that may be considered)

Task 3

Total cost = 59.8 + (1.48 × output)

Output is 4,400, ie 44 (hundreds)

∴ Total cost	=	59.8 + (1.48 × 44)
	=	124.92 (£ hundred)
∴ Predicted cost	=	£12,492

Chapter 3
OVERHEADS

1 Solution

Task 1

Overhead analysis sheet for 20X2

Expense	Basis of alloc'n	Machining £	Assembly £	Finishing £	Total £
Indirect wages	allocated	120,354	238,970	89,700	449,024
Factory rent	floor space	5,708,475	4,439,925	2,537,100	12,685,500
Rates	floor space	1,552,905	1,207,815	690,180	3,450,900
Heat/light	floor space	443,408	344,872	197,070	985,350
Machine power	horse power	1,878,890	72,265	939,445	2,890,600
Plant dep'n	machine value	375,000	45,000	180,000	600,000
Canteen sub'y	no of employees	100,000	120,000	36,000	256,000
		10,179,032	6,468,847	4,669,495	21,317,374

Task 2

Overhead absorption rates

Machining $\dfrac{£10,179,032}{200,000}$ = £50.90 per machine hour

Assembly $\dfrac{£6,468,847}{140,000}$ = £46.21 per direct labour

Finishing $\dfrac{£4,669,495}{90,000}$ = £51.88 per machine hour

2   Solution

Task 1

Item	Basis	Total	Residential	Catering	House–keeping	Mainten–ance
		£	£	£	£	£
Consumable materials	Allocated	73,000	14,000	23,000	27,000	9,000
Staff costs	Allocated	46,500	16,500	13,000	11,500	5,500
Rent/Rates	Floor area	37,500	20,625	10,125	4,500	2,250
Contents insurance	Value of equipment	14,000	6,533	4,667	1,400	1,400
Heat/Light	Floor area	18,500	10,175	4,995	2,220	1,110
Depreciation on equipment	Value of equipment	37,500	17,500	12,500	3,750	3,750
		227,000	85,333	68,287	50,370	23,010
Apportion	Maintenance	–	11,505	6,903	4,602	(23,010)
Apportion	Housekeeping	–	38,480	16,492	(54,972)	–
		227,000	135,318	91,682	Nil	Nil

Task 2

Absorption rates:

Residential (per guest – night):

$$\frac{\text{Costs}}{\text{Guest - nights}} = \frac{£135,318}{2,800} = £48.33$$

Catering (per meal)

$$\frac{\text{Costs}}{\text{Meals}} = \frac{£91,682}{16,000} = £5.73$$

Task 3

Residential:

		£
Amount absorbed (3,050 × £48.33)	=	147,406.50
Cost incurred	=	144,600.00
Over absorption	=	2,806.50

Catering:

		£
Amount absorbed (15,250 × £5.73)	=	87,382.50
Cost incurred	=	89,250.00
Under absorption	=	£1,867.50

Task 4

The hotel might consider the use of alternative methods of accounting for its overhead costs by trying to identify them with particular activities. They may also consider the introduction of a standard costing system for some parts of their organisation (where there are clearly definable common tasks involved).

3   Solution

Task 1

Profit and loss accounts for period 1 and 2 under marginal costing.

		Period 1		Period 2	
	£	£		£	£
Sales		327,000			246,750
Less: Cost of sales					
Opening stock (W1)				13,800	
Production	168,500			125,500	
Less: Closing stock (W1)	(13,800)			(22,800)	
		(154,700)			(116,500)
Contribution		172,300			130,250
Less: Fixed overheads		(110,000)			(82,000)
Profit		62,300			48,250

Task 2

Profit and loss accounts for period 1 and 2 based on absorption costing.

		Period 1		Period 2	
	£	£		£	£
Sales		327,000			246,750
Less: Cost of sales					
Opening stock (W2)	–			22,800	
Production	278,500			207,500	
Less: Closing stock (W2)	(22,800)			(37,800)	
		(255,700)			(192,500)
Profit		71,300			54,250

Task 3

Stock levels are rising over period one and two thus, total absorption costing, which includes a share of fixed costs in the stock valuation gives a higher reported profit than marginal costing which charges the fixed costs against profit in the period in which they are incurred.

Thus, the reported profit under total absorption costing is £15,000 more over the two periods as £9,000 of fixed costs are 'carried forward' from period 1 to 2, and a net £6,000 are 'carried forward' from period 2 to 3.

WORKINGS

		Alpha	Beta	Total
(W1)		MC per unit	45	32

Period 1

Closing stock	units	200	150	
	value (£)	9,000	4,800	13,800

Period 2

Closing stock	units	400	150	
	value (£)	18,000	4,800	22,800

(W2)   TAC per unit

MC	45	32

Overheads

Period 1

$$\frac{£110,000}{(3 \times 2,500) + (2 \times 1,750)} = £10 \text{ per labour hour} \qquad 30 \qquad 20$$

	75	52

Period 1

Closing stock	units	200	150	
	value (£)	15,000	7,800	22,800

MC	45	32

Period 2

Overheads

$$\frac{£82,000}{(3 \times 1,900) + (2 \times 1,250)} = £10 \text{ per hour} \qquad 30 \qquad 20$$

TAC	75	52

Closing stock	units	400	150	
	value (£)	30,000	7,800	37,800

4   Solution

Task 1

$$\text{Machine hour absorption rate} = \frac{£10,430 + £5,250 + £3,600 + £2,100 + £4,620}{(120 \times 4) + (100 \times 3) + (80 \times 2) + (120 \times 3)}$$

$$= \frac{£26,000}{1,300} = £20/\text{machine hour.}$$

The total costs for each product are thus:

	A £	B £	C £	D £
Direct materials	40	50	30	60
Direct labour	28	21	14	21
Production overhead	80	60	40	60
Per unit	£148	£131	£84	£141
Total (W4)	£17,760	£13,100	£6,720	£16,920

Task 2

Cost driver rates

Machine dept costs (m/c hour basis)	=	£10,430/1,300		=	£8.023/hr
Set up costs	=	£5,250/21	(W1)	=	£250/run
Stores receiving	=	£3,600/80	(W2)	=	£45/requisition
Inspection/quality control	=	£2,100/21	(W1)	=	£100/run
Material handling despatch	=	£4,620/42		=	£110/order

Total costs	*A* £	*B* £	*C* £	*D* £
Direct materials	4,800	5,000	2,400	7,200
Direct labour	3,360	2,100	1,120	2,520
Machine dep costs	3,851	2,407	1,284	2,888
Set up costs	1,500	1,250	1,000	1,500
Stores receiving	900	900	900	900
Inspection/quality control	600	500	400	600
Materials handling despatch	1,320	1,100	880	1,320
	£16,331	£13,257	£7,984	£16,928

Task 3

Per unit costs

Product	*A* £	*B* £	*C* £	*D* £
Traditional machine hour method	148.00	131.00	84.00	141.00
ABC method (W3)	136.09	132.57	99.80	141.07
Difference	11.91	(1.57)	(15.80)	(0.07)

The most significant differences concern products A and C. The ABC approach, in theory, attributes the cost of resources to each product which uses those resources on a more appropriate basis than the traditional method. The implication is that product A is more profitable than the traditional approach implies whereas C is less profitable. Alternatively the price of C should be increased whereas that of A could be reduced.

WORKINGS

(W1)	$(120 + 100 + 80 + 120)/20 = 21$
(W2)	$4 \times 20 = 80$
(W3)	Cost/quantity of each product.
(W4)	Unit cost × quantity of each product.

Chapters 4 – 5

PRESENTATION OF INFORMATION

1   **Solution**

Answer plan

(1)   Factors criterion discussion of alternatives conclusion.
(2)   Source stratification example.

Task 1

(i)   When determining the method to be used to collect data as part of a survey the key considerations are the cost of collecting the data and the sensitivity of the accuracy of the results.

(ii)   The newspaper is described as being local, covering an area of 100 square miles this indicates that its budget for surveys and data collection is likely to be small and consequently cost considerations are highly important.

(iii) The use of personal interviews requires much labour time together with travelling expenses which is costly, this method is rejected because of its high cost. The use of telephone interviews introduces bias by restricting respondents to those who have a telephone. However, the survey is concerned with the use of supplements which are of most interest to groups who tend to have a telephone. This bias is therefore considered to be irrelevant, and this method is significantly cheaper than the use of personal interviews. The cheapest option is the use of postal services but these are likely to have the lowest response rate, and the reliability of the results collected by this method is questionable.

(iv)   In conclusion, the use of telephone interviews is recommended because it represents a balance between cost and the likelihood of reliable results.

Task 2

(i)   When using telephone interviews as the means of collecting data, the source of information (or sampling frame) is the telephone directories for the area. This introduces bias by the exclusion of ex–directory numbers, but to include these would be too costly.

(ii)   The respondents selected should be stratified according to the criteria set out by the market research. Some of these are easier to achieve than others, particularly when using telephone interviewing to collect the data. Regions may be identified from the telephone directory and gender may be satisfied by the use of a quota system. Age is more difficult because people will tend not to wish to divulge their age, but this problem can be solved by careful interviewing. Stratification by annual income will be the most difficult, and is likely to be the least reliable of the criteria and for these reasons is probably best ignored.

(iii) The overall sample size will depend on the newspaper's budget for this exercise, but, using 1% of the market (ie, 5,000) as a sample size, the quotas for the suburban area (30%) would be:

Under 25	150
25 – 34	225
35 – 44	300
45 – 54	300
55 – 64	300
65 plus	225
Total	1,500

These would be divided equally between male and female respondents for each age range.

2 Solution

Task 1

Month	Sales 20X1	Sales 20X2	(a) Cumulative monthly sales 20X2	(b) Moving annual totals 20X2
Jan	29	54	54	490
Feb	30	55	109	515
Mar	30	55	164	540
Apr	34	55	219	561
May	37	50	269	574
June	39	46	315	581
July	40	43	358	584
Aug	40	41	399	585
Sep	40	40	439	585
Oct	45	40	479	580
Nov	49	42	521	573
Dec	52	44	565	565

Calculation of the moving annual totals. For Jan 20X2 take the 'current' Jan 20X2 figure and add in the previous year.

MAT, Jan 20X2 = sum of Feb 20X1 to Jan 20X2 (incl).

Similarly, MAT for Feb 20X2 is calculated as the sum of March 20X1 to Feb 20X2 (incl).

(*Tutorial note:*

Moving annual totals may be obtained quickly by updating the previous moving annual total.

MAT   Jan 20X2 = 490

MAT   Feb 20X2 = 490 – 30 + 55 = 515
                                ↑   ↑
                         Feb 20X1   Feb 20X2

To update this Jan 20X2 MAT, the new February figure (20X2) needs to be included in the total and the old February figure (20X1) excluded.

Similarly, for March 20X2

MAT = 515 – 30 + 55 = 540
                ↑   ↑
        Mar 20X1   Mar 20X2

and so on.

The cumulative figure for December will always equal the December MAT figure. This is a good checking point for accuracy.

Task 2

Z Chart: Unit sales 20X2 (Source: exam question)

Unit sales

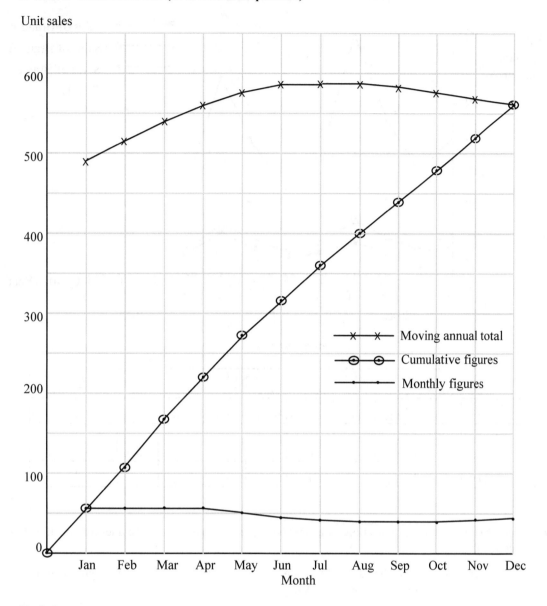

Task 3

(i)   The monthly sales remain fairly steady between January and April, indicating that the March television advertising campaign has no effect on the sales.

(ii)   From May to October, monthly sales fell probably due to the heavy price cutting by the competitors.

(iii)   The moving annual total, which indicates the trend, shows that from Jan–Sep sales were higher than that same time the previous year, despite the price cutting by the competitors. However, from Oct–Dec, despite rising monthly sales, the trend in sales was less than that same time the previous year.

3   Solution

Quarterly sales of brands A, B & C

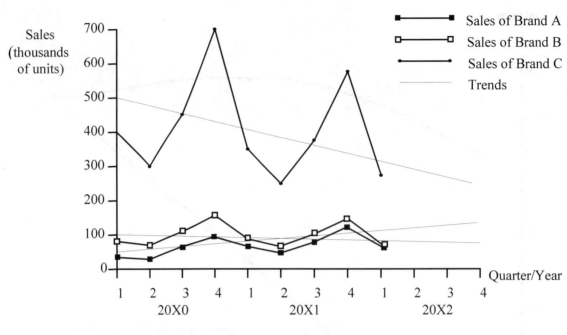

Summary table

	A			B			C			Total		
	20X0	20X1	20X2*	20X0	20X1	20X2*	20X0	20X1	20X2*	20X0	20X1	20X2*
Annual sales ('000 units)	237	317	397	400	400	400	1,850	1,530	1,210			
Annual contribution (£'000)	23.7	31.7	39.7	40	40	40	185	153	121	248.7	224.7	200.7
% of total for group	9.5	14.1	19.8	16.1	17.8	19.9	74.4	68.1	60.3			

* Estimated.

(Tutorial note: there is no time in the examination for a detailed time series analysis and the question specifically stated that this was not required.

The values for 20X2 were therefore predicted by the crude method of assuming the same difference in the annual values from 20X1 to 20X2 as there was from 20X0 to 20X1.

The fact that the first quarter sales for 20X2 show the same trend as the previous first quarters for each brand (this can be seen from the graph) indicate that this is a reasonable assumption.*

Points to note (at least five are required)

(i)   Each brand has a strong seasonal variation.
(ii)   The seasonal variation occurs at the same time for each brand, being lowest in Q_2 and highest in Q_4.
(iii)   Brand A has an increasing trend of approximately 80,000 units per year.
(iv)   Brand B has a constant trend (ie, no increase or decrease).
(v)   Brand C has a decreasing trend of approximately 320,000 units per year.
(vi)   The total market is decreasing by approximately £24,000 per year.
(vii)   Brand C at present has the largest share of the market, but this is decreasing.
(viii)   Brands A and B have an increasing share of a decreasing market.
(ix)   Sales of Brand A will probably overtake those of Brand B in 20X2.
(x)   The forecasts of performance for 20X2, as given in the summary table.

Chapters 6 – 7

TIME SERIES AND INDEX NUMBERS

1   Solution

Task 1

Year	Sales ('000)	Sums in 3's	Moving average trend
X0	50		
X1	59	155	51.7
X2	46	159	53.0
X3	54	165	55.0
X4	65	170	56.7
X5	51	176	58.7
X6	60	181	60.3
X7	70	186	62.0
X8	56	192	64.0
X9	66	198	66.0
X10	76		

Task 2 – Brand Y

Annual sales of Brand Y and trend
20X0–20X10

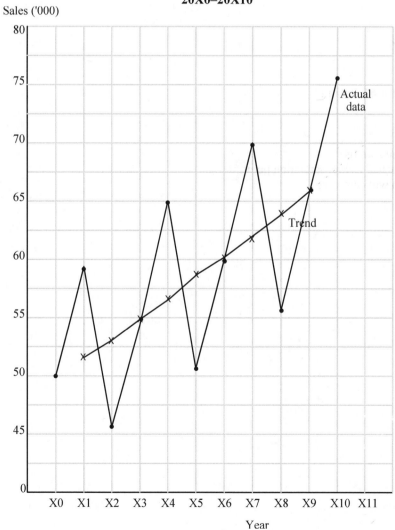

Task 3

The annual sales data shows a marked cyclical pattern of 3 years.

20X11 sales would be expected to be less than the trend assuming this pattern continues.

Looking at the sales–trend values for corresponding years in this cycle:

$$20X8 \quad 56 - 64 \qquad = -8$$
$$20X5 \quad 51 - 58.7 \qquad = -7.7$$
$$20X2 \quad 46 - 53 \qquad = -7$$

$$\text{Mean cyclical movement} \quad = \quad \frac{-8 - 7.7 - 7}{3}$$

$$= \quad \frac{-22.7}{3}$$

$$= \quad -7.6$$

Sales forecast for 20X11 = Trend + cyclical variation.

(Assuming an additive model.)

The trend value for 20X11 can be estimated from the graph by extending the trend line in the direction of the last pair of points. (This is shown by the dotted line on the graph.)

$T = 69.5$

$$\text{Forecast} \quad = \quad 69.5 - 7.6$$
$$= \quad 61.9$$

The sales forecast for 20X11 is 61,900 units.

The assumptions made are:

(i)   The trend will continue to rise.
(ii)   Brand Y has not reached market saturation point.
(iii)   The cyclical pattern will continue.

2   Solution

Task 1

Year	Quarter	(000s) Sales	Moving total	Moving average	Centred average	Actual trend
20X1	4	14		(W1)	(W2)	(W3)
20X2	1	16				
			100	25		
	2	30			25.5	+4.5
			104	26		
	3	40			26.0	+14.0
			104	26		
	4	18			26.5	−8.5
			108	27		
20X3	1	16			27.5	−11.5
			112	28		
	2	34			27.5	+6.5
			108	27		
	3	44			27.0	+17.0
			108	27		
	4	14			27.5	−13.5
			112	28		
20X4	1	16			29.0	−13.0
			120	30		
	2	38				
	3	52				
	4					

WORKINGS

(W1)   The moving average is found by dividing each four period total by 4.

> eg $100 \div 4 = 25$
> $104 \div 4 = 26$
> etc

(W2)   The centred moving average is calculated by taking pairs of data and finding their average.

> eg $(25 + 26)/2 = 25.5$
> $(26 + 26)/2 = 26.0$
> $(26 + 27)/2 = 26.5$
> $(27 + 28)/2 = 27.5$
> etc

Task 2

Graph showing sales of ice cream

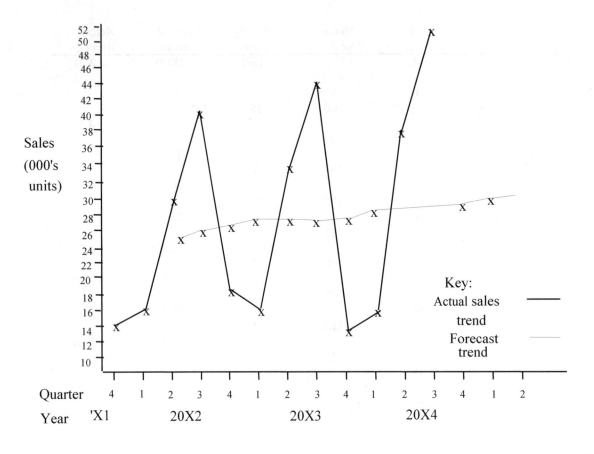

Task 3

(Note: the question did not state whether the additive or multiplicative model should be used. Presumably, full marks would be obtained for either model. The additive model has been illustrated here.*)*

WORKING

(W3) If   Actual = Trend + Seasonal variation
       then   Seasonal variation = Actual − Trend

| Year | Actual − Trend | | | | Total |
	Q1	Q2	Q3	Q4	
20X2	−	+4.5	+14.0	−8.5	
20X3	−11.5	+6.5	+17.0	−13.5	
20X4	−13.0				
Total	−24.5	+11.0	+31.0	−22.0	
	÷2	÷2	÷2	÷2	
Average	−12.25	+5.5	+15.5	−11.0	−2.25
Adjustment	+0.75	+0.5	+0.5	+0.5	+2.25
Seasonal Variation	−11.5	+6.0	+16.0	−10.5	0

Task 4

Forecast = Trend + Seasonal variation

The trend has been obtained by extrapolating the trend line on the time series graph.

		Trend	*+ SV*	*Sales Forecast*
20X4	Q4	30.0	−10.5	= 19.5, ie 19,500 units
20X5	Q1	30.5	−11.5	= 19.0, ie 19,000 units

3   Solution

Task 1

Date	*Deflated production industries index (20X1 = 100)*
20X1	$\dfrac{100}{107} \times 107 =$ 100.0
February 20X2	$\dfrac{104.9}{111.5} \times 107 =$ 100.7
May 20X2	$\dfrac{108.1}{115.0} \times 107 =$ 100.6
August 20X2	100.9
November 20X2	101.9
February 20X3	101.7
May 20X3	100.2
August 20X3	100.0
November 20X3	101.8
February 20X4	102.3
May 20X4	103.6
August 20X4	103.9
November 20X4	104.0

We can see from the above that the average earnings of the production industries sector were fairly constant in real terms throughout 20X2 and the start of 20X3. They rose somewhat in 20X2 and declined gently to August 20X3, but not markedly in either case.

After August 20X3 real average earnings in the production industries sector started to grow quite briskly and continued to grow in real terms until November 20X4, though the rate of growth had by then appeared to tail off.

Task 2

The pensioner starts with £5,000 a year in May 20X2.

In November 20X2 it is uprated to $£5,000 \times \dfrac{112.7}{107.2} = £5,257$

In November 20X3 it is uprated to $£5,000 \times \dfrac{123.0}{107.2} = £5,737$

In November 20X4 it is uprated to $£5,000 \times \dfrac{129.7}{107.2} = £6,049$

The real values of these pensions can be considered by deflating the above numbers by the RPI numbers.

Month	Pension £	RPI	Real pension	£
May 20X2	5,000	115.0		5,000
November 20X2	5,257	118.5	$5,257 \times \dfrac{115}{118.5} =$	5,102
November 20X3	5,737	130.0	$5,737 \times \dfrac{115}{130} =$	5,075
November 20X4	6,049	135.6	$6,049 \times \dfrac{115}{135.6} =$	5,130

We can see that the value of the pension in real terms has grown since May 20X2. The growth in November 20X2 in real terms was relatively large. In November 20X3 the real value fell back slightly, but still exceeded the £5,000 starting figure. In November 20X4 the real value increased again to a highest figure yet compared with the £5,000 starting figure.

Chapters 8 – 10
BUDGETS

1   Solution

(a)   **Assumptions**

Sales forecast (units):

January	2,500
February	3,000
March	4,000
April	3,500
May	3,800
June	4,500

Finished stock at the beginning of each month to be equal to 50% of that month's sales.

Each unit of the finished product to require 5 kgs of material X which costs £3/kg.

Material stocks at the beginning of the month to be equal to 25% of that month's production requirements.

(b) & (c)

Budgets for March – May

	A	B	C	D	E	F
1						
2		PRODUCTION BUDGET				
3		March	April	May	June	
4	Sales	4,000	3,500	3,800	4,500	
5	Opening stock	B4*.5	C4*.5	D4*.5	E4*.5	
6	Closing stock	+C5	+D5	+E5		
7	Production	+B4-B5+B6				
8						
9		PURCHASES BUDGET				
10	Production usage	B7*5	C7*5	D7*5		
11	Opening stock	B10*.25	C10*.25	D10*.25		
12	Closing stock	+C11	+D11	+E11		
13	Purchase quantity	+B10-B11+B12				
14	Purchase price	3.00	3.00	3.00		
15	Purchase value	+B13*B14				

(*Note:* In practice, the spreadsheet would include additional columns for each month showing actual performance and variance from budget.)

2 Solution

Task 1

Production budget (cases)

	June	July	August	Sept
Sales	6,000	7,500	8,500	7,000
Add: Closing stock				
(10% next months sales)	750	850	700	650
Less: Opening stock	(750)	(750)	(850)	(700)
Production	6,000	7,600	8,350	6,950

Task 2

Ingredients purchase budget (kgs)

	June	July	August	Total
Usage (prod × 2.5)	15,000	19,000	20,875	54,875
Add: Closing stock				
(50% next months usage)	9,500	10,438	8,688	8,688
Less: Opening stock	(5,800)	(9,500)	(10,438)	(5,800)
Purchases	18,700	19,938	19,125	57,763

Task 3

Budgeted gross profit for the quarter June to August

Total sales (cases)	=	6,000 + 7,500 + 8,500 =	22,000
Standard profit per unit	=	£25 – £15	= £10
Budgeted gross profit	=	22,000 × £10	= **£220,000**

(*Tutorial note:* The wording of the requirement implies that a total figure for the quarter only is required. Monthly figures would be as follows:

June :	6,000 × £10 =	£60,000
July:	7,500 × £10 =	£75,000
August:	8,500 × £10 =	£85,000
		£220,000*)

Task 4

Flexible budgeting is a system of budgeting whereby the original fixed budget is adjusted prior to comparison with actual results. The adjustments will take account of the expected changes resulting from the actual operating activity level differing from that originally budgeted.

At the simplest level, the adjustment may be in the form of a pure flexing exercise, whereby fixed costs are assumed to remain constant at all activity levels (ie as budgeted) and variable costs are assumed to vary in direct proportion to activity level (ie variable cost per unit is assumed to remain constant as per original standard cost)

If fixed costs increase on a stepped basis, and/or variable costs per unit change through overtime, bulk discounts etc, at certain activity levels the budget may also be adjusted for these effects.

The result of this exercise is that the actual results will be compared with a budget that is applicable to the actual activity level achieved, and will thus produce more equitable and meaningful variances. It will focus attention on the relevant causes of costs and areas for cost–reduction.

It will also provide more relevant information for decision–making.

3   Solution

Task 1

(a)

Sales budget
Year ended 31 December 20X4

Quarter	Units	£'000
1	40,000	6,000
2	50,000	7,500
3	30,000	4,800
4	45,000	7,200
	165,000	25,500

(b)

Production budget
Year ended 31 December 20X4

	Quarters (units)				
	1	2	3	4	Total
Required by sales	40,000	50,000	30,000	45,000	165,000
Closing stock	5,000	3,000	4,500	4,000	4,000
	45,000	53,000	34,500	49,000	169,000
Opening stock	(9,000)	(5,000)	(3,000)	(4,500)	(9,000)
Production	36,000	48,000	31,500	44,500	160,000

(c)

Material usage budget
Year ended 31 December 20X4

	Quarters (units)				
	1	2	3	4	Total
Component R	144,000	192,000	126,000	178,000	640,000
Component T	108,000	144,000	94,500	133,500	480,000
Shell S	36,000	48,000	31,500	44,500	160,000

(d)

Production cost budget
Year ended 31 December 20X4

		Quarters				
		1	2	3	4	Total
		£'000	£'000	£'000	£'000	£'000
Direct material:	R	1,152	1,689.6	1,108.8	1,566.4	5,516.8
	T	540	792	519.75	734.25	2,586
	S	1,080	1,440	945	1,335	4,800
Direct labour		1,080	1,440	945	1,388.4	4,853.4
Variable overhead		360	480	315	445	1,600
Fixed overhead		54	72	47.25	66.75	240
		4,266	5,913.6	3,880.80	5,535.8	19,596.2

◈ FOULKS*lynch*

Task 2

The principal budget factor is the factor which limits the organisation within the budgeting period. This may be one or more production resources which limit production or it may be demand for its products, ie, sales.

When this factor has been identified this budget must be prepared first and the other budgets derived from it.

Assuming sales to be the limiting factor a forecast of likely sales demand must be made for the budget period. Such forecasts may use both external and internal data.

External data would include:

- feedback from existing customers, and
- the results of market research.

These could be entered onto a database or statistics package on a computer and analysed by consumer group, age and various other classifications.

Internal data will be based on past records of sales volumes and prices. These may be analysed using time series techniques to identify seasonal and underlying trends. Such trends may be compared with other internal and external data to establish any correlation which may exist.

Again this analysis can be improved by using statistical and modelling (ie, spreadsheet) packages on a microcomputer. This analysis can be used to predict future sales based on trends.

4   Solution

Task 1

(a)   Sales budget

		Product		
	A	B	C	Total
Sales (units) (W1)	500	1,000	2,000	
Selling price (£)	215	250	300	
Sales value (£)	107,500	250,000	600,000	957,500

(b)   Production budget

		Product	
	A	B	C
Required by sales	500	1,000	2,000
Required closing stock	270	630	1,440
	770	1,630	3,440
Less opening stock	(300)	(700)	(1,600)
Production required	470	930	1,840

(c)   Material usage budget

		Product		
	A	B	C	Total
Copper frames	470	930	1,840	3,240
Component D	2,350	930	5,520	8,800
Component E	470	6,510	9,200	16,180
Component F	1,880	4,650	1,840	8,370

(d)   Material purchases

	Copper Frames	Components D	E	F
Required by production	3,240	8,800	16,180	8,370
Required closing stock	900	3,600	9,000	3,600
	4,140	12,400	25,180	11,970
Less opening stock	(1,000)	(4,000)	(10,000)	(4,000)
Purchases quantity	3,140	8,400	15,180	7,970
Purchase price	£20	£8	£5	£3
Purchase value	£62,800	£67,200	£75,900	£23,910

(e)   Manpower budget

	Skilled (machining)	Unskilled (assembly)
Hours required – Product A	940	940
– Product B	1,395	1,860
– Product C	2,760	5,520
	5,095	8,320
Hours per man per period (4 × 37.5)	150	150
Number of workers required	34	56

Task 2

The stock of components would be significantly reduced if this proposal were adopted thus freeing storage space for alternative uses (or possible cost savings). However, the holding of fewer stocks will lead to a greater number of orders being placed, albeit of lesser values, and consideration must be given to the total cost of the inventory function from ordering, handling and storage.

The risk is that stocks will not be replenished when required leading to production being stopped or the need to make best use of the materials which are available by switching to other products. In order to reduce this risk there must be increased communication with suppliers so that they are aware of the materials required. This requires closer control of production planning.

WORKINGS

(W1)

	A £	B £	C £
Selling price	215	250	300
Variable costs			
Frame	20	20	20
Component D	40	8	24
Component E	5	35	25
Component F	12	15	3
Skilled labour	12	9	9
Unskilled labour	9	9	13.5
Variable overhead	5	4	3.5
	103	100	98
Contribution per unit	112	150	202

Contribution per batch of sales:

		£
A:	1 × £112 =	112
B:	2 × £150 =	300
C:	4 × £202 =	808
		1,220

	£
Contribution required	
Production overhead	728,000
Selling and distribution	364,000
Administration	338,000
Profit	6,500,000
	7,930,000

$$\text{Sales batches required} = \frac{£7,930,000}{£1,220} = 6,500 \text{ per annum}$$

$$\text{Period 1} = \frac{6,500}{13} = 500$$

Sales units are therefore:

A   500 × 1 = 500
B   500 × 2 = 1,000
C   500 × 4 = 2,000

5   Solution

Task 1

Flexible budget for period 9

Budget centre	Total cost (W1) £
Cleaning	12,875
Laundry	15,506
Reception	13,025
Maintenance	10,980
Housekeeping	20,150
Administration	7,670
Catering	22,065
General overheads	11,250

(W1)   Flexed budget

Cleaning	
Fixed cost = £13,250 – £2.50 × 2,000 =	8,250
Variable cost per unit = £2.50	
Flexed variable cost £2.50 × 1,850 =	4,625
Total	12,875

Laundry

Fixed cost £15,025 – £1.75 × 4,300 =	7,500
Variable cost per unit = £1.75	
Flexed variable cost £1.75 × 4,575 =	8,006
Total	15,506

Reception

Fixed cost =	12,100

$$\text{Variable cost per unit } \frac{£13,100 - 12,100}{2,000} = 50\text{p}$$

Flexed variable cost 50p × 1,850 =	925
Total	13,025

Maintenance

Fixed cost £11,100 – 80p × 2,000 =	9,500
Variable cost per unit = 80p	
Flexed variable cost 80p × 1,850	1,480
Total	10,980

Housekeeping

Fixed cost	11,000

$$\text{Variable cost per unit } \frac{19,600 - 11,000}{4,300} = £2$$

Flexed variable cost £2 × 4,575	9,150
Total	20,150

Administration

Fixed cost 7,700 – 20p × 2,000	7,300
Variable cost per unit 20p	
Flexed variable cost 20p × 1,850	370
	7,670

Catering

Fixed cost £21,460 – £2.2 × 4,300	12,000
Variable cost per unit £2.2	
Flexed variable cost £2.2 × 4,575	10,065
	22,065

General fixed overheads	11,250

Task 2

Individual expenditure variances

Budget centre	Flexed budget £	Actual £	Variance £	Favourable/ Adverse
Cleaning	12,875	13,292	(417)	A
Laundry	15,506	14,574	932	F
Reception	13,025	13,855	(830)	A
Maintenance	10,980	10,462	518	F
Housekeeping	20,150	19,580	570	F
Administration	7,670	7,930	(260)	A
Catering	22,065	23,053	(988)	A
General overheads	11,250	11,325	(75)	A
	113,521	114,071	(550)	

Task 3

Advantages of a budgeting system:

(a)   budgets motivate staff because they clarify responsibilities and provide targets and yardsticks against which actual performance can be measured

(b)   budgets improve the co–ordination between the various parts of a business

(c)   budgets increase control over costs and make employees more cost conscious

(d)   budgets improve communication and provide authorisation for expenditure without continuous reference to top management.

Chapters 11 – 12

STANDARD COSTING AND VARIANCES

1   Solution

Task 1

A fixed budget is a budget showing costs, revenues, or both for a single level of activity. In contrast a flexible budget recognises that costs have different behavioural patterns and in so doing shows costs, revenues, or both for a number of activity levels. It therefore allows costs to be predicted for any level of activity.

Budgetary control is the process of comparing actual results with a target. If efficiency is to be measured it is important to compare actual performance with that which should be achievable in respect of the actual activity. In order to do this cost behavioural factors must be considered therefore a flexible budget should be used.

Task 2

The standard direct labour cost is the product of two separate elements:

(a)   the standard time allowance per unit, and
(b)   the standard hourly wage rate.

The standard time allowance will be determined having regard to past results or in the case of a new product by using work measurement techniques. These techniques include timing employees performing particular tasks which may be used as the basis of standard time allowances.

The standard hourly wage rate will have regard to the skills of the employees who perform the tasks their present hourly wage rate the wage rate paid by local competitors the rate of inflation and the likely wage increase for future period.

Once these separate elements have been determined they are multiplied together to produce the standard direct labour cost per unit.

Task 3

	Standard cost	Actual cost	Variance
(a)	2,150 × £8.40 = £18,060	£18,100	£18,060 – £18,100 = £40 (A)
(b)	2,150 × £7.60 = £16,340	£14,980	£16,340 – £14,980 = £1,360(F)
(c)	2,150 × £3.90 = £8,385	£8,160	£8,385 – £8,160 = £225 (F)
(d)	2,150 × £5.10 = £10,965	£9,950	£10,965 – £9,950 = £1,015 (F)

2   Solution

Task 1

		Major		Minor	
		£		£	
Direct materials @£15/kg	2.2 kgs	33.00	1.4 kgs	21.00	
Direct labour:					
Machining @ £6/hr	4.8 hrs	28.80	2.9 hrs	17.40	
Assembly @ £5/hr	3.6 hrs	18.00	3.1 hrs	15.50	
Standard prime cost		79.80		53.90	
Overhead:					
Machining @ £16/machine hr	3.5 hrs	56.00	0.9 hrs	14.40	
Assembly @ £9.50/labour hr	3.6 hrs	34.20	3.1 hrs	29.45	
Standard production cost		170.00		97.75	

Task 1

Machining department:

Major:

650 units should cost £28.80 each	=	£18,720
Actual cost	=	£18,239
Total variance	=	£481 (F)

2,990 hours should cost £6 each	=	£17,940
Actual cost	=	£18,239
Rate variance	=	£299 (A)

650 units should take 4.8 hrs each	=	3,120 hours
Actual time taken	=	2,990 hours
Time saved	=	130 hours
Efficiency variance = 130 hours × £6/hr	=	£780 (F)

Minor:

842 units should cost £17.40 each	=	£14,650.80
Actual cost	=	£15,132.00
Total variance	=	£481.20 (A)

2,480 hours should cost £6 each	=	£14,880
Actual cost	=	£15,132
Rate variance	=	£252 (A)

842 units should take 2.9 hours each	=	2,441.8 hours
Actual time taken	=	2,480.0 hours
Excess time	=	38.2 hours

Efficiency variance = 38.2 hours × £6/hr = £229.20 (A)

Machining department summary

	£
Rate variance	551.0 (A)
Efficiency variance	550.8 (F)
Total variance	0.2 (A)

Assembly department:

Major:

650 units should cost £18.00 each	=	£11,700
Actual cost	=	£11,700
Total variance	=	£Nil

2,310 hours should cost £5 each	=	£11,550
Actual cost	=	£11,700
Rate variance	=	£150 (A)

650 units should take 3.6 hours each	=	2,340 hours
Actual time taken	=	2,310 hours
Time saved	=	30 hours

Efficiency variance = 30 hours × £5/hr   =   £150 (F)

Minor:

842 units should cost £15.50 each	=	£13,051
Actual cost	=	£12,975
Total variance	=	£76 (F)

2,595 hours should cost £5 each	=	£12,975
Actual cost	=	£12,975
Rate variance	=	£Nil

842 units should take 3.1 hours each	=	2,610.2 hours
Actual time taken	=	2,595.0 hours
Time saved	=	15.2 hours

Efficiency variance = 15.2 hours × £5/hr   =   £76 (F)

Assembly department summary

	£
Rate variance	150.0 (A)
Efficiency variance	226.0 (F)
Total variance	76.0 (F)

Task 3

Rate variances reflect differences between the hourly wage rate paid and that anticipated to be paid. These differences may be caused by inaccuracies in the standard or by using different grades of labour than anticipated.

Efficiency variances measure the effectiveness of the labour used compared to the standard time allowed.

The analysis by department and product identifies a consistent rate variance in the machining department between products which may indicate that the standard hourly rate is no longer valid. The divergence of efficiency variances could indicate that the standard time allowance for each product unit is also invalid.

In the assembly department the variances for the Major product could indicate that a higher grade of labour was used. This has led to an adverse rate variance but has also resulted in time being saved. The efficiency variance for the Minor product may be the result of an invalid standard.

3   Solution

Task 1

Production cost budget (marginal) for ARF Ltd

	Per tonne £	In total £
		(4,500 tonnes)
Materials		
A (2.50 × 400)	1,000	4,500,000
B (4.00 × 600)	2,400	10,800,000
Labour		
(6.00 × 20)	120	540,000
Variable overhead		
(4.00 × 20)	80	360,000
	3,600 × 4,500 =	16,200,000

Task 2

		Actual cost £	Standard cost (of actual output) £	Variance £
(a)	Material A	4,870,000	5,000,000	130,000 F
	Material B	13,125,000	12,000,000	1,125,000 A
	Total			995,000 A
(b)	Labour	580,000	600,000	20,000 F
(c)	Variable overhead	437,000	400,000	37,000 A
(d)	Fixed overhead	475,000	500,000	25,000 F

4   Solution

(*Tutorial note:* part (a) is based on an understanding of a flexible budget and the variances relating to fixed and variable overhead. Care is needed since mistakes in early parts of the answers would make it more difficult to arrive at the answer to subsequent parts.)

Task 1

Calculation of:

(a)   Budgeted variable overhead cost per tonne

	Expenditure £	Output tonnes
High	108,000	7,000
Low	72,000	3,000
Difference = variable	£36,000	4,000

Variable overhead per tonne

$$\frac{£36,000}{4,000} = £9$$

(b)   Total budgeted fixed cost per month

	£
Total budgeted expenditure at 7,000 tonnes	108,000
Less: Variable overhead 7,000 × £9	63,000
Budgeted fixed overhead	£45,000

(c)   Budgeted output on which standard rate is based

	£
Standard absorption rate (ie total overhead)	18
Less: Variable overhead absorption rate	9
Fixed overhead absorption rate	9

$$\text{Fixed overhead absorption rate} = \frac{\text{Budgeted fixed overhead}}{\text{Budgeted tonnes}}$$

$$£9 = \frac{45,000}{\text{Budgeted tonnes}}$$

$$\therefore \text{ Budgeted tonnes} = \frac{45,000}{9} = 5,000 \text{ tonnes}$$

(d)   Budgeted overhead allowance for the actual output in April

	£
Budgeted fixed overhead	45,000
Budgeted variable overhead for 5,500 tonnes £9 × 5,500	49,500
Budgeted overhead allowance	£94,500

◆ FOULKS*lynch*

(e)   Total overhead absorbed for April

Amount absorbed
= overhead absorption rate × actual tonnes produced
= £18 × 5,500 =   £99,000

(f)   Variable production overhead expenditure variance for April

	£
Actual expenditure	52,000
Budgeted variable overhead for actual output of 5,500 tonnes	49,500
Variable overhead expenditure variance	£2,500 adverse

(g)   Fixed production overhead expenditure variance for April

	£
Actual expenditure	53,750
Budgeted fixed overhead (ie per original budget)	45,000
Fixed overhead expenditure variance	£8,750 adverse

(h)   Fixed production overhead volume variance for April

	Tonnes
Budgeted volume on which absorption rate is based	5,000
Actual volume	5,500
Volume difference	500

∴ Fixed overhead volume variance
∴ (over recovery)
500 tonnes at £9 =   £4,500 favourable

Task 2

A flexible budget is a budget which, by recognising different cost behaviour patterns, is designed to change as volume of activity changes. Consequently a comparison of the flexed budget with actual will result in identifying expenditure changes which need investigating.

If comparison were made between a fixed budget and an actual, part of the difference would be because of the fact that variable costs are affected by volume changes.

Task 3

Typical production costs which would be classified as variable production overhead expenses

(a)   Electricity consumed by plant and machinery.
(b)   Cooling oil used on, for example, lathes.
(c)   Depreciation if this is incurred on the basis of usage (machine hour basis).

(Only two were needed.)

Task 4

An attainable standard is a standard which can be attained if a standard unit of work is carried out efficiently, a machine properly operated or a material properly used. Allowances are made for normal losses, waste and machine downtime.

This represents a standard which, as the name suggests, should be achieved. Consequently for operational performance an attainable standard is preferable, any adverse variances would indicate performance is below what it should be. Managers are likely to be motivated to achieve an attainable standard.

An ideal standard is a standard which can be attained under the most favourable conditions, with no allowance for normal losses, waste and machine downtime. Also known as potential standard.

Consequently adverse variances will arise when an ideal standard is used. These variances serve as a constant reminder that better performance is possible but are difficult to interpret when trying to evaluate performance and are likely to demotivate managers. They are therefore not recommended.

5   Solution

Task 1

Standard cost of 18,000 units of Jay

	£
Direct material (£48 × 18,000)	864,000
Direct labour (£35 × 18,000)	630,000
Variable production overhead (£10 × 18,000)	180,000
Fixed production overhead (£50 × 18,000)	900,000
	2,574,000

Task 2

Cost item	Standard cost £	Variances Adverse £	Favourable £	Actual cost £
Direct materials	864,000			836,000
Price variance (W1)			76,000	
Usage variance (W2)		48,000		
Direct labour	630,000			604,800
Rate variance (W3)		16,800		
Efficiency variance (W4)			42,000	
Variable production overhead	180,000			172,000
Expenditure variance (W5)		4,000		
Efficiency variance (W6)			12,000	
Fixed production overhead	900,000			1,030,000
Expenditure variance (W7)		30,000		
Volume variance (W8)		100,000		
	2,574,000	198,800	130,000	2,642,800

Task 3

Such a report identifies the extent of the difference between standard and actual costs, and how it may be attributed to the effects of price and resource utilisation.

The report provides the starting point for managers to investigate why the variance occurred and improve future performance. However, it does not identify managerial responsibilities or controllability. Changing the report to identify these aspects would allow the report to be directed to the appropriate manager.

WORKINGS

(W1)

	£
76,000 kgs should cost £12/kg	912,000
Actual cost	836,000
	76,000 F

(W2)		kgs
18,000 units should use 4 kgs each		72,000
Actual usage		76,000
		4,000 A
4,000 kgs × £12/kg		£48,000 A

(W3)		£
84,000 hours should cost £7/hour		588,000
Actual cost		604,800
		16,800 A

(W4)		Hours
18,000 units should use 5 hours each		90,000
Actual time taken		84,000
		6,000 F
6,000 hours × £7/hour		£42,000 F

(W5)		£
84,000 hours should cost £2/hour		168,000
Actual cost		172,000
		4,000 A

(W6)		Hours
18,000 units should use 5 hours each		90,000
Actual time taken		84,000
		6,000 F
6,000 hours × £2/hour		£12,000 F

(W7)		£
Budget cost = 20,000 × £50/unit		1,000,000
Actual cost		1,030,000
		30,000 A

(W8)		Units
Budget volume		20,000
Actual volume		18,000
		2,000 A
2,000 units × £50/unit		£100,000 A

Chapters 13 – 14

IMPROVING PERFORMANCE

1   Solution

Task 1

In general terms, the suggestions made by the MD reflect a mistaken view of quality and how it is assured. His emphasis is 'reactive' rather than 'pro–active', is 'feedback' based rather than 'feedforward', and is concerned with quality control rather than quality assurance.

Specifically:

(i)   His initial statement that 'something drastic has to be done about quality' does not seem to be based on any kind of systematic analysis or measurement. Nor does it suggest that the MD understands the meaning of quality, which according to Crosby is 'conformity to requirements'.

(ii)   His statement that 'quality is the responsibility of your department' ignores the fact that quality is the responsibility of all staff at all stages, in all departments and at all levels.

(iii)   The 'tougher line' suggests a punishment orientated approach which contradicts the advice of Deming 'to drive out fear', and to seek co–operation.

(iv)   'Raising quality standards' without targeting particular areas, and without understanding why such quality improvement is necessary, is likely to be a costly and unproductive exercise.

(v)   'Increasing inspection rates' and 'giving greater authority to quality control inspectors' reinforces the 'control' approach, and the 'specialist' emphasis discussed earlier.

Task 2

An alternative approach involves viewing quality control as part of a more strategic approach to quality – quality assurance. This requires:

(i)   An analysis of existing quality performance and problems. Such an analysis should involve all levels and all departments, and should concern itself with the customers, with the competition, with suppliers as well as the activities of the firm itself. Crosby advocates the creation of 'quality committees' composed of members drawn from different departments.

(ii)   Calculating the 'cost of quality', which involves measuring the costs of not 'getting it right first time', and includes 'prevention costs', 'appraisal costs', and 'failure costs'.

(iii)   The careful selection and monitoring of suppliers, perhaps involving an 'active' rather than a passive relationship.

(iv)   The design of the product, to ensure an appropriate level of quality.

(v)   The installation of quality information systems which measure and feedback quality performance to those involved, and which can serve as the basis for targets.

(vi)   Quality improvement, perhaps involving the creation of quality circles.

(vii)   Quality staff, which involves investment in recruitment, selection, training, development, appraisal and reward.

In conclusion, such an approach is essentially long term, and requires a shift in thinking about quality at all levels. The essential ingredient in this cultural shift is a 'right first time' mentality which encompasses all activities that impinge on quality. In short, the MD and other staff need to be educated in 'total quality management'.

2   Solution

(Tutorial notes:

Overall

On reading the requirements at the start, Task 3 refers to gross profit, therefore this should be included in your answer to Task 1 to save time, and Task 4 asks for alternative action which should be borne in mind as you work through the question.

The key in answering Task 1 is to focus on the requirements which ask for two things ie:

(i)   Presentation of the information in a more meaningful way to aid decision making, and

(ii)   Include statistics or indicators of performance which are considered useful.

The answer should therefore be geared to providing information which is as specific as possible to the individual departments so as to identify where profits are being earned/losses incurred. The answer should consider the rate at which profit is being earned and should focus on the principal budget factor which is floor area.

Initial points on first read of question:

(i)   The store is currently making a loss!

(ii)   No figures given showing the amount of profit/loss of each department.

(iii)   Two proposals put forward as possible ways to improve the situation.*)*

Task 1

Results for year ended 31 January 20X0

	£'000	£'000	£'000	£'000	£'000	£'000	£'000	£'000	£'000	£'000	£'000	£'000
Sales		800		400		2,200		1,400			200	5,000
Cost of sales:												
Purchases	506		220	1,290		1,276		167				
Stock												
(Increase/decrease)	(10)	(496)	20	(240)	30	(1,320)	(100)	(1,176)	(1)	(166)		(3,398)
Gross profit		304		160		880		224		34		1,602
Allocable direct fixed costs:												
Wages	96		47		155		59		26		383	
Expenses	38		13		35		20		10		116	
Sales and promotion	10		5		30		75		–		120	
		(144)		(65)		(220)		(154)		(36)		(619)
Profit/(loss)		160		95		660		70		(2)		983

Other costs:	
Office wages	70
Delivery	200
Directors' salaries and fees	120
Store capacity costs	488
Interest	20
Discounts allowed	25
Bad debts	15
Miscellaneous expenses	75
	(1,013)
Loss	(30)

Performance Indicators

	Ladies	Mens	General	Toys	Restaurant

Gross profit %

$\dfrac{\text{Gross profit}}{\text{Sales}} \times 100$	$\dfrac{304}{800} \times 100$	$\dfrac{160}{400} \times 100$	$\dfrac{880}{2,200} \times 100$	$\dfrac{224}{1,400} \times 100$	$\dfrac{34}{200} \times 100$
	$= 38\%$	$= 40\%$	$= 40\%$	$= 16\%$	$= 17\%$

Gross profit per 1% of floor space

	$\dfrac{304}{20}$	$\dfrac{160}{15}$	$\dfrac{880}{20}$	$\dfrac{224}{35}$	$\dfrac{34}{10}$
£'000	$= 15.2$	$= 10.67$	$= 44$	$= 6.4$	$= 3.4$

(Gross profit – direct fixed costs) per 1% of floor space

	$\dfrac{160}{20}$	$\dfrac{95}{15}$	$\dfrac{660}{20}$	$\dfrac{70}{35}$	$\dfrac{(2)}{10}$
£'000	$= 8$	$= 6.33$	$= 33$	$= 2$	$= (0.2)$

Sales per 1% of floor space

£'000	40	26.67	110	40	20

Task 2

(Tutorial note: care should be taken to show and explain the effect.)

Effect on profit for a full year of closing Toys Department

	– £'000	+ £'000
Lost sales	1,400	
Saving in cost of sales		1,176
Saving in – Wages		59
– Expenses		20
– Sales and promotions		75
	1,400	1,330
	1,330	
Net reduction in profit	70	

The department store would show a loss of £100,000 if the Toys Department is closed as it is making a £70,000 contribution to overheads.

Assumptions

The whole of the department expenses and sales and promotion costs can be avoided by closing the department.

The aim here is to show the incremental effect of closing the department. Hence store capacity costs are omitted as it is assumed they will be unaffected by the closure.

Task 3

Calculation of increase in sales needed to maintain gross profits

	Ladies Wear		Mens' Wear	
Effect on gross profit %	%		%	
Selling price	100 – 5 =	95	100 – 5 =	95
Cost of sales	62	62	60	60
Gross profit	38	33	40	35

$$\text{Revised gross profit \%} = \frac{33}{95} \times 100 \qquad\qquad \frac{35}{95} \times 100$$

$$= 34.7\% \qquad\qquad\qquad\qquad = 36.8\%$$

Hence sales value needed to maintain gross profit

$$= \text{Gross profit} \times \frac{100}{\text{gross profit \%}} \qquad = 304 \times \frac{100}{34.7} = 876 \qquad 160 \times \frac{100}{36.8} = 435$$

Original sales		800	400
(a)	Increase in sales value £'000	76	35

(b)   Increase in sales as % of 20X0 sales.

$$\frac{76}{800} \times 100 \qquad\qquad \frac{35}{400} \times 100$$

$$= 9^{1}/_{2}\% \qquad\qquad\qquad = 8^{3}/_{4}\%$$

Task 4

(Tutorial note

This part of the question requires discipline.

The answer should cover the proposals and any other points which may have occurred to you as you worked through the question. Reference where appropriate should be made to the figures prepared in Task 1 ie, use your answer.*)*

(i)   **Closure of Toys Department**

The working in Task 2 indicates that profits would be reduced by this closure. The calculations are slightly unrealistic in that alternative uses for the space presently occupied by the department have been ignored.

(ii)   **Reduce selling prices in Ladies Wear and Mens' Wear**

This proposal is dependent on being able to assess the effect of the reduction in selling prices on demand if the effect is greater than $9^{1}/_{2}\%$ and $8^{3}/_{4}\%$ then this proposal will result in an improvement in profits.

(iii)   **Alternative action**

The following should be evaluated:

(1)   The most profitable department is the General department. Can this be expanded?

(2)   The restaurant is not promoted at present. Advertising may boost turnover and consequently increase the number of people entering the store. The fact that the restaurant is likely to attract people into the store is a strong argument for keeping it open at existing sales volumes even though there is at present a loss incurred on its operation.

Chapters 15 – 16

DECISION MAKING PRINCIPLES

1 Solution

Task 1

Conditional and expected profit table

The figures in the body of the table represent the profits made for each combination of order size and demand, calculated as:

Sales (= lower of demand and order size) × £60 - Order size × £30

		Order size (cases)			
Demand (cases)	Prob	20	21	22	23
20	0.20	£600	£570	£540	£510
21	0.40	£600	£630	£600	£570
22	0.30	£600	£630	£660	£630
23	0.10	£600	£630	£660	£690
Expected profit*		£600	£618	£612	£588

* Calculated for each order size by multiplying each possible profit by the corresponding probability and summing the results

Task 2

Ordering 21 cases a day maximises expected long–run profitability (£618 per day) assuming that past records of demand are a good indicator of future demand levels.

Task 3

If there were no prior knowledge of demand pattern (for example if the wholesaler is just starting up his business) it will be difficult to estimate the optimum stock purchase quantity. The wholesaler will have to make assumptions such as:

(a)   His pricing strategy – whether he will keep his prices constant regardless of demand levels experienced, or whether he may try to stimulate demand by lowering prices during the day if this seems necessary. The latter strategy will be more flexible, allowing him to order slightly higher levels (and thus benefit from high levels of demand) knowing that he can more easily dispose of them if sales turn out to be lower than expected.

(b)   His costs – whether the price paid per case will depend upon the amounts ordered. If so, he may be able to afford to order slightly higher quantities, again to get the benefit from higher levels of demand, without significantly increasing costs.

2   Solution

Task 1

(a)   Breakeven point in sales value

$$= \frac{\text{Fixed cost}}{(\text{Sales} - \text{Variable costs})} \times \text{Sales}$$

$$= \frac{78}{(288 - 171)} \times £288{,}000$$

$$= 0.667 \times £288{,}000$$

$$= £192{,}000$$

Breakeven point in units

$$= \frac{\text{B/E point in sales value}}{\text{Selling price per unit}}$$

$$= \frac{192{,}000}{32}$$

$$= 6{,}000 \text{ units}$$

(b)   **Contribution/volume or profit volume graph**

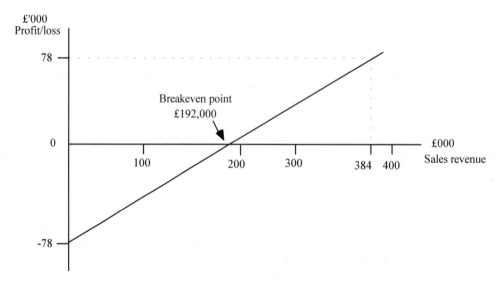

(c)   Anticipated profit at full capacity (ie, sales of 12,000 × £32 = £384,000) from the graph is £78,000

Task 2

		(a) £		(b) £
Sales	10,800 × £28	302,400	12,000 × £27.20	326,400

		£		£	
Less:	Direct materials (W1)	64,800		72,000	
	Direct wages (W2)	86,400		96,000	
	Production overhead variable (W3)	21,600		24,000	
	Selling overhead variable (W4)	32,400		36,000	
			205,200		228,000
Contribution			97,200		98,400
Fixed overhead (42,000 + 36,000)			78,000	(42,000 + 36,000 +5,000)	83,000
Profit			19,200		15,400

The respective profits are:

Original plan	£39,000
Alternative (a)	£19,200
Alternative (b)	£15,400

Management should continue with its original budget, operating at 75% of capacity, as this produces the greatest profit.

Task 3

(a)

	£
Sales 12,000 at £32	384,000
Less: Marginal cost (from Task 2 part (b))	228,000
Contribution	156,000
Fixed overhead	93,000
Profit	63,000

This proposal would generate a greater profit than any of the others and should be implemented.

(b)   A major reservation is in the reliability of the forecast. This would depend on the track record of the company carrying out the market research study. More useful information may be given if the probability of the success of this campaign could be forecast.

WORKINGS

(W1)	Cost/unit	=	£54,000/9,000	=	£6	£6 × 10,800	=	£64,800
						£6 × 12,000	=	£72,000

(W2)	Cost/unit	=	£72,000/9,000	=	£8	£8 × 10,800	=	£86,400
						£8 × 12,000	=	£96,000

(W3)	Cost/unit	=	£18,000/9,000	=	£2	£2 × 10,800	=	£21,600
						£2 × 12,000	=	£24,000

(W4)	Cost/unit	=	£27,000/9,000	=	£3	£3 × 10,800	=	£32,400
						£3 × 12,000	=	£36,000

3   Solution

Task 1

	Reasons	£
Paper	– Book value is irrelevant because it is a sunk cost, as there is no other use replacement would not occur so the opportunity cost or scrap sale proceeds is the relevant value.	2,500
Ink	– Since this involves a future cost if the work is undertaken the purchase price should be used. Since the remaining stock has no foreseeable use it has no value so the entire purchase cost is used.	3,000
Skilled labour	– Since the weekend working is caused if the work is undertaken the full cost is relevant:	

$$125 \text{ hours @ £4/hr} = \quad £500$$
$$125 \text{ hours @ £5/hr} = \quad £625 \qquad 1,125$$

Unskilled labour	– The weekend work results in 50 hours time off in lieu, this with the 75 other hours worked totals 125 hours which is less than the 200 hours of idle time which are already being paid for, thus there is no incremental cost.	Nil
Variable overhead	– This is a future cost which will be incurred if the work is undertaken	1,400
Printing press	– The depreciation is a past cost and should be ignored, however, the use of the press has an opportunity cost. If this work is undertaken then the press is not available for hire. The opportunity cost is the contribution which would be earned from hiring:	

$$200 \text{ hours @ (£6 – £3)} \qquad 600$$

Production fixed costs	– As these costs are unaffected by the decision they should be ignored	Nil
Estimating costs	– These costs are past or sunk costs and should be ignored.	Nil
MINIMUM PRICE		£8,625

Task 2

Contribution is the difference between sales and variable costs, both of which are dependent on activity. Fixed costs, which tend to be independent of activity, are ignored.

Since most decisions involve changes in the level of activity the relevant costs and revenues are those affected by changes in the level of activity. Thus the net effect of these relevant costs and revenues is contribution.

Task 3

An opportunity cost is the value which represents the cost of the next best alternative or the benefit forgone by accepting one course of action in preference to others when allocating scarce resources.

If there is only one scarce resource, decisions can be made by ranking alternatives according to their contributions per unit of the scarce resource. However, in reality there will be many scarce resources, and different alternatives will use alternative combinations of those scarce resources. In these situations opportunity costs are used to identify the optimum use of those resources.

4   Solution

Task 1

(a)

	Sales £	Cost of sales £
Highest	90,000	55,000
Lowest	80,000	50,000
	10,000	5,000

$$\text{Variable cost} = \frac{£5,000}{£10,000} = 50\% \text{ of sales}$$

By substitution:

Lowest:	Variable cost = 50% × £80,000	=	£40,000
	Fixed cost (balance)	=	£10,000
	Total cost	=	£50,000

(b)

	Sales £	Sell/Dist £
Highest	90,000	9,000
Lowest	80,000	8,000
	10,000	1,000

$$\text{Variable cost} = \frac{£1,000}{£10,000} = 10\% \text{ of sales}$$

By substitution:

Lowest:	Variable cost = 10% × £80,000	=	£8,000
	Fixed cost (balance)	=	£Nil
	Total cost	=	£8,000

(c)

	Sales £	Admin £
Highest	90,000	15,000
Lowest	80,000	15,000
	10,000	Nil

$$\text{Variable cost} = \frac{£\text{Nil}}{£10,000} = \text{Nil}$$

By substitution:

Lowest:	Variable cost	=	£Nil
	Fixed cost (balance)	=	£15,000
	Total cost	=	£15,000

Task 2

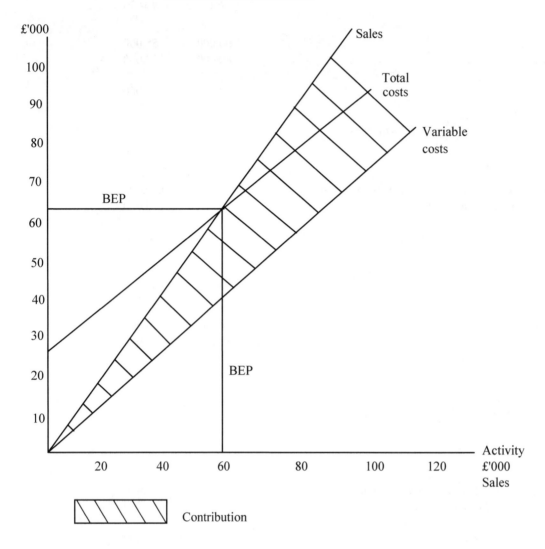

Z plc
Contribution breakeven chart

Break-even point = £62,500 of sales

Task 3

Breakeven value = £62,500/month
Margin of safety = 30%
Average monthly sales = £62,500 × 1.3 = £81,250

If sales = £81,250:

Variable costs = 60% of sales	=	£48,750
Fixed costs	=	£25,000
Total costs	=	£73,750

Monthly profit averages £81,250 – £73,750 = £7,500

Annual profit = £7,500 × 12 = £90,000

Task 4

Contribution from existing outlet per month
= 40% of sales
= 40% of £81,250
= £32,500

This is an annual contribution of £32,500 × 12 = £390,000.

By opening the second outlet 10% of this is transferred ie, £39,000.

Therefore to make the same overall profit the contribution from the second outlet must equal:

Contribution transferred	£39,000
Fixed costs of new outlet	£100,000
	£139,000

Since contribution = 40% of sales, the sales required are:

$$\frac{£139,000}{40\%} = £347,500$$

Task 5

A retail organisation needs to identify the costs and revenues associated with each of its products (or at least product ranges) in order to determine their profitability. This is measured relative to their consumption of resources (eg, space occupied).

For multi–site retail organisations costs and revenues should be separately recorded for each site. Managers will then have responsibility for the costs and revenues which they can control at their respective sites. In this regard it is important to clearly identify controllable and non–controllable items in any performance reports, which will probably be linked to budgets.

Chapters 17 – 18

DECISION MAKING TECHNIQUES

1   **Solution**

Task 1

Assuming the fixed overhead costs are not changed in total because of the decision.

Relevant manufacturing cost = £54 – £20 (fixed cost) = £34

This is lower than the price offered by Trigger plc, therefore the unit should be manufactured, *not* purchased.

Task 2

(a)   The benefit from manufacturing, using relevant costs is £50 – £34 = £16 per unit.

If there is an additional fixed cost of £56,000 to be incurred per annum, the benefit from manufacturing applies provided the annual production volume exceeds 3,500 units. (£56,000/£16).

At lesser volumes the unit should be purchased.

(b)   The present component earns a net saving (compared to purchase) of £16/4 hours = £4/hour.

The alternative product earns a contribution of £40/unit (£90 – £10 – £24 – £16). This is equal to £40/8 hours = £5/hour. Greater benefit is obtained by buying the component and using the labour on the alternative product.

Task 3

MEMO

To: Production director

From: Cost accountant

Date: X–X–20XX

Subject: Special grinding equipment

The original cost of the equipment is a past or sunk cost which cannot be recovered in the future. Consequently it is irrelevant to the decision being made. The book value of £80,000 will have to be set against profits of the current/future years irrespective of the decision made.

2   Solution

Task 1

Budgeted profit

	Product A £	Product B £	Product C £	Total £
Revenue (W1)	700,000	800,000	500,000	2,000,000
Variable costs (W2)	175,000	287,500	175,000	637,500
Contribution	525,000	512,500	325,000	1,362,500
Fixed costs – attributable	65,000	140,000	95,000	300,000
Attributable profit	*460,000*	*372,500*	*230,000*	*1,062,500*
– apportioned	280,000	320,000	200,000	800,000
Profit	180,000	52,500	30,000	262,500

WORKINGS

(W1)   Revenue

	Product A	Product B	Product C
Volume (units)	8,750	12,500	5,000
Price per unit	£80	£64	£100
Revenue (£)	700,000	800,000	500,000

(W2)   Variable costs

	Product A	Product B	Product C
Volume (units)	8,750	12,500	5,000
Cost per unit	£20	£23	£35
Costs (£)	175,000	287,500	175,000

Task 2

Revised budgeted profit

	Product A £	Product B £	Total £
Revenue	700,000	800,000	1,500,000
Variable costs	175,000	287,500	462,500
Contribution	525,000	512,500	1,037,500
Fixed costs – attributable	65,000	140,000	205,000
Attributable profit	*460,000*	*372,500*	*832,500*
– apportioned (Working)	336,000	384,000	720,000
Profit/(loss)	124,000	(11,500)	112,500

WORKING

New total general fixed costs = 90% × £800,000 = £720,000

Apportioned between A and B in the same ratios as before:

$$A: \frac{280}{600} \times 720 = £336,000 \qquad B: \frac{320}{600} \times 720 = £384,000$$

Task 3

The overall effect on the profits of DNP Limited of the elimination of product C is a reduction of £150,000 – being the loss of 'attributable profit' from C of £230,000, net of the savings in general fixed costs, £80,000.

Using the 'bottom line' profit figure for product C shown in (a), £30,000, as a measure of the loss of profits is misleading, as this assumes all costs shown against product C would be saved. This is not true of the apportioned general fixed costs – only £80,000 is saved, the remaining £120,000 being re–apportioned between the remaining products (resulting in product B now showing a 'loss').

On the basis of these calculations, it would appear to be inadvisable to eliminate product C (or indeed any other product, as all show healthy 'attributable profits').

3 Solution

Task 1

12,000 capacity

		£'000	£'000
Fees (12,000 × £300)			3,600
Variable costs			
Materials	(12,000 × £115)	1,380	
Wages	(12,000 × £30)	360	
Variable overhead	(12,000 × £12)	144	
			1,884
Contribution			1,716
Fixed overhead	(12,000 × £50)		600
Profit			1,116

Task 2

18,000 tests with additional shift

		£'000	£'000
Fees	(18,000 × £300)		5,400
Variable costs			
Materials	$(1,380 \times {}^{18}\!/_{12} \times 80\%)$	1,656	
Wages	(360 + 6 × £30 × 150%)	630	
Variable overhead	$(144 \times {}^{18}\!/_{12})$	216	
			2,502
Contribution			2,898
Fixed overhead	(600 + 700)		1,300
Profit			1,598

Task 3

Additional factors to consider

(1) The duration of the higher level of demand. If it is expected to continue over several periods, it may be worth employing extra staff rather than paying overtime premiums. In addition, the commitment to extra fixed overheads may extend over a longer period than the extra demand.

(2)   The pricing policy. The urgency of the need for extra tests may mean that fees can be increased without significantly affecting demand (ie, price inelastic).

(3)   The quality of the work done, materials used etc. Increasing activity by 50% using current resources may well lead to a drop in the quality of output – ie, unreliable test results – which could have a knock–on effect on future demand.

4   Solution

Task 1

Unit costs		Product X £	Product Y £	Product Z £	Total £
Direct materials		50	120	90	
Direct labour:	A	70	40	75	
	B	24	18	30	
	C	32	16	60	
Variable overhead		12	7	16	
		188	201	271	
Selling price		210	220	300	
Contribution per unit		22	19	29	
Sales volume (units)		7,500	6,000	6,000	
Total contribution (£)		165,000	114,000	174,000	453,000
Less fixed costs					300,000
Profit					153,000

Task 2

	X	Y	Z
Contribution/unit	£22	£19	£29
Department B hours/unit	4	3	5
Contribution/hr	£5.50	£6.33	£5.80
Ranking	(3)	(1)	(2)

Maximum Dept B hours

$$= (7,500 \times 4) + (6,000 \times 3) + (6,000 \times 5)$$
$$= 78,000 \text{ hours}$$

$\therefore$ Manufacture:

7,500 units of Y uses	22,500 hours
8,000 units of Z uses	40,000 hours
3,875 units of X uses	15,500 hours (W1)
	78,000

This yields a contribution of:

		£
X: 3,875 × £22 =		85,250
Y: 7,500 × £19 =		142,500
Z: 8,000 × £29 =		232,000
		459,750
Less fixed costs		300,000
Profit		159,750

Task 3

(1)   It has been assumed that the fixed costs are not affected by the increased volume of products Y and Z and reduction in volume of product X.

(2)   It relies on the sales director's demand estimates.

(3)   It ignores the effects of reducing the production of X such as the effect on customers' goodwill, and the position of the company in the market for X.

WORKINGS

(W1)   This is the balancing number of department B hours available.

5   Solution

Task 1

	Total sales from 1 module £	Total sales from 2 modules £	Incremental sales from 2nd module £
Range A	6,750	2 × 6,250 = 12,500	5,750
Range B	3,500	2 × 3,150 = 6,300	2,800
Range C	4,800	2 × 4,600 = 9,200	4,400
Range D	6,400	2 × 5,200 = 10,400	4,000
Range E	3,333	2 × 3,667 = 7,334	4,001

Note that the sales figures in the question are per module. For instance for Range A if there is only 1 module the sales are £6,750. If there are 2 modules the sales are £6,250 per module, ie, £12,500 in total, of which £6,750 comes from the 1st module, therefore £5,750 (the remainder) must come from the 2nd module.

Modules	Sales £	C/S Ratio	Contribution per module £	Priority
Range A – No 1	6,750	20%	1,350	3rd
No 2	5,750	20%	1,150	5th
Range B – No 1	3,500	40%	1,400	2nd
No 2	2,800	40%	1,120	6th
Range C – No 1	4,800	25%	1,200	4th
No 2	4,400	25%	1,100	7th
Range D – No 1	6,400	25%	1,600	1st
No 2	4,000	25%	1,000	
Range E – No 1	3,333	30%	999.9	
No 2	4,001	30%	1,200.3	

Note that although the 2nd module for range E provides a contribution of £1,200.3, in order to open the 2nd module, the first must also be opened. The net result is an increase in contribution of £2,200.2, in effect an average increase of £1,100.1 per module. This increase is not as good as Range B module 2 and Range C module 2.

Task 2

Operating costs are £5,600 per week for 7 modules = £800 per week per module.

Range	Contribution £	Operating costs £	Profit £
A	2,500	1,600	900
B	2,520	1,600	920
C	2,300	1,600	700
D	1,600	800	800
			3,320

Task 3

A limiting factor is that factor which prevents a company from achieving the level of activity that it would wish. Examples of possible limiting factors include sales demand, machine capacity, availability of skilled labour, etc.

When preparing a budget or any other plan, the starting point is usually the limiting factor as this sets the overall level of activity for the business. For instance, for most companies the limiting factor is sales demand and the sales budget would therefore be the starting point for the budgeting process. Once the sales budget has been completed the company will then be able to determine the required production and thus the required material usage, etc.

With limiting factor decisions, the 'rule' is to maximise the contribution per unit of scarce resource. If a resource is in short supply, it makes sense to ensure the greatest return from each unit of that resource.

Chapters 19 – 20

PRICING AND COST ESTIMATION

1   **Solution**

Task 1

Week	Production	Total costs
	x	£
1	85	4,625
2	64	3,579
3	50	2,980
4	38	2,529
5	40	2,600
6	73	4,006
7	91	4,956
8	60	3,400
9	82	4,465
10	100	5,480
11	120	6,760
12	140	8,200
13	21	1,988
14	15	1,825
15	20	1,960

Graph of total costs

Total costs = materials + power etc + £1,480

This is graphed from the above data.

Graph of revenue

Revenue $= 65x$ is a linear function

Only 2 points need to be found to graph a linear function

$$x = 15 \qquad R = 65 \times 15 \quad = \quad £975$$
$$x = 100 \qquad R = 65 \times 100 \quad = \quad £6,500$$

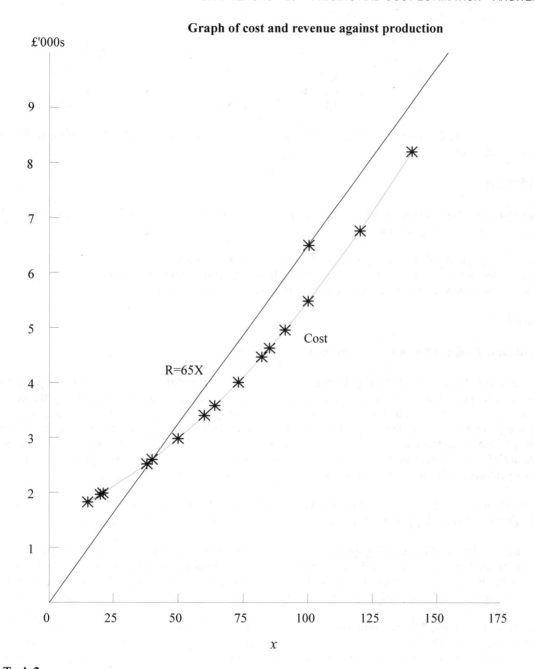

Graph of cost and revenue against production

Task 2

Break–even point occurs where costs = revenue

From the graph: production level = 40 at the break–even point

   revenue = 65 × 40 = £2,600
   costs = £2,600

Task 3

The recommended level of output would be the level which maximised profit:

   Profit = revenue – costs

This maximum value can be estimated from the graph by finding the maximum vertical distance between the cost and revenue lines.

The greatest distance between the two lines appears to occur over the range:

$$100 < x < 140$$

x	R	C	Profit $(R - C)$
100	6,500	5,480	1,020
120	7,800	6,760	1,040
140	9,100	8,200	900

This appears to be a maximum when $x = 120$, but a more detailed analysis would be required to find the true profit maximisation point.

2   Solution

Tutorial note: this question involves identifying what is wrong with the method used for calculating the cost of jobs. The main things to note are that

(1)   a single 'blanket' recovery rate (47.5%) is used for all overheads

(2)   the fact the company uses total cost as the lowest acceptable selling price and

(3)   a recession is imminent making (2) a dangerous approach to use.

Task 1

Criticism of method for estimating costs

The essential feature of job costing is that all jobs are potentially different. The cost is therefore likely to differ. The method used for charging costs to jobs should aim at reflecting the incidence of the costs ie the costs caused by the job. In this case all overheads are charged to products on the basis of a single blanket recovery rate of 47.5% of direct materials and direct labour. It is extremely unlikely that such a direct method will provide an accurate basis for charging overheads eg if higher priced higher quality material is used the amount of variable overhead may be less if, for example, less labour time is needed to work on the better quality material. The above absorption rate would result in a higher overhead charge.

Similarly it may be that direct labour rates vary in which case higher wage rates would **not** necessarily result in higher overheads being incurred whereas with this method more overhead is charged to the job.

Another weakness of the existing system is that no attempt is made to split cost between fixed and variable. With the imminent recession it will be extremely important for managers to know the variable cost of jobs so that, with increased competition, it is possible to quote lower prices which will still generate contribution. If the existing total cost plus pricing system is continued the company is likely to start losing jobs to competitors.

As shown for job no. 878 the current system is to use total cost ie fixed cost and variable costs, as the lowest acceptable price. This is misleading since the lowest price should be as mentioned above the variable cost. This is because a price above variable cost will generate contribution which will increase profit/reduce losses. In a time of recession the firm may be forced to accept very low prices in order to win orders from customers.

A further criticism is the method for calculating the mark up of 47.5%. This is based on the actual costs for the year first ended.

$$\left(\text{ie } \frac{383,000 + 118,500 + 192,000}{1,000,000 + 460,000} \times 100 = 47.5\% \right)$$

There are several factors which will result in costs being different in the current period from the previous period:

(i)   The level of activity may be lower – this will cause average fixed overheads to increase as a proportion of direct costs.

(ii)   Inefficiency may have arisen in the previous year which is not expected to recur.

(iii)   Inflation would cause the level of costs to alter.

(iv)   Changes in production method may have occurred.

Task 2

In this circumstance it would be more accurate to calculate separate production overhead recovery rates for each of the production departments ideally based on budgeted figures. Direct labour hours or machine hours would be suitable bases for recovery but the information given means direct labour hours must be used below:

Based on last year's actual figures   *Grinding*   *Finishing*

Direct labour hours $\dfrac{200,000}{5} = 40,000$ $\dfrac{260,000}{6} = 43,333$

Overhead recovery rates

$= \dfrac{\text{Overhead}}{\text{Direct labour cost}} \times 100$ $\dfrac{175,000}{40,000}$ $\dfrac{208,000}{43,333}$

$= £4.375 \text{ per hour}$ $= £4.80 \text{ per hour}$

Administration and selling costs, as a percentage of production costs

$$\dfrac{118,500 + 192,000}{1,000,000 + 460,000 + 383,000} \times 100$$

$= 16.85\%$

Mark up $= \dfrac{\text{net profit}}{\text{sales}} \times 100$ $= \dfrac{246,500}{2,400,000} \times 100$

$= 10.27\%$

Revised estimate for job 878

		£	£
Direct material			9,000
Direct labour			3,800
Production overhead:			
Grinding:	400 × 4.375 =	1,750	
Finishing:	300 × 4.80 =	1,440	3,190
			15,990
Admin. and selling costs			
16.85% × 15,990 =			2,694
Revised total cost			18,684
Mark up 10.27% × 18,684 =			1,919
Revised selling price			20,603

or if based on 'preferred return'

Cost	83 1/3
Mark up	16 2/3
Selling price	100

$$\text{Selling price} = 18,684 \times \dfrac{100}{83\,1/3} = £22,421$$

Task 3

The following changes should be made to improve the accounting information:

(a)   Preparation of budgets. This would include calculation of predetermined overhead recovery rates and a separation of fixed and variable costs. The latter will be needed to identify the minimum acceptable selling price for each job. This will enable adoption of a more flexible attitude to pricing (ie, not just use a margin of $16^{2}/3\%$) which will be particularly important in the recession when prices may need to be determined by demand.

(b)   When actual costs are available for each job these should be compared with budget to identify variances. These variances may indicate that current activities must be amended or that it is necessary to vary future estimates.

(c)   It could be beneficial to obtain information about competitors eg costs, profits, quality of product and selling prices charged.

(d)   It may be possible to establish more accurate job costs by using activity based costing.

3   Solution

(Note: this question needs careful thought. Consider what the costs relate to, eg per page or per hour.*)*

Task 1

		£	£
Photography			
64 pages @ £150 per page			9,600
Set–up			
Labour	64 plates × 4 hours × £7	1,792	
Material	64 plates × £35	2,240	
Overheads	64 plates × 4 hours × £9.50	2,432	
			6,464
Printing			
Material – paper (see working)		39,184	
– other (£7 × 100,000/500)		1,400	
Labour and overheads $\dfrac{100,000}{1,000}$ hours × £62		6,200	
			46,784
Binding			
Labour and overheads $\dfrac{100,000}{2,500}$ hours × £43			1,720
Total costs			64,568
Selling price	£64,568 ÷ 90%		71,742

WORKINGS

(W1)   Material cost

1 catalogue requires 32 sheets
Number of sheets of output required for 100,000 catalogues
= 100,000 × 32 = 3,200,000 sheets

This represents 98% of **input** required (2% of input is lost).

$$\therefore \text{ Input required } = 3,200,000 \times \frac{100}{98}$$

$$= 3,265,306$$

Cost is £12 per thousand sheets

$\therefore$ Total cost of sheets

$$= \frac{3,265,306}{1,000} \times £12$$

$$= £39,184$$

Task 2

Estimate hours in set–up   = 64 plates $\times$ 4 hours
                             = 256

If efficiency is 90%, then **actual** hours

$= 256 \times \dfrac{100}{90}$ = 284.4 hours

Extra hours   = 284.4 – 256
                             = 28.4 hours

Labour & overhead cost per hour   = £7 + £9.50
                                  = £16.50 per hour

$\therefore$ Additional costs   = 28.4 hours $\times$ £16.50
                             = £469.3

Chapters 21 – 22

INVESTMENT APPRAISAL

1 Solution

Tutorial note: note in Task 1 that you are not required to total the costs over the seven–year period, so do not waste time doing so.

Task 1

Maintenance costs – company providing its own maintenance

Year	Regular costs (increasing by 5% pa) £	Overhaul £	Total £
1	10,500		10,500
2	11,025		11,025
3	11,576		11,576
4	12,155	25,000	37,155
5	12,763		12,763
6	13,401		13,401
7	14,071		14,071

Task 2

Present value of maintenance costs

Year	Costs £	Factor	Present value £
1	10,500	0.909	9,544
2	11,025	0.826	9,107
3	11,576	0.751	8,694
4	37,155	0.683	25,377
5	12,763	0.621	7,926
6	13,401	0.564	7,558
7	14,071	0.513	7,218
		Present value =	75,424

Task 3

Present value of supplier's maintenance contract

Cumulative present value of £1, payable at the end of each year for seven years, at a discount rate of 10%: 4.868.

Present value is therefore £13,000 × 4.868 = £63,284.

Task 4

On the basis of the calculations above, the supplier's maintenance contract appears preferable. It costs only £63,284 in present value terms, compared with a cost of £75,424 for the in–house option. Additional advantages of the supplier's contract include:

- certainty of the level of costs
- possible insurance against unforeseen breakdowns.

2   Solution

Task 1

Time	Flow	Discount factor at 15%	PV at 15%	Discount factor at 20%	PV at 20%
0	(10,000)	1	(10,000)	1	(10,000)
1	500	0.870	435	0.833	416.5
2	2,000	0.756	1,512	0.694	1,388
3	3,000	0.658	1,974	0.579	1,737
4	4,000	0.572	2,288	0.482	1,928
5	5,000	0.497	2,485	0.402	2,010
6	2,500	0.432	1,080	0.335	837.5
7	2,000	0.376	752	0.279	558
8	2,500	0.327	817.5	0.233	582.5
			1,343.5		−542.5

Net present value at 15% is £1,343.5

Task 2

$$IRR = A\% + \frac{NPV_A}{NPV_A - NPV_B} \times (B - A)\%$$

where   A% = 15 NPV_A = 1,343.5
          B% = 20 NPV_B = −542.5

$$IRR \cong 15\% + \frac{1,343.5}{1,343.5 + 542.5} (5\%)$$

$$\cong 18.6\%$$

Task 3

The project has a positive Net Present Value and an IRR which is higher than the cost of capital and thus will increase shareholder wealth and should be undertaken.

Other factors to consider are:

Risk – how certain are the cash flows and how reliable are the estimates on which they were based?

Changes in the cost of capital – will the cost of capital remain at 15% throughout the life of the project?

The effects of inflation or tax – will inflation or tax change the cash flows?

The effects on other projects – will doing this project affect the company's ability to complete other projects because of, for example, a shortage of skilled labour or factory space?

3   Solution

Task 1

Year end	Current cashflows £m	New pump cashflows £m
0 (Now)	–	(0.75)
1	0.5	1.0
2	0.5	1.0
3	0.5	1.0
4	0.5	1.0
5	0.5	1.0 + 0.1 = 1.1
6	0.5	–
7	0.5	–
8	0.5	–
9	0.5	–
10	0.5	–

Task 2

Discount tables may be used to find cumulative discount factors and discount factors.

The current situation

$NPV = 0.5 \times 6.710 = \underline{£3.355m}$

(6.710 comes from annuity table, 8% for 10 years.)

The new pump

$NPV = (0.75) + 1.0 \times 3.312 + 1.1 \times 0.681$
$= (0.75) + 3.312 + 0.749$
$NPV = \underline{£3.311m}$

(Tutorial note:

£(0.75)m is the cash outflow **now**, so is already a present value. There follows an annuity of £1.0m a year for 4 years hence discounted by the cumulative present value factor of 3.312. The final cash flow of £1.1m is discounted back over 5 years at 8%, discount factor = 0.681.)

The company should continue operating with their existing equipment and work the well for the next 10 years. At today's values, it is financially advantageous to follow this course of action as it yields the higher NPV.

Task 3

Recalculating the NPVs (@ 12%)

Existing equipment

$NPV = 0.5 \times 5.650 = \underline{£2.825m}$

New pump

$NPV = (0.75) + 1.0 \times 3.037 + 1.1 \times 0.567$

$NPV = \underline{£2.911m}$

If the cost of capital were to change to 12%, the new pump should be installed as this option now gives the higher NPV.

The higher the cost of capital, the smaller the present value of long term future cashflows. Therefore a shorter life project is the better option.

PRACTICE CENTRAL
ASSESSMENT ACTIVITIES

ANSWERS

FOULKS*lynch*

ASSESSMENT ACTIVITIES – CONTENTS

AAT Assessments

◈ FOULKS*lynch*

266

UNIT 8 – SECTION 1 – JUNE 1997

Task 1.1

(a)   Calculation of the material and labour variances

	Material variances	£	
(i)	Actual usage at standard price (78,000 litres × £20)	1,560,000	
	Actual usage at actual price (given in May data)	1,599,000	
	Material price variance	39,000	(Adverse)

		Litres	
(ii)	Standard usage (9,500 units produced × 8 litres)	76,000	
	Actual usage (given in May data)	78,000	
	Excess litres used	2,000	
	Material usage variance (2,000 litres × £20)	£40,000	(Adverse)

	Labour variances	£	
(iii)	Actual hours at standard rate (39,000 hours × £6)	234,000	
	Actual hours at actual rate (given in May data)	249,600	
	Labour rate variance	15,600	(Adverse)

		Hours	
(iv)	Standard hours (9,500 units × 4 hours)	38,000	
	Actual hours (given in May data)	39,000	
	Excess hours used	1,000	
	Labour efficiency variance (1,000 hours × £6)	£6,000	(Adverse)

(b)

Standard marginal costing statement for Beta production – May 1997

	£	
Actual marginal cost of production	1,848,600	
Material price variance	(39,000)	(A)
Material usage variance	(40,000)	(A)
Labour rate variance	(15,600)	(A)
Labour efficiency variance	(6,000)	(A)
Standard marginal cost of production (9,500 units × £184)	1,748,000	

Key: A = adverse

Task 1.2

(a)   Calculation of variances attributable to the special order   *Litres*

Material purchased (1,500 units × 8 litres × $\frac{1}{0.8}$)   15,000

Standard usage (1,500 units × 8 litres)   12,000

Excess usage (litres)   3,000

Material price variance (15,000 litres × [£22 − £20])   £30,000 (Adverse)
Material usage variance (3,000 litres × £20)   £60,000 (Adverse)
Labour rate variance (1,500 units × 4 hours × £6 × 50%)   £18,000 (Adverse)

(b)   Revised standard price based on current index

          £

(i)   Revised standard price (247.2/240.0) × £20   20.60
        Original standard (given in data)   20.00

        Difference   0.60

(ii)   Effect on original material price variance
        ([78,000 − 15,000] litres × £0.60)*   £37,800 (Adverse)

*Actual purchase = 78,000 litres. Purchases for special order = 15,000 litres.

(c)
Revised standard marginal costing statement for Beta production – May 1997

	£	£
Actual marginal cost of production		1,848,600
Variances from factors outside divisional control		
Special order		
Material price variance	30,000 (A)	
Material usage variance	60,000 (A)	
Labour rate variance	18,000 (A)	
	108,000 (A)	
Amended standard for material prices	37,800 (A)	145,800 (A)
Variances from factors within divisional control		
Material price variance (39,000 − 30,000 − 37,800)	28,800 (F)	
Material usage variance (40,000 − 60,000)	20,000 (F)	
Labour rate variance (15,600 − 18,000)	2,400 (F)	
Labour efficiency variance	6,000 (A)	
		45,200 (F)
Standard marginal cost of production		1,748,000

Key: A = adverse, F = favourable

(d)

MEMO

To: Richard Hill   From: The Management Accountant

Date: 18 June 1997

Subject: Variances arising outside your control

Introduction

This memo justifies my treatment of the variances arising from factors outside your control in the attached standard costing statements, and suggests further action that should be taken by the company.

Justification for showing the variances separately

Within the original divisional adverse variance of £100,600, £108,000 arose because of the acceptance of the special order by the sales director and £37,800 arose because of a general increase in material prices. Although these originated in your division, neither were *caused* by the division. Because you have no responsibility for these variances, you cannot control them and so they are reported separately from those variances you can control and be held responsible for.

Possible action to be taken

The adverse variance arising from the general increase in prices suggests that the standard cost of the materials needs revising. Before doing this, however, the company should check that the index is an appropriate one for the material used in Beta production and that there is not a cheaper and better alternative source of supply.

The adverse variance arising from the special order should first be compared with the overall profitability of that order. If, after charging the variances to the order, it was still profitable then the variances, by ignoring the revenue aspect, might be sending out a false signal. If the adverse variances made the special order unprofitable then the consequences of this should be made known to the sales director to prevent similar losses being incurred in the future. Secondly, it might be useful to discuss with the sales director whether advance warning of extra orders could be given in the future as this would, at least, enable materials to be sourced from the normal supplier at the normal cost.

UNIT 8 – SECTION 1 – DECEMBER 1997

Task 1.1

(a)	**Labour hours**		*Budgeted*	*Actual*
	Labour cost		£48,000	£42,240
	Budgeted and actual rate		£8	£8
	(i),(ii)	Labour hours (labour cost ÷ £8)	6,000	5,280
		Tonnes produced	3,000	2,400
	(iii),(iv)	Hours per tonne (labour hours ÷ tonnes produced)	2	2.2

(b)   **Fixed overhead variances**

Workings

Budgeted fixed overheads	£81,000
Budgeted tonnes	3,000
Budgeted fixed overhead per tonne (£81,000 ÷ 3,000)	£27.00
Budgeted labour hours	6,000
Budgeted fixed overhead per labour hour	£13.50

			£
(i)	Actual cost of fixed overheads		90,000
	Budgeted cost of fixed overheads		81,000
	Fixed overhead expenditure variance		9,000 (Adverse)

			Tonnes
(ii)	Budgeted tonnes		3,000
	Actual tonnes		2,400
	Volume variance (tonnes)		600 (Adverse)
	Fixed overhead volume variance [600 × £27.00]		£16,200 (Adverse)

(Tutorial note: Alternatively:

		Hours
Budgeted hours [3,000 tonnes × 2 hours]		6,000
Actual hours produced [2,400 × 2 hours]		4,800
Volume variance (hours)		1,200 (Adverse)
Fixed overhead volume variance [1,200 × £13.50]		£16,200 (Adverse))

			Hours
(iii)	Budgeted hours		6,000
	Actual hours worked		5,280
	Capacity variance (hours)		720 (Adverse)
	Fixed overhead capacity variance [720 × £13.50]		£9,720 (Adverse)

		Hours
(iv)	Actual hours worked	5,280
	Actual hours produced (2,400 tonnes × 2 hours)	4,800
	Efficiency variance (hours)	480 (Adverse)
	Fixed overhead efficiency variance [480 × £13.50]	£6,480 (Adverse)

Task 1.2

MEMO

To: Claude Debussy   **From**:   The Company Accountant

Date: 19 August 1998

Subject: **Fixed overhead variances**

(a)   Fixed overhead costs and changes in activity

Fixed overheads are fixed in the sense that they do not vary with changes in output over the relevant range. Instead, they tend to vary with time. The longer the time period, the greater the cost. Examples include rent and rates, which have to be paid irrespective of the number of tonnes of fertiliser made. Because of this, it is inappropriate to excuse automatically the increase in fixed costs simply because volume has increased. Fixed costs, however, are only fixed over the 'relevant range'. For a taxi with five passenger seats, the relevant range would be from one to five passengers resulting in a sixth passenger requiring an additional taxi. Providing Debussy Ltd's production for the year has not exceeded this relevant range, then fixed costs should not have increased as a result of volume increases. Any increase must be due to the fixed overheads costing more than budgeted.

(b)   Possible reasons for the fixed overhead variances

Fixed overhead expenditure variance
          Inflation
          Non–standard supplier for power and insurance
          Inappropriate standard

Fixed overhead capacity variance
          Reduced demand compared with budget
          Inappropriate standard

Fixed overhead efficiency variance
          Poor quality materials slowing down production
          Workforce working slower than normal
          Inappropriate standard

Task 1.3

The notes should include the following:

(a)   **Revised quarterly power budgets**

	Quarter 1	Quarter 2	Quarter 3	Quarter 4
Seasonal variation (%)	+5%	−10%	− 20%	+25%
	£	£	£	£
Current budget	30,000	30,000	30,000	30,000
Seasonal variation	1,500	(3,000)	(6,000)	7,500
Revised budget	31,500	27,000	24,000	37,500

(b)   **Use in variance analysis**

Although the power budget does not vary with changes in volume, it does vary with the different outside temperatures of each quarter. Allowing for these seasonal variations will give a more accurate budget figure against which to compare actual costs for control purposes. For example, the existing system shows an adverse expenditure variance for power of £6,000 but with the revised variance this becomes a favourable variance of £1,500. Allowing for the extra £7,500 of expenditure on power causes the budget for quarter 4 to increase by that amount to £88,500.

There is, however, a problem in using the revised budget of £88,500 when calculating the fixed overhead volume variance. Using that figure to calculate fixed overhead absorption rates will cause the volume variance to appear larger than before while reducing any variances in quarters when the seasonal variation is negative. This will result in the same volume variance in tonnes having different monetary values in different quarters and this is likely to be misleading to managers. Given that the seasonal variations will balance out over the four quarters, it would seem reasonable to calculate the volume variance using annual fixed overhead absorption rates.

UNIT 8 – SECTION 1 – DECEMBER 1998

Task 1.1

M E M O

To: Richard Jones   From: Accounting Technician

Date: 2 December 1998

Subject: Variances in kit costs

(a)   (i)   The standard cost per kit was based on an exchange rate of \$9.80 to the pound. Because of this, the UK standard cost became £5,535 (\$54,243/9.80). The detailed costs and variances are calculated below.

Month	Workings	September	October	November
Number of kits		2,000	2,100	2,050
Contract cost in \$	*number of kits × \$54,243*	\$108,486,000	\$113,910,300	\$111,198,150
Exchange rate		\$9.00	\$10.00	\$10.25

(ii)

Contract cost in £	*\$ cost/exchange rate*	£12,054,000	£11,391,030	£10,848,600
Contract cost in £	*as above*	£12,054,000	£11,391,030	£10,848,600
Standard cost	*Cost in Erehwon \$/\$9.8*	£11,070,000	£11,623,500	£11,346,750

(iii)

Price variance		£984,000 (A)	£232,470 (F)	£498,150 (F)
Cost in £	*as above*	12,054,000	11,391,030	10,848,600
Actual cost	*given in task*	12,059,535	11,385,495	10,848,600

(iv)

Usage variance		5,535 (A)	5,535 (F)	nil

(b)   The price variances due to exchange rate differences are unlikely to be of help to the production manager of Pronto Ltd as they are not controllable by him and should, therefore be excluded.

Task 1.2

(a)   Budgeted data

      (i)   Budgeted overheads per machine (or track) hours £840,000/140 = £6,000 per hour.

      (ii)   Budgeted number of cars produced per machine (or track) hour = 560/140 = 4 per hour.

      (iii)   Standard hours of production = 500/4 = 125 hours.

(b)   Variances

      (i)   Fixed overhead expenditure variance = £840,000 – £842,000 = £2,000 (adverse).

      (ii)   Fixed overhead volume variance = (125 hours – 140 hours) × £6,000 = £90,000 (adverse).

      (iii)   Fixed overhead efficiency variance = (125 hours – 126 hours) × £6,000 = £6,000 (adverse).

      (iv)   Fixed overhead capacity variance = (126 hours – 140 hours) × £6,000 = £84,000 (adverse).

(c)

Reconciliation statement between fixed overheads incurred and fixed overheads absorbed week ended 28 November 1998

		£
Fixed overheads incurred		842,000
Expenditure variance		2,000 (A)
Efficiency variance		6,000 (A)
Capacity variance		84,000 (A)
Fixed overheads absorbed	125 × £6,000	750,000

UNIT 8 – SECTION 1 – JUNE 1999

Task 1.1

(a)   **Calculation of quantities**

(i)	Actual litres used	£338,283/£40.20	8,415
(ii)	Actual hours worked	£110,330/£5.90	18,700
(iii)	Standard litres for 1,700 tins of Zed	1,700 × 5 litres	8,500
(iv)	Standard labour hours for 1,700 tins of Zed	1,700 × 10 hours	17,000
(v)	Standard hours of fixed overheads charged to budgeted production	1,750 × 10 hours	17,500
(vi)	Standard hours of fixed overheads charged to actual production	1,700 × 10 hours	17,000

(b)   **Calculation of variances**

(i)   **Direct Material Price Variance**   **F/(A)**

(Standard price – Actual price) actual usage

(£40 – £40.20) 8,415 litres =   £(1,683)

(ii)   **Direct Material Usage Variance**

(Standard usage – Actual Usage) standard price

(8,500 – 8,415) £40 =   £3,400F

(iii)   **Direct Labour Rate Variance**

(Standard rate – Actual rate) actual hours

(£6 – £5.90) 18,700 =   £1,870 F

(iv)   **Direct Labour Efficiency Variance**

(Standard hours produced – Actual hours worked) standard rate per hour

(17,000 – 18,700) £6 =   £(10,200)

(v)   **Fixed Overhead Expenditure Variance**

This is simply the difference between Budget and Actual Fixed Cost

	£
Budget	420,000
Actual	410,000
	£10,000 F

This is an under–spend, or over–recovery due to expenditure.

(vi)   **Fixed Overhead Volume Variance**

(Standard hours produced – Budget standard hours) FORR
FORR = Fixed overhead recovery rate per standard hour

(17,000 – 17,500) £24 =   £(12,000)

This is an under–recovery due to the fall in volume.

Note: The volume variance sub–divides to the concepts of capacity and efficiency.

(vii)   **Fixed Overhead Capacity Variance**

(Budget standard hours – actual hours worked) FORR

(17,500 – 18,700) £24   £28,800 F

This is an over–recovery due to the excess capacity utilised.

(viii)   **Fixed Overhead Efficiency Variance**
         (Standard hours produced − actual hours worked) FORR
         (17,000 − 18,700) £24 =   £(40,800)

         This is an under–recovery due to efficiency of labour.

         (See also direct labour efficiency adverse variance.)

(c)   **Reconciliation statement Zed production May 99**

      Standard to actual cost of production:

                                                                    £
      Actual cost of production   858,613
                                                                    ‾‾‾‾‾‾‾

Summary of variances	**F/(A)**	
Direct material price	(1,683)	
Direct material usage	3,400 F	
	‾‾‾‾‾	
		1,117 F
Direct labour rate	1,870 F	
Direct labour efficiency	(10,200)	
	‾‾‾‾‾	
		(8,330)
Fixed overhead expenditure	10,000 F	
Fixed overhead volume	(12,000) *1	
	‾‾‾‾‾	
		(2,000)
		‾‾‾‾‾
		(8,613)
		‾‾‾‾‾

      Standard cost of actual production   £850,000 *2
                                                                   ‾‾‾‾‾‾‾

      * 2 1,700 tins × £500.00/tin
      * 1 Fixed overhead capacity variance   £28,800 F
           Fixed overhead efficiency variance   £(40,800)
                                                                   ‾‾‾‾‾‾‾
      Thus: Volume   £(12,000)
                                                                   ‾‾‾‾‾‾‾

Task 1.2

MEMO

To: **Production director**   **From:** **Management accountant**

Subject: Material variances   **Date:**   **16 June 1999**

I note your comments on the material variances calculated in my reconciliation statement for Zed production.

(a)   If we had updated the material price to incorporate the change in the index, the revised standard would have been:

          $£40,000 \times (125.86/124.00) = £40.60$ per litre

     It is possible to subdivide the material price variance into two elements, that due to the increased standard cost as measured by the index and that due to the efficiency of the purchasing department. The original price variance of £1,683 (A), £5,049 (A) was due to a failure to estimate accurately the original standard price whilst a favourable variance of £3,366 arose from efficiencies within the purchasing department. The workings for this are shown below.

Revised standard price/litre	£40.60	Revised standard price/litre	£40.60
Original standard price/litre	£40.00	Actual price/litre	£40.20
	———		———
Variance	£0.60 (A)	Variance	£0.40 (F)
Actual quantity (litres)	8,415	Actual quantity (litres)	8,415
Price variance due to revised price	£5,049 (A)	Price variance due to purchasing	£3,366 (F)

(b)   There are a number of reasons why a favourable usage variance is experienced. These include:

     (i)   incorrect setting of the standard usage

     (ii)   data error input as when a clerk misreads a figure

     (iii)   some drums of material contain in excess of 50 litres resulting in more material being used than recorded as being used

     (iv)   errors in the automatic weighing system. In May, 8,415 litres of material were used to produce 1,700 tins of Zed. This is equivalent to 4.95 litres per tin. The lowest acceptable error is only 0.5% or 4.975 per tin. This suggests that there might be a problem with the settings of the measuring machine.

(c)   Considering the above factors, we must investigate favourable variances if the production system is to be kept under control.

UNIT 8 – SECTION 1 – DECEMBER 1999

SECTION 1

Task 1.1

(a)   **Budget data**

(i)	Actual number of meals: 4 meals × 7 days × 648 guests =		18,144
(ii)	Standard number of meals: 3 meals × 7 days × 648 guests =		13,608
(iii)	Actual hourly rate for catering staff: $5,280 cost ÷ 1,200 hours =		$4.40
(iv)	Standard hours allowed to serve three meals:		
	(648 ÷ 12) × 3 meals × 7 days =		1,134
(v)	Standard overhead per guest:		
	$38,340 budgeted overheads ÷ 540 budgeted guests =		$71.00
(vi)	Standard cost of providing for 648 guests:		
	Meals: $3.00 × 13,608 meals =		$40,824
	Catering staff: $4.00 × 1,134 hours =		£4,536
	Fixed overheads: $71.00 standard overhead per guest × 648 guests =		$46,008
	Total		$91,368

(b)   **Variances**

(i)   **Material Price Variance**   **F/(A)**

(Standard cost/meal – actual cost/meal) actual meals

($3 – $2.75) 18,144 = $4,536 F

(ii)   **Material Usage Variance**

(Standard meals – actual meals) standard cost/meal

(13,608 – 18,144) $3 = $(13,608)

(iii)   **Labour Rate Variance**

(Standard rate per hour – actual rate per hour) actual hours

($4 – $4.4) 1,200 = $(480)

(iv)   **Labour Efficiency Variance**

(Standard hours produced – actual hours worked) standard rate

(1,134 – 1,200) $4 = $(264)

(v)   **Fixed Overhead Expenditure Variance**

	$
Budgeted fixed cost	38,340
Actual fixed cost	37,800
	$540 F

This represents an under–spend.

(vi)   **Fixed Overhead Volume Variance**

(Budgeted no of guests – actual number of guests) Fixed overhead rate/guest

= (540 - 648) $71 = $7,668 F

(c)   **Bare Foot Hotel**
Reconciliation statement, standard to actual cost – meals
Seven days ended 27 November 1999

	F/(A)
	$
Standard cost for 648 guests	91,368

Summary of variances:

Material price	4,536 F
Material usage	(13,608)
Labour rate	(480)
Labour efficiency	(264)
Fixed overhead expenditure	540 F
Fixed overhead volume	7,668 F
Actual cost of meals, 648 guests	$92,976

Task 1.2

MEMO

To:	**Alice Groves**	From:	**Assistant management accountant**
Subject:	**Issues arising from the reconciliation statement**	Date:	**1 December 1999**

(a)   The labour efficiency variance can be analysed to that part due to guests taking, on average, four meals per day and that part due to other efficiency reasons. Thus:

Standard cost of standards hours – 3 meals per guest	$4,536
Standard cost of standard hours – 4 meals per guest	
[(648 ÷ 12) × 4 meals × 7 days] × $4	$6,048
Variance due to guests taking extra meals per day	$1,512 (A)
Standard cost of standard hours – 4 meals per guest	$6,048
Standard cost of actual hours	$4,800
Variance due to other factors	$1,248 (F)

(b)   **Fixed overhead capacity and efficiency variances**

The capacity variance is a sub–analysis of the volume variance.

Volume can be influenced by either capacity or efficiency.

If volume is favourable then fixed overhead will be over–recovered, the underlying reason for such a situation would be either favourable efficiency or favourable capacity or a combination of both.

(c)   **Feasibility of applying these variances**

It is clear that the volume variance can be expressed in terms of the unit – guests per day. But in order to express meaningfully the capacity and efficiency variances we would need to identify the total hours of activity, planned and actual not just that for preparing meals.

◆ **FOULKS***lynch*

UNIT 8 – SECTION 1 – JUNE 2000

Task 1.1

(a)   (i)   Budgeted labour hours of production of NGJ Ltd

Labour hours	Budgeted hours per unit	Budgeted production	Budgeted hours
Basic	6	10,000	60,000
Grand	1	70,000	70,000
Super	1	70,000	70,000
Total budgeted labour hours			200,000

(ii) Standard factory fixed overhead rate per labour hour (£600,000/200,000 hours)	£3.00
(iii) *Basic* budgeted factory fixed overhead (£600,000 × [60,000/200,000])	£180,000
Basic actual factory fixed overhead (£630,000 × [60,000/200,000])	£189,000
(iv) Actual material cost per metre (£872,298/69,230)	£12.60
Actual labour hourly rate (£343,735/70,150)	£4.90
(v) Standard absorption cost of actual *Basic* production	
Material (£12 × 6 metres × 11,500 *Basics*)	£828,000
Labour (£5 × 6 hours × 11,500 *Basics*)	£345,000
Factory fixed overheads (£3 × 6 hours × 11,500 *Basics*)	£207,000
	£1,380,000
(vi) Actual absorption cost of actual *basic* production	
Material	£872,298
Labour	£343,735
Factory fixed overheads	£189,000
	£1,405,033

(b)   **Variances**

		F/(A)
(i) **Direct Material Price Variance**		
(Standard price – actual price) actual usage		
(£12 – £12.60) 69,230 =		£(41,538)
(ii) **Direct Material Usage Variance**		
(Standard usage – actual usage) standard price		
(69,000 – 69,230) £12 =		£(2,760)
(iii) **Direct Labour Rate Variance**		
(Standard rate – actual rate) actual hours		
(£5 – £4.90) 70,150 =		£7,015 F
(iv) **Direct Labour Efficiency Variance**		
(Standard hours produced – actual hours) standard rate		
(69,000 – 70,150) £5 =		£(5,750)

(v)   **Fixed Overhead Variance**

	£
Budgeted fixed cost	180,000
Actual fixed cost	189,000
	£(9,000)

This represents an over–spend.

(vi)   **Fixed overhead volume variance**
        (Standard hours produced – budget standard hours) FORR
        (69,000 – 60,000) £3 =   £27,000 F

(vii)   **Fixed overhead capacity variance**
        (Budget standard hours – actual hours) FORR
        (60,000 – 70,150) £3 =   £30,450 F

(viii) **Fixed overhead efficiency**
        (Standard hours produced – actual hours worked) FORR
        (69,000 – 70,150) £3 =   £(3,450)

(c)   **Basic Production**
      Reconciliation statement, standard to actual cost of production period ended 31 May 2000

	F/(A)
	$
Standard cost of actual production	1,380,000

Summary of variances:

Material price	(41,538)
Material usage	(2,760)
Labour rate	7,015 F
Labour efficiency	(5,750)
Fixed overhead expenditure	(9,000)
Fixed overhead capacity	30,450 F
Fixed overhead efficiency	(3,450)
	(25,033)
Actual cost of production	£1,405,033

Task 1.2

MEMO

To: *Basic* **product line manager**   From: **Management accountant**

Subject:Material price variances and fixed overheads   **Date: 21 June 2000**

I enclose my comments on the issues relating to *Basic* production.

(a)   Market price = £12.60 × (100/90) =   £14.00

(b)   Subdivision of material price variance:
        due to contracted price differing from market price
           (£14.00 − £12.60) × 69,230   £96,922 (F)
        due to other reasons (£12.00 − £14.00) × 69,230   £138,460 (A)
                                                                          ————————
        Total material price variance   £41,538 (A)
                                                                          ————————

(c)   The value added from the purchasing manager's actions is the benefit of continuing production from
        guaranteed supplies of materials.

(d)   Traditional absorption costing focuses on the recovery of fixed overheads rather than the control of such costs.

        ABC however recognises the activities which drive costs and directs the overheads to those products
        generating cost.

(e)   An analysis of fixed overheads shows that £202,000 of budgeted fixed overheads arose because of the
        complexities of the mechanised production of the *Grand* and *Super*. Most of the depreciation relates to the
        manufacture of those products as both require expensive machines. As *Basic* production only uses a small
        part of the factory, it is also possible that most of the rent and rates relating to production are driven by the
        manufacturing needs of the *Grand* and the *Super*. It is highly likely that ABC would have reduced both the
        budgeted and actual fixed overheads attributable to *Basic* production.

UNIT 8 – SECTION 1 – DECEMBER 2000

Task 1.1

(a)　(i)　Standard price of fuel per litre
　　　　　£497,664/1,244,160 = £0.40

　　(ii)　Standard litres of fuel for 5,760 ferry crossings
　　　　　1,244,160 × (5,760/6,480) = 1,105,920 litres

　　(iii)　Standard labour rate per hour
　　　　　£466,560/93,312 = £5.00

　　(iv)　Standard labour hours for 5,760 ferry crossings
　　　　　93,312 × (5,760/6,480) = 82,944 hours

　　(v)　Standard fixed overhead per budgeted operating hour
　　　　　£466,560/7,776 = £60.00

　　(vi)　Standard operating hours for 5,760 crossings
　　　　　5,760 × (7,776/6,480) = 6,912 hours

　　(vii)　Standard fixed overhead cost absorbed by the actual 5,760 ferry crossings
　　　　　6,912 hours × £60.00 = £414,720

(b)　**Variances**

			F/(A)
(i)	**Material Price Variance**		
	(Standard price – actual price) actual usage		
	(£0.40 – £0.46) 1,232,800 litres =		(73,968)
(ii)	**Material Usage Variance**		
	(Standard usage – actual usage) standard price		
	(1,105,920 – 1,232,800) £0.40 =		(50,752)
(iii)	**Labour Rate Variance**		
	(Standard rate – actual rate) actual hours		
	(£5.00 – £5.25) 89,856 =		(22,464)
(iv)	**Labour Efficiency Variance**		
	(Standard hours allowed – actual hours worked) standard rate		
	(82,944 – 89,856) £5 =		(34,560)

(v)　**Fixed Overhead Expenditure Variance**

	£
Budget fixed overhead	466,560
Actual fixed overhead	472,440
	£(5,880)

(vi)　**Fixed overhead volume variance**
(Budget standard hours – standard hours allowed) FORR
(7,776 – 6,912) £60 =　　　　　　　　　　　£(51,840)

(vii)　**Fixed overhead capacity variance**
(Budget standard hours – actual hours) FORR
(7,776 – 7,488) £60 =　　　　　　　　　　　(17,280)

(viii)   **Fixed overhead efficiency variance**
(Standard hours allowed − actual hours) FORR
(6,912 − 7,488) £60 =   (34,560)

(c)   **Travel Ferries Ltd: Reconciliation statement for the year to 30 November 2000**

		$
Actual cost of actual operation		£1,511,272
Material price variance	(73,968)	
Material usage variance	(50,752)	
Labour rate variance	(22,464)	
Labour efficiency variance	(34,560)	
Fixed overhead expenditure variance	(5,880)	
Fixed overhead capacity variance	(17,280)	
Fixed overhead efficiency variance	(34,560)	(239,464)
Standard cost of actual operation [1]		£1,271,808

[1]	Material: 1,105,920 litres × £0.40 =	£442,368
	Labour: 82,944 hours × £5.00 =	£414,720
	Fixed overhead: 6,912 hours × £60.00 =	£414,720
		£1,271,808

Task 1.2

MEMO

To: **Chief Executive**	**From:** **Management accountant**
Date: **6 December 2000**	
Subject: Explanation of variances	

You recently made a number of observations regarding the adverse variances for Travel Ferries' operations in the year to 30 November 2000. In order to assist, my analysis I have:

- further analysed the material price variance
- identified uncontrollable variances and
- suggested variances which are controllable and, therefore, should be investigated.

(a)   Material price variance

    Actual market price: £0.40 × 1.2 =   £0.48
    Actual price paid: £567,088/1,232,800 litres =   £0.46

        Price variance due to failing to revised the standard (£0.40 × £0.48) × 1,232,800 litres =   £98,624 (A)
        Price variance due to efficient purchasing policy (£0.48 × £0.46) × 1,232,800 litres =   £24,656 (F)

    Total price variance   £73,968 (A)

(b)   The labour efficiency variance has arisen due to the extra time taken as a result of the adverse weather conditions and is therefore uncontrollable and not worthy of investigation.

    For 5,760 crossings, the ferries should have operated for 6,912 hours. However due to conditions, the operating time was 7,488 hours.   The time taken was $8\frac{1}{3}\%$ more than standard. The standard labour hours for 5,760 crossings should have been 82,944 hours. However, 89,856 labour hours were worked. Therefore the adverse labour efficiency variance was entirely due to the adverse weather conditions.

(c)   Two controllable variances are the labour rate variance and the material price variance. Neither can be automatically explained by the adverse weather conditions.

UNIT 8 – SECTION 2 – JUNE 1997

Task 2.1

The Cam Car Company	Yearly performance indicators		
	Workings	Van division	Car division
Return on capital employed	1	40.00%	2.53%
Profit margin	2	26.67%	4.21%
Asset turnover	3	1.5 times	0.6 times
Profit per employee	4	£11,200	£4,000
Wages per employee	5	£11,000	£11,500
Output (Vehicles) per employee	6	5	7
Labour cost per vehicle	7	£2,200	£1,643
Added value per employee	8	£32,500	£29,167

WORKINGS

1	£112m/£280m
2	£112m/£420m
3	£420m/£280m
4	£112m/10,000
5	£110m/10,000
6	50,000/10,000
7	£110m/50,000
8	(£420m – £95m)/10,000

Task 2.2

MEMO

To: Peter Ross   From: The Management Accountant

Date: 19 August 1998

Subject: Wage negotiations and performance

(a)   **The meaning of productivity and added value**

    (i)   Productivity is a ratio of input to output. Normally, this is expressed in physical terms such as hours of labour to units produced. However, sometimes productivity is expressed in financial terms where unit information is either not available or not appropriate.

    (ii)   Companies buy in raw materials and services. They then convert these to finished products by adding labour and overheads. These are then sold, hopefully, at a profit. Through these stages, the worth or value attached to the original raw materials is increased. Added value measures the overall increase in value added to those original raw materials by the actions of the organisation. In that sense, it is a monetary measure of the skills added by the organisation. Formally, added value is defined as the difference between sales value and the cost of bought–in material and services. (An alternative definition is conversion costs plus profit.) Often this is expressed as a relative measure by dividing by the number of employees.

(b)   **Performance indicators supporting the employees' claims**

    (i)   *Profitability*
        Return on capital employed
        Profit margin
        Profit per employee
        Wages per employee

    (ii)   *Productivity*
        Asset turnover
        Added value per employee

(c)   **Performance indicators questioning the employees' claims**

    Although the wages paid to the employees in the van division are lower than those paid to the car division, what matters to the company is labour cost per unit. Each employee of the van division only produces 5 vehicles per annum whereas the output per employee in the car division is 7. In addition, the labour cost per vehicle is higher for vans than for cars.

    The employee representatives might argue that these indicators result from the van division having a smaller and older investment in building, plant and machinery. With more modern and more efficient equipment output per employee is likely to be higher.

(d)   **Possible overstatement of the performance statistics**

    The depreciation for land and buildings in the profit and loss account is 2% of the original cost for both divisions. For plant and machinery, it is 10% in both cases. Given straight–line depreciation, this suggests the following average ages of fixed assets:

	Workings	Van division Buildings £m	Van division Plant £m	Car division Buildings £m	Car division Plant £m
Cost	(1)	500	400	1,200	800
Depreciation this year	(2)	10	40	24	80
Depreciation rate	(2) ÷ (1)	2%	10%	2%	10%
Accumulated depreciation	(3)	400	320	240	240
Average age of assets (years)	(3) ÷ (2)	40	8	10	3

Task 2.2 *continued*

The van division's fixed assets are considerably older than those for the car division. Both divisions record their fixed assets at historical cost and this may cause the value or replacement cost of the assets to be understated. This is likely to apply more to the van division as its fixed assets are significantly older. The result is that the capital employed is likely to be understated and, with understated depreciation, profit overstated. The overall return on capital employed is therefore likely to be overstated compared with that in the car division.

In addition, the added value of the car division is less, simply because it buys more of its components from outside suppliers rather than because its activities are less valuable.

UNIT 8 – SECTION 2 – DECEMBER 1997

Task 2.1

Maximum occupancy [365 days $\times$ 80 bedrooms]		29,200 room–nights
Actual occupancy		
Accommodation turnover =	£1,635,200	
Cost per bedroom =	£80	
Number of room–nights sold [1,635,200 ÷ £80] =	20,440	
Occupancy rate [20,440 ÷ 29,200] $\times$ 100% =		70%
Gross margin: accommodation [(327,040 ÷ 1,635,200) $\times$ 100] =		20%
Gross margin: restaurant [(157,680 ÷ 630,720) $\times$ 100] =		25%
Operating profit [33,296 + 80,000] =		£113,296
Sales margin [113,296 ÷ 2,265,920] =		5%
Return on capital employed [113,296 ÷ 1,416,200] =		8%
Asset turnover [2,265,920 ÷ 1,416,200]		1.6 times

Task 2.2

Green and Co
Accountants and Registered Auditors

Claire Hill   19 August 1998
The Grand Hotel
Dear Ms Hill,

Thank you for your recent letter enclosing details of your proposals. I have evaluated these and my comments are detailed below.

(a)   **Operating profit to give a 20% return on capital employed**
       With net assets (= capital employed) of £1,416,200, this implies an operating profit of £283,240.

(b)   **Revised profit if plans achieved**

	£	£
Increase in occupancy rate		
Revised contribution [£327,040 × (80/70)]	373,760	
Existing contribution	327,040	
Increase in profit		46,720
Change in restaurant prices and costs		
Increase in turnover [£630,720 × 5%]	31,536	
Decrease in variable costs [£473,040 × 5%]	23,652	55,188
Increase in profit		101,908
Current operating profit		113,296
Revised profit		215,204

(c)   **Revised performance indicators**

	£	
Return on capital employed [£215,204/£1,416,200]		15.20%
Revised turnover from accommodation [£1,635,200 × (80/70)]	1,868,800	
Revised turnover from restaurant [£630,720 × 105%]	662,256	
Revised turnover	2,531,056	
Asset turnover [£2,531,056 ÷ £1,416,200]		1.787 times
Sales margin [215,204 ÷ £2,531,056]		8.50%

(d)   **Findings**

The current plan results in an increase in operating profit of £101,908. This almost doubles the return on capital employed to 15.2% but it is still below the 20% average for that type of hotel.

(i)   With an increase in contribution of £46,720 coming from the increased occupancy rate, this suggests that 45.8% of the improvement comes from a more intensive use of assets. Similarly with an increase of £55,188 from the change in the restaurant costs and prices, 54.2% of the improvement is traceable to improved sales margins in the restaurant.

(ii) Even before the planned changes in the pricing and cost structure, the restaurant was achieving better gross margins than the sector average. With the improvements planned and with full capacity in the restaurant, it is unlikely that additional profit can be generated from that source.

The occupancy rate for the accommodation is planned to be the same as the sector average. However, the 20% gross margin for accommodation is still below the sector average, suggesting some improvement is possible. This should be investigated as an increase in prices with no further change in volume will improve the asset turnover ratio as well as the overall sales margin. Given the circumstance of the hotel, the only other possible area of investigation relates to the fixed overheads. Some of these – such as rates and insurance – are difficult to reduce. However, the level of administration is a possible source of further cost reductions. If the overheads can be reduced, this will have the effect of improving the return on capital employed through improving the sales margin of the hotel.

Yours sincerely,

A. Technician

Green and Co.

UNIT 8 – SECTION 2 – DECEMBER 1998

Task 2.1

(a)	Return on capital employed	£975/£4,875 × 100	20%
(b)	Asset turnover	£3,900/£4,875	0.8 times
(c)	Sales (or operating profit) margin	£975/£3,900 × 100	25%
(d)	Average age of debtors	(£325/£3,900 × 12	1 month
(e)	Average age of finished stock	(£140/£840) × 12	2 months

Task 2.2

Briefing notes considering the use of wider performance indicators

Prepared for Angela Frear
Prepared by Financial Analyst
Date: 2 December 1998

(a) Return on capital employed

The return on capital employed might be misleading for a number of reasons. A great deal of the overheads are discretionary costs, that is they could be reduced without immediately affecting output. However, marketing, customer support, research and development, and training could all be viewed as investments in the future even though they are treated as revenue expenditure for accounting purposes. Without these expenses, the return on capital employed would have looked much higher.

(b) Manipulation of the sales margin

It is possible to manipulate the sales margin in a number of ways. The obvious ones are to reduce expenditure on the discretionary costs identified in (a). Other ways include choosing a longer time period over which to depreciate the assets and choosing a different way of valuing stock if this gave a higher closing stock figure. All of these would show short–term improvements although probably at the expense of long–term viability.

(c) Average delay in fulfilling orders

Orders during the year	£4,550,000
Turnover during the year	£3,900,000
	—————
Unfulfilled orders	£650,000
Average delay = (£650/£3,900) × 12	2 months

(d) Other measures of customer satisfaction

continued/

There are at least two other measures of customer satisfaction:

- repeat custom (£3,120/£3,900) = 80%
- the amount of customer support per customer or per £ of sales.

(e)   Internal perspective indicators

There are a number of indicators which would support the performance of the company from an internal perspective. One would be the level of training as a percentage of manufacturing cost. There are, however, two which can be measured directly. These are:

- the percentage of returns (100/4,000) = 2.5%
- the percentage of reworking (37.2/930) = 4%

The objective should be for these to be as small as possible – unlike the amount of training.

(f)   Innovation and learning

Two possible measures are:

- the percentage of turnover derived from new products (1,560/3,900) = 40%
- the amount spent on research and development, perhaps expressed as a percentage of sales or production.

UNIT 8 – SECTION 2 – JUNE 1999

Task 2.1

Performance indicators for ALV (West) Ltd

(a)	Asset turnover	£2,520/£2,100	1.2 times
(b)	Net profit margin	(£378/£2,520) × 100	15%
(c)	Return on capital employed	£378/£2,100 × 100	18%
(d)	Wages per employee	£260,000/20	£13,000
(e)	Production labour cost per unit	£260,000/30,000	£8.67
(f)	Output per employee	30,000/20	1,500
(g)	Added value	£2,520,000 − £1,020,000 = £1,500,000	
	Added value per employee	£1,500,000/20	£75,000
(h)	Profit per employee	£378,000/20	£18,900

Task 2.2

REPORT ON THE EFFICIENCY AND PRODUCTIVITY
OF ALV (EAST) AND ALV (WEST)

Prepared for: **Jill Morgan, Chief executive**

Prepared by: **Accounting technician**

Date: **16 June 1999**

Introduction

This report seeks to distinguish between the meaning of productivity and efficiency and relate these concepts to the performance of ALV (East) and ALV (West). It then highlights productivity and efficiency within each company. Finally, a further measure of productivity is considered to explain the apparent inconsistency between the measures.

(a)   **Productivity and efficiency**

These terms are concerned with relating outputs from a given input such as number of cars produced per person.

(i)   Productivity is a measure of outputs related to inputs usually in partially or wholly physical terms or in terms of value added.

(ii)   Efficiency is concerned with the financial value of the inputs and outputs. Only if the financial value of the output is greater than the financial cost of the inputs can an activity be described as being efficient – and the greater the difference, the greater the efficiency.

(b)   **Two performance indicators to measure efficiency**

The prime measure of efficiency in 'for profit' organisations is the return on capital employed. This might then be followed by the net profit margin, although profit and employees might also be of significance. Comparing the performance of the two companies, it is clear that ALV (East) shows a more favourable result.

Indicator	ALV (East)	ALV (West)
Return on capital employed	42.00%	18%
Net profit margin	20.00%	15%

(c)   **Two performance indicators to measure productivity**

Two major indicators used by ALV Ltd to measure productivity would be output per employee and the added value per employee, although profit per employee might also be used as a measure of productivity. Comparing the performance of the two companies and using output per employee and added value per employee as the indicators, it is clear that ALV (West) is the company with higher productivity.

Indicator	ALV (East)	ALV (West)
Output per employee	556 units	1,500 units
Added Value per employee	£27,778	£75,000

(d)   **An alternative measure of productivity**

	ALV (East)	ALV (West)
Net fixed assets	£360,000	£2,100,000
Output	10,000	30,000
Net fixed assets per unit	£36.00	£70.00

(e)   **Why productivity and efficiency measures give different rankings**

There are two reasons for the difference in the rankings between efficiency and productivity.

(i)   ALV (West) has a far greater amount of fixed assets employed in manufacturing.

(ii)   ALV (East) has more ageing fixed assets. The plant and machinery for both companies is depreciated at 10% per year. The plant and machinery for ALV (East) appears to be, on average, eight years old ($240/300 \times 10$ years). The plant and machinery for ALV (West), however, only has an average age of 2 years. The fixed asset, buildings are of a similar age.

With much greater capital invested in fixed assets and their much younger age, it is expected that output per employee be greater for ALV (West) even if the employees in each company work equally as hard.

The same applies to ALV (East) which appears to be more efficient in financial terms. With much of its fixed assets already written off, its capital employed is lower. Likewise, with much older capital equipment, the depreciation charge in the profit and loss account is likely to be much lower, boosting profits.

UNIT 8 – SECTION 2 – DECEMBER 1999

Task 2.1

(a)   Return on capital employed
$(£48,000 \div £200,000) \times 100\% = 24\%$
Scorecard: financial perspective

(b)   Sales margin percentage
$(£48,000 \div £240,000) \times 100 = 20\%$
Scorecard: financial perspective and possibly internal perspective as partly measuring unit cost

(c)   Asset turnover
$£240,000 \div £200,000 = 1.2$ times
Scorecard: internal perspective, demonstrating intensive use of assets and, hence, unit cost

(d)   Research and development as percentage of production
$(£15,900 \div £53,000) \times 100\% = 30\%$
Scorecard: innovation and learning perspective

(e)   Training as percentage of labour costs
$(£5,200 \div £26,000) \times 100\% = 20\%$
Scorecard: innovation and learning perspective or possibly the internal perspective (TQM)

(f)   Average age of finished stocks
$(£13,000 \div £52,000) \times 12 = 3$ months
Scorecard: customer perspective as the greater the amount of finished stock, the less time customers have to wait for delivery

Task 2.2

Notes on performance: prepared by financial analyst

Date: 1/12/99

I wish to make the following comments on the issues raised:

(a)   The four indicators currently used by the St Nicolas Police Force :

- % cash expenditure to allocated funds – 97%
- Average police hours/crime investigated – 8 hours
- Average police hours/crime solved – 20 hours
- Clear–up rate – 40%

(b)   Limitation on clear up rate

- Timing differences, carry over from one year to the next
- Are all reported crimes investigated
- Definition of crime. If one person is responsible for 40 break–ins when convicted, is this 40 or 1 crime.

(c)   Performance measures

    (i)   % of cash expenditure to allocated funds, accounts only for revenue and not capital measures.

        It focuses on keeping within budget and ignores output or value added.

    (ii)   Clear up rate is an inadequate measure as it fails to account for crime prevention activities. This has an effect on level of crime and therefore a higher clear up rate.

(iii)   The number of hours spent may possibly be a measure effort. However, it could point to inefficiency.

(iv)   A number of measures might focus on innovation and learning perspective. An objective is community safety and therefore a measure could therefore be the cost of crime prevention in relation to decrease in recorded crime.

A further measure could be the level of investment into training initiatives both capital and manpower.

UNIT 8 – SECTION 2 – JUNE 2000

Task 2.1

(a)	Return on capital employed ($1,188,000/$11,880,000) × 100%	10.00%
(b)	Asset turnover $29,700,000/$11,880,000	2.50 times
(c)	Sales (or net profit) margin $1,188,000/$29,700,000 × 100%	4.00%
(d)	Actual number of return flights per year 6 × 360	2,160
(e)	Actual number of return passengers per year $29,700,000/$275	108,000
(f)	Average seat occupancy 108,000/(2,160 × 80) × 100%	62.50%
(g)	Actual number of passenger–miles 108,000 × 300	32,400,000
(h)	Cost per passenger mile $28,512,000/32,400,000 miles	$0.88
	(Total cost = turnover − profit = $29,700,000 = $1,188,000 = $28,512,000)	

Task 2.2

MEMO

To: Carol Jones   From: Management accountant

Subject: Competitive advantage   Data: 21 June 2000

The following is a summary of the forecast number of passengers, the net profit and the return on capital employed for the year to 31 May 2001. I have identified where SeaAir has a competitive advantage and one existing cost which does not add value.

(a)   Forecast number of passengers 9 flights × 80 seats × 55.00% occupancy × 360 days = 142,560.

(b)   Forecast net profit for the year to 31 May 2001

	$000
Revenue 142,560 flights × $275	39,204
Fuel and aircraft maintenance $14,580,000 × 9/6	21,870
Take off and landing fees at Waltonville $2,160,000 × 9/6	3,240
Aircraft parking at Waltonville $2,880,000 × 50%	1,440
Depreciation of aircraft	600
Salaries of flight crew $380,000 + $58,000	438
Home airport costs	8,112
Net profit	3,504

(c)   Revised return on capital employed   31%

(d)   SeaAir has a competitive advantage over LandAir arising from its route to Waltonville being over the sea. SeaAir cannot be threatened with competition from rail or road, allowing our airline to charge a higher price for a route of a similar distance. A further competitive advantage arises from the 55 percent seat occupancy. With a lower set occupancy than LandAir, SeaAir's passengers might be willing to pay a higher fare as they are more likely to obtain a seat on any desired flight.

(e)   One major expense which does not add value from a customer perspective is the cost of aircraft parking at Waltonville.

◆ **FOULKS**lynch

UNIT 8 – SECTION 2 – DECEMBER 2000

Task 2.1

(a)	Gross profit margin	£221,760/£633,600 × 100%	35%
(b)	Net profit margin	£76,032/£633,600 × 100%	12%
(c)	Return on capital employed	£76,032/£95,040 × 100%	80%
(d)	Asset turnover	£633,600/£95,040	6.67 times
(e)	Number of passengers in the year	£633,600/£1	633,600 passengers
(f)	Total cost per mile	(£633,600 × £76,032)/356,400	£1.56
(g)	Number of journeys per day	356,400/(18 miles × 360 days)	55 journeys
(h)	Maintenance cost per mile	£28,512/356,400	£0.08
(i)	Passengers per day	633,600/360	1,760 passengers
(j)	Passengers per journey	1,760/55	32 passengers
(k)	Number of drivers	£142,000/£14,200	10

MEMO

To:	Chief Executive	From:	Management accountant
Date:	6 December 2000		
Subject:	Performance of Travel Bus Ltd		

You recently raised a number of observations relating to the performance of Travel Bus Ltd. My analysis and comments are:

(a) **Relationship of productivity to profitability**

Productivity is a measure of outputs derived from inputs, generally measured in non–financial terms. One example is output per production employee. An increase in productivity does not always lead to an increase in profitability. Profitability may fall if costs are not controlled and product sales mix alters.

(b) **Driver productivity**

A measure of driver productivity is number of passengers carried per driver year.

1999	**2000**
540,000/8	633,600/10
= 67,500	= 63,360

This does not support the drivers claim for extra productivity.

(c) **One possible reason for the improved profitability of Travel Bus Ltd**

The increase in passenger volume and the additional revenue per passenger journey together with greater recovery of fixed costs due to volume.

(d) **Possible indicators of passenger needs being satisfied**

   (i) Last year, the number of journeys per day was 50. This year, 55. The provision of an improved number of services is a measure of satisfying passenger needs as the waiting time between buses will have been reduced.

   (ii) Indicators are not provided for timetable adherence, departures and arrivals nor cancellation of services. Such information would indicate the level of passenger service, 'value–added'.

(e) **Possible safety indicators**

   (i) In 1999 the maintenance cost per mile was £0.10. This year, it reduced to £0.08 per mile. This might imply that safety is being compromised, especially as the fleet of buses is not one year older.

   (ii) A further indicator to safety would be accidents per year, or time delay between fault report and maintenance correction.

UNIT 9 – SECTION 1 – JUNE 1997

Task 1.1

(*Tutorial note:* The format of your report should be guided by responsibility accounting, i.e. in responsibility accounting, costs and revenues are traced to the person (manager) responsible for their incurrence, so that each manager is both responsible and accountable for the costs under their control. Concurrent with responsibility accounting is the classification into controllable and non–controllable, therefore a classification along these lines is expected. The layout could also be further classified into variable and fixed or direct and indirect but the optimum presentation would require a controllable/non–controllable classification. Additionally, cost per tonne figures could be added to highlight efficiency.)

	Actual	Flexed budget		Variance		Comments*
Reclamation Division Performance Report – 4 weeks to 31 May 1997						
Production (tonnes)	200	200		–		
	£	£		£		
Controllable						
Wages, etc	46,133	43,936	(W1)	2,197	(A)	Overtime payments, one off event
Fuel	15,500	15,000	(W2)	500	(A)	Poor energy efficiency–investigate
Consumables	2,100	2,000	(W3)	100	(A)	
Power	1,590	1,500	(W4)	90	(A)	
Divisional overheads	21,000	20,000		1,000	(A)	Additional employee, no action
Sub–total	86,323	82,436		3,887	(A)	
Non–controllable						
Plant maintenance	6,900	5,950		950	(A)	
Central services	7,300	6,850		450	(A)	
Sub–total	14,200	12,800		1,400	(A)	
Total	100,523	95,236		5,287	(A)	

*These are examples of comments.

WORKINGS

(W)   6 employees × 4 teams × 42 hours/week × £7.50/hour × 4 weeks = £30,240
        + 40% = 12,096 = £42,336 + (200 tonnes × £8/tonne) = £1,600 = £43,936

(W)   200 tonnes × £75/tonne

(W)   200 tonnes × £10/tonne

(W)   £500 + (200 tonnes × £5/tonne)

◆ FOULKS*lynch*

Task 1.2

MEMO

To:	Management Board	**Date:**	19 August 1998
From:	Deputy Financial Controller		
Subject:	**Budgeting**		

The following report covers the questions raised at the recent management meeting. The report format is in the same sequence as that of the questions raised.

(a)   Queries raised regarding the original report.

   (i)   The use of two–year–old figures can only be justified on the basis that the company is operating in an environment which has remained unchanged and this is unlikely. Budgeting is concerned with planning and therefore any plan should be prepared from current knowledge of the company's environment. Past knowledge in the form of the original budget may be a guide to the future but it will not be a substitute for using up to date information.

   A reconciliation of both budgets (original and revised) may serve a purpose in assessing the accuracy of the original proposal, but it would have limited use in planning.

   (ii)   For planning purposes the budget data should be based on what we are proposing to do in a future period. This will act as a target for the managers and it might motivate them to achieve the overall plan. The budget would also serve to co–ordinate the various activities of the company.

   For control purposes the budgeted figures should be focused on what we actually produced and the expenses which should have been incurred in producing it to enable a meaningful comparison.

   (iii)   Using fixed budgets, the variable costs also appear fixed, and any changes in volume actually achieved are ignored. Had the division produced nothing then savings would have been shown for the variable costs which would render the information meaningless. The same would apply if the original tonnage was exceeded in this case an overspend on the variable costs would be reported which would be another meaningless figure when higher actual tonnage had been achieved. As regards the fixed costs these will tend to be unaffected. Using flexible budgeting, the variable costs reflect the changes in the volume of activity. A more balanced assessment of the division's performance would result from the inclusion of sales revenue.

   (iv)   The basis for charging plant maintenance to the division is flawed since the method of apportionment is not related to the likely use of maintenance resources nor is it a reasonable approximation. A new division will have significant capital costs but it will require less maintenance. As regards the charging of any overspend on the maintenance department to a user department this procedure is likely to mask any inefficiencies in that department.

   (v)   The comments explaining the variances are very negative in tone with every adverse variance being reinforced and no praise being given for favourable variances. This may affect the motivation of the managers. The comments do not identify the reasons for the variances arising nor the actions which might be taken to resolve them.

   (vi)   The decision to investigate variances will depend on a number of factors their absolute or relative size (cost/benefit of investigation), whether they are one–off or continuing, whether they have been resolved or whether they are just commencing.

Task 1.2 (cont'd)

(vii)   The inclusion of central service charges in a divisional report will not help control these costs as they are not being reported to the managers who control them. However, the reporting of these charges to the divisional managers ensures that they are aware of the other costs incurred in running a business. A degree of control may also be exercised by the divisional managers on these costs when the level of divisional charges is perceived to be excessive.

            One of the objectives of budgeting is to motivate managers to achieve the goals of the organisation, and the inclusion of central expenses over which the manager has no control in a divisional performance report may be demotivating.

(b)   The main objective of my revised report is to provide meaningful feedback. By providing feedback it should be possible to establish whether the plan is being achieved or whether the plan should be changed because it cannot be achieved as circumstances have changed.

    My report has the following advantages over the original report:

(i)   it follows the technique of responsibility accounting by classifying costs into controllable and non–controllable

(ii)   it is prepared on a flexible budget basis, thus comparing like with like

(iii)   the non–controllable expenses are included so that the manager is aware of the other costs which may be incurred in the running of the total organisation

(iv)   the comments column contains the underlying reasons for the variance from plan and the actions necessary to return to the plan.

UNIT 9 – SECTION 1 – DECEMBER 1997

Task 1.1

(a)   Centred Four–Point Moving Average Trend Figures

Year	Quarter	Visitors	Moving Annual Total	Moving average	Centred average (trend)	Seasonal variations	
1996	1	5,800					
	2	9,000					
			35,200	8,800			
	3	6,000			8,900	–2,900	
			36,000	9,000			
	4	14,400			9,100	+5,300	Total = 0
			36,800	9,200			
1997	1	6,600			9,300	–2,700	
			37,600	9,400			
	2	9,800			9,500	+300	
			38,400	9,600			
	3	6,800					
	4	15,200					

(b)

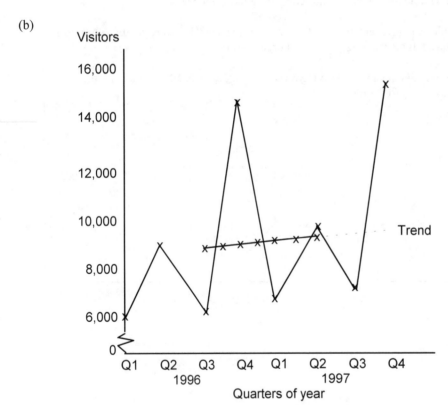

(c)   The figures should be:

1998   Quarter 1 $10,100 - 2,700 = 7,400$
              2         $10,300 + 300\ \ = 10,600$
              3         $10,500 - 2,900 = 7,600$
              4         $10,700 + 5,300 = 16,000$

(d)   The notes should include the following:

(i)   A number of methods could be used to forecast visitor numbers: they could be internal or external, primary or secondary. However, the initial step would need to be the gathering of the data which would be used as input.

Internal sources could be extracted from whatever information is currently being gathered eg, visitor number by quarter these could be further analysed by month, week or date. This internal data could be analysed using time series analysis in order to establish a trend, as above. However, this method assumes that the past will be repeated and ignores random and cyclical fluctuations. It also ignores the product life cycle, which again follows a trend.

External information would need to be sourced from past, current, or potential visitors.

Primary and secondary sourcing of data could be used in forecasting some primary sources are outlined above. Secondary sources would include: leisure–based data, tourist data, industry data, etc. However this data would tend to be less useful in forecasting, in this case, as it is not likely to be focused on the industry or on the location required.

(ii)   Both methods would use random or selective sampling. However, telephone sampling would be preferred for the following reasons:

–   telephone sampling would tend to avoid misunderstandings by clarifying the questions
–   a higher response rate would be achieved
–   all the questions would be answered
–   the questions could be extended and adapted if the interviewer believed more thorough answers might be useful
–   additional questions could be asked where the interviewee raises issues which were not considered in the original design.

(iii)   The concept of the product life cycle of start–up, growth, maturity and decline could be applied to any area, including a museum. The start–up phase requires investment this would have been the situation several years ago when the museum was first opened, the investment being in working exhibits, marketing, staff etc. The next phase would have been the growth phase, with the rapid growth in visitors reflecting this. They would have been attracted to the museum by investment in marketing, special offer tickets, special weekend attractions, etc. The maturity stage would be reflected in the number of visitors reaching a peak and levelling off. The final phase would be that of decline which appears to have been the case in recent years.

To achieve sustained growth, there would need to be investment every year, so that each investment would have its own product life cycle which would overlap with the previous investment resulting in the sustained growth. It can be seen that with the recent investment, the museum has completed the start–up phase and is now at the beginning of the growth phase after years of decline.

Task 1.2

MEMO

To: **John Derbyshire**

From: **Accounting Technician**

Date: **19 August 1998**

Subject: Motivational issues

(a)   **Motivational implications of imposing the budget reduction from £35,000 to £29,000**

Budgets are usually the best estimates of the figures for an organisation when they are submitted to management. However, in some cases, there will be an amount of slack built in, i.e. additional expenses or reduced income in order to improve the chances of meeting the budget. Top management need to remove this slack so they make an estimate of what it is, then ask the manager for this reduction. Where slack has not been built in, this request would tend to demotivate the managers as the whole budgeting process will have to be started again and expenses reduced to the levels required. As a result, the manager will not be inclined to own the budget because it has been imposed.

The size of the reduction will also have an effect on morale, with a small reduction having a minor effect and a large reduction, as in this case, having a large effect.

The reduction to £29,000 appears to have been made for political reasons and not realistic reasons, therefore the effect on the manager is likely to be negative.

(b)   **Arguments for and against using a top–down budgeting approach for the museum**

Top–down budgeting is the name given to an approach where the manager decides what the budget should be and then issues it to the staff of the organisation. There is no discussion of the figures.

Bottom–up budgeting is where all the staff of the organisation are involved in the budgeting process and they all participate in the preparation of it.

Top–down budgeting is generally used in start–up situations and with small organisations, whereas bottom–up budgeting is used in more mature organisations, of medium to large size.

For the Eskafeld Museum a bottom–up approach is preferable as it combines participation with motivation and results in a budget which is believed in.

UNIT 9 – SECTION 1 – DECEMBER 1998

Task 1.1

Amber Ltd production budget for next three weeks

	Week	1	2	3	4
	Sales (units)	23,520	27,440	28,420	32,340
	Good production required (units)	27,440	28,420	32,340	
	Loss = 2/98 × good production	560	580	660	
(a)	Gross production required (units)	28,000	29,000	33,000	
		£	£	£	
	Weekly paid labour	21,280	21,280	21,280	
(b)	Overtime (33,000 – 30,400) × £2			5,200	
	total labour cost	21,280	21,280	26,480	
	Material[1]	140,000	145,000	165,000	
	Production overhead[2]	63,000	65,250	74,250	
(c)	Cost of production	224,280	231,530	265,730	

Notes:

1   Gross production volume × £5

2   Production overhead per gross unit = £3,792,825/1,685,700 = £2.25

      Production overhead per week = Gross production volume × £2.25

Task 1.2

Amber Ltd Revised production budget and savings for next three weeks

	Week	1	2	3
	Planned production units (gross)	28,000	29,000	33,000
	Maximum production possible	30,400	30,400	30,400
	Surplus/(deficit)	2,400	1,400	(2,600)
	Change in planned production	1,200	1,400	(2,600)
(a)	Revised production plan (units)	29,200	30,400	30,400
	Savings		£	£
	Overtime saved			5,200
	Finance cost week 1: (20p × 1,200 units × 2 weeks)		480	
	Finance cost week 2: (20p × 1,400 units × 1 week)		280	760
(b)	Net savings			4,440

UNIT 9 – SECTION 1 – JUNE 1999

Task 1.1

(a)   **Production budget – quarter ended 17 September 1999**

	Alphas	Betas
Budgeted sales in units	2,000	2,400
Add closing stock [1]	200	480
Less opening stock (given)	(500)	(600)
Production of completed units	1,700	2,280

	Alphas	Betas
[1] Sales this quarter	2,000	2,400
Add 20% seasonal variation	400	480
Budgeted sales next quarter	2,400	2,880
Closing stock ($5/60 \times 2,400 = 200$) ($10/60 \times 2,880 = 480$)	200	480

(b)   **Material purchases budget – quarter ended 17 September 1999**

	kilograms
Material required for Alpha production ($8kg \times 1,700$)	13,600
Material required for Beta production ($12kg \times 2,280$)	27,360
	40,960
Add closing material stock [2]	16,384
Less opening material stock (given)	(12,000)
Material purchases	45,344

[2] Closing stock of materials	
Production this period	40,960
Add 20%	8,192
Material required for production next period	49,152
Stock required ($20/60 \times 49,152$)	16,384

(c)   **Cost of material purchases** ($45,344 \times £10$)   £453,440

(d)   **Labour budget – quarter ended 17 September 1999**

	Hours
Labour hours required for Alpha production (3 hours $\times$ 1,700)	5,100
Labour hours required for Beta production (6 hours $\times$ 2,280)	13,680
Total hours required before efficiency adjustment	18,780
Efficiency adjustment ($^{20\%}/_{80\%}$)	4,695
Total labour hours	23,475
Normal hours (50 employees $\times$ 35 hours $\times$ 12 weeks)	21,000
Overtime hours	2,475

(e)

Normal hours (50 employees $\times$ 12 weeks $\times$ £210)	£126,000
Overtime (2,475 hours $\times$ £9)	£22,275
Cost of labour	£148,275

Task 1.2

MEMO

To: **Margaret Brown**

Subject: **Sales forecasting**

From: **Management accounting**

Date: **16 June 1999**

I wish to make the following observations regarding your concerns about the accuracy of sales forecasting.

(a)   **Limitations of linear regression as a forecasting technique**

- Linear regression uses a sample of historic data to establish a trend. If the sample size is small then the resulting formula may provide an inaccurate forecast.

- The technique also assumes that there is a linear relationship. It might be that there is a clear pattern in the data but if this pattern is curvilinear – eg, 20% growth per quarter – then linear regression will not accurately identify this trend.

- The data used to establish the trend is historical data and assumes the trend will continue into the future. The demand for a product, however, can suddenly change for a variety of reasons. New products might make existing ones less popular and therefore the product mix may change.

- Any seasonal variations included in the forecast may change if the seasons are abnormal. For example, a high pound may attract more visitors abroad for holidays.

(b)   **Other ways of forecasting**

In light of these limitations, it may be useful to consider other ways of forecasting.

- If the company has a limited number of customers, it may be possible to seek information regarding their plans. This particularly applies if Wilmslow has formed long–term relationships with its customers.

- Wilmslow might also consider the possibility of there being leading indicators such as when a change in demand for a product in one period results in a change in demand for another product in a later period.

- A third way of deriving sales demand is to use market research. This can be in the form of both primary and secondary research techniques as interviews, questionnaires or generic consumer surveys by trade associations.

UNIT 9 – SECTION 1 – DECEMBER 1999

Task 1.1

(a)   (i)   Number of production days in quarter 1: 12 weeks × 5 days = 60 days

(ii)   Units of closing finished stock:
Exe (8 days/60 days) × 930 units = 124 units
Wye (9 days/60 days) × 1,320 units = 198 units

(iii)   Labour hours in quarter before overtime: 12 weeks × 35 hours × 46 employees = 19,320 hours

(b)   (i)   **Production budget for 12 weeks ending 24 March 2000**

	Exe	Wye
Budgeted sales	930	1,320
Add closing stocks	124	198
Less opening stocks (given)	(172)	(257)
Production of good units	882	1,261
Faulty production (Exe = 2/98 × 882, Wye = 3/97 × 1,236)	18	39
Total production (units)	900	1,300

(ii)   **Material purchases budget for 12 weeks ending 24 March 200**

	litres
Material required for Exe production (6 litres × 900 Exe)	5,400
Material required for Wye production (9 litres × 1,300 Wye)	11,700
Total material required for production	17,100
Add closing raw material stock (5 days/60 days × 17,100 litres)	1,425
Less opening raw material stock (given)	(1,878)
Material purchases (litres)	16,647
Total material cost (16,647 × £15)	£249,705

(iii)   **Production labour budget for 12 weeks ending 24 March 2000**

	hours
Budgeted hours required for Exe production (12 hours × 900 Exe)	10,800
Budgeted hours required for Wye production (7 hours × 1,300 Wye)	9,100
Total labour hours required	19,900
Hours available before overtime	19,320
Overtime hours	580
Cost of normal hours (19,320 × £6)	£115,920
Cost of overtime (580 × £6 × 130%)	£4,524
Total labour cost	£120,444

(c)   **Finance and other savings per quarter**

Exe ([172 – 124] × £4)	£192
Wye ([257 – 198] × £5)	£295
Raw material ([1,878 – 1,425] × £1)	£453
	£940

Task 1.2

(a)   **Sales per quarter**

Demand per quarter before seasonal variations = 20,000 ÷ 4 = 5,000

	Quarter 1	*Quarter 2*	*Quarter 3*	*Quarter 4*
Quarterly demand before seasonal variations	5,000	5,000	5,000	5,000
Seasonal variations	+1,000	+1,500	-500	-2,000
Budgeted volume	6,000	6,500	4,500	3,000

(b)   **Spreadsheet formulae**

A	B	C	D	E	F
1	Unit selling price	£90			
2	Annual volume	20,000			
3	Seasonal variations	20%	30%	-10%	-40%
4		Quarter 1	Quarter 2	Quarter 3	Quarter 4
5	Seasonal variations (units)	= (C2/4)*C3	= (C2/4)*D3	= (C2/4)*E3	= (C2/4)*F3
6	Quarterly volume	= (C2/4)+C5	= (C2/4)+D5	= (C2/4)+E5	= (C2/4)+F5
7	Quarterly turnover	= C1*C6	= C1*D6	= C1*E6	= C1*F6

UNIT 9 – SECTION 1 – JUNE 2000

Task 1.1

(a) **Closing stocks quarter 3**
Delta: 3,300 boxes × (6/60)   330 boxes
Omega: 2,640 boxes × (8/60)   352 boxes

(b) **Labour hours available**
52 employees × 36 hours × 12 weeks   22,464 hours

(c) **Production budget**

	Delta	Omega
Sales demand quarter 3	3,000	2,400
Add: closing stocks	330	352
Less: opening stocks (given)	(630)	(502)
Good production	2,700	2,250
Add: scrap (1/9)	300	250
Total production	3,000	2,500

(d) **Material budget**   kg
Material for Delta production 12 kg × 3,000 boxes   36,000
Material for Omega production 15 kg × 2,500 boxes   37,500

Material used in production   73,500
Add: closing stock   21,340
Less: opening stock   13,560

Material purchases   81,280

Cost of purchases £7 × 81,280   £568,960

(e) **Labour budget**   hours
Labour hours for Delta production 3 hours × 3,000 boxes   9,000
Labour hours for Omega production 6 hours × 2,500 boxes   15,000

Labour hours required   24,000
Labour hours before overtime   22,464

Overtime hours   1,536

Cost of labour
Wages £180 × 52 employees × 12 weeks   £112,320
Overtime £7.50 × 1,536 hours   £11,520

                                                                      £123,840

Task 1.2

(a)   **Trend and seasonal derived variations**

Year	Quarter	Actual	4 quarter total	4 quarter average	Centred trend	Seasonal variation
1997	3	142				
	4	142				
			584	146		
1998	1	150			146	4
			584	146		
	2	150			148	2
			600	150		
	3	142			150	-8
			600	150		
	4	158			152	6
			616	154		
1999	1	150			154	-4
			616	154		
	2	166			156	10
			632	158		
	3	142			158	-16
			632	158		
	4	174			160	14
			648	162		
2000	1	150				
	2	182				

(b)   **Adjusted seasonal variations**

	Quarter 1	Quarter 2	Quarter 3	Quarter 4	Residual
1998	4	2	-8	6	
1999	-4	10	-16	14	
	—	—	—	—	
Total	0	12	-24	20	
Average	0	6	-12	10	4
Adjustment for residual	-1	-1	-1	-1	-4
Seasonal variations	-1	5	-13	9	0

(c)   **Forecast demand – quarter 2**

Trend (160 + 2 + 2)	164
Seasonal variation	5
	—
Forecast	169
Actual (estimate)	182
	—
Residual	13

(d)   **Reasons why there might be a difference**

Random errors
Seasonal variations might be multiplicative not additive
The actual data was only an estimate
Sales volume data ignores other factors influencing demand such as changes in prices.

UNIT 9 – SECTION 1 – DECEMBER 2000

Task 1.1

(a)

Production budget in units	Period 1	Period 2	Period 3	Period 4	Period 5
Demand	5,700	5,700	6,840	6,460	6,080
Less opening stock	1,330	855	1,026	969	912
Add closing stock	855	1,026	969	912	
Production	5,225	5,871	6,783	6,403	

(b)

Material budget (litres)		Period 1	Period 2	Period 3	Period 4
Production (units)		5,225	5,871	6,783	6,403
Material required (production × 6 litres)	(a)	31,350	35,226	40,698	38,418
Maximum material available	(b)		34,000	34,000	34,000
Shortfall of material available (a − b)			1,226	6,698	4,418
Reschedule purchases		1,226	-1,266		
Material purchases from Contrax plc	(c)	32,576	34,000	34,000	34,000
Material purchases from outside supplier	(d)			6,698	4,418

(c)

Material purchases budget (£)	Period 1 £	Period 2 £	Period 3 £	Period 4 £
Material purchases from Contrax plc (c) × £8	260,608	272,000	272,000	272,000
Material purchases from outside supplier (d) × £12		80,376	53,016	
	260,608	272,000	352,376	325,016

(d)

Labour hours budget	Period 1	Period 2	Period 3	Period 4
Production (units of Omega)	5,225	5,871	6,783	6,403
Standard hours required (units × 2 hours)	10,450	11,742	13,566	12,806
Inefficiency (5/95 × standard hours)	550	618	714	674
Total labour hours required	11,000	12,360	14,280	13,480
Basic hours (78 employees × 4 weeks × 40 hours)	12,480	12,480	12,480	12,480
Overtime	nil	nil	1,800	1,000

(e)

Labour budget (£)	Period 1 £	Period 2 £	Period 3 £	Period 4 £
Basic wage (£160 × 78 employees × 4 weeks)	49,920	49,920	49,920	49,920
Overtime (overtime hours × £6)			10,800	6,000
	49,920	49,920	60,720	55,920

Task 1.2

MEMO

To: **Adrian Jones**   **From:**   **Management Accountant**
Date: **7 December 2000**
Subject: **Cost Savings**

In response to your recent concerns about the level of overtime and the need to purchase material from another supplier. I have identified a possible immediate cost saving. The material constraint, however, appears long–term, although further cost savings are possible in the longer term.

(a) and (b) Immediate cost savings

> In period 1, the material available from Contrax plc is 34,000 litres, against our planned requirement 32,576 litres. Therefore there is a surplus of 1,424 litres available from Contra plc in that period. A saving is possible in one of two ways. By bringing production forward to period 1, there will be an immediate saving of £5,696 from reducing purchases from the alternative supplier [1,424 × (£12.00 – £8.00)]. The same saving is possible simply by buying the 1,424 litres in advance. The extra purchases in period 1 could then be used in period 2. Any resulting surplus in period 2 could then, in turn, be used in period 3, so reducing the purchases at the higher price.

(c)   Continuing difficulties

> If the minimum demand for Omegas is 5,700 per four–week period, this suggests that the material requirements, even without stocks, will be 34,200 litres (5,700 × 6 litres) and the labour requirements, with the current 5 per cent inefficiency, will be 12,000 hours (5,700 × 2 hours × 100/95). The constraint, therefore, appears to be a longer term problem, although, with 12,480 labour hours available, the labour constraint is merely short–term.

(d)   Possible longer–term cost savings

> In the longer term, it may be possible to renegotiate the stock level requirements with Advanced Industries plc. However, we would have to assure them that we would still be able to supply their requirements on time if the forecast requirements were inaccurate. One possible way of reducing stock levels while still meeting the actual requirements is to introduce flexible labour working. This would involve employees working unpaid overtime when necessary and being given time off in lieu when production requirements fell. This would also result in elimination of overtime payments.

UNIT 9 – SECTION 2 – JUNE 1997

Task 2.1

(a)   **Materials Purchases Budget for September 1997 (to the nearest £)**

£

        September 1997   3,368

(WORKINGS

80,000 cans × 100/95 (damage adjustment) × 100kg/1,000 cans × 100/50 (waste) × £200/tonne= £3,368)

(b)   **Monthly Labour Budget – number of Employees**

        September 1997   3.69 (say 4 employees)

(WORKINGS

80,000 cans × 100/95 (damage adjustment) × 6 hours/1,000 cans × 100/90 (absenteeism) × 1/38 (hours per employee) × 1/4 (weeks per month) = 3.69)

(c)   **Materials Purchases budget (adjusted for price indices)**

£

September 1997   3,508

(WORKINGS

3,368 × 125/120 = 3,508)

Task 2.1

Task 2.2

MEMO

To: Production Manager   **Date:**   19 August 1998
From: Assistant Cost Accountant

Subject: Budgeting for materials and labour

The following memo covers the issues raised by yourself and follows the same sequence.

Material prices are usually forecast for the year ahead and a single average value is chosen for convenience. Unfortunately prices of materials in the market will vary so that the average price used may reflect the movement in prices over the period but it is not likely to reflect the prices on a smaller time scale e.g. a month. Therefore the accuracy of prices is weakened as a result. The solution that we chose was to base the price changes on last year's figures, which is an improvement on the use of a single average price. Unfortunately the confidence in these figures may not be high as the price may be affected by Political, Economic, Social and Technological (P.E.S.T.) factors.

As regards an alternative method of predicting prices, we could use time series analysis. This may be a more accurate method as it would take into account trends, seasonal variations and cycles. Again this method would be affected by P.E.S.T. factors but possibly to a lesser extent.

The type of labour information which should be supplied is:

Daily   Attendance, absenteeism, production, damaged goods, productive hours, productivity.

Weekly   Weekly summaries of the daily figures, total wages cost plus comparisons with planned figures, labour costs/1,000 cans.

Monthly   Monthly performance reports expressing the weekly figures in monetary terms, including variance analysis. The monthly figures would prove the overall control of the labour costs but any deviation from the plan would be identified from the daily and weekly figures.

UNIT 9 – SECTION 2 – DECEMBER 1997

Task 2.1

(a)   The purchases budget for materials is 20,000 kilograms at £5 per kg ie, a value of £100,000.

(b)   The next step is to calculate the materials issued to production figure this is 19,400 kg, i.e.

	Kg
Purchases	20,000
Opening stock	6,000
Closing stock	(6,600)
Materials issued to production	19,400

(c)   Given the limit on materials purchases and usage, the next step is to decide which products should be produced and sold. This would depend on product contribution per limiting factor in this case, materials.

	Alpha £	Beta £
Sales price/unit	36	39
Materials cost/unit	10	7.50
Labour cost/unit	10	11.14
Variable cost/unit	20	18.64
Contribution/unit	£16	£20.36
Limiting factor (materials)	2 kg	1.5 kg
Contribution/limiting factor	£8	£13.57
Ranking	2	1

Given that 9,000 units of Beta will be produced, requiring 13,500 kg of materials, the balance of materials usage for the Alpha is 5,900 kg, which equates to 2,950 units of product. This represents the decrease in the Alpha production of 3,950 units (6,900 – 2,950). If the closing stock remains the same, the budgeted sales must also be reduced by this amount. Alpha sales will therefore be 6,500 – 3,950 = 2,550 units.

The revised sales budget would be:

	Units	Selling price £	Turnover £
Alpha	2,550	36.00	91,800
Beta	7,800	39.00	304,200
			396,000

(d)   The revised labour budget would be:

	Hours
Alpha 2,950 units × 2.5 hours =	7,375
Beta (as original labour budget)	25,065
Total labour hours	32,440
Labour cost (× £4/hour) =	£129,760

(e)   Using a 13 week period and a 35–hour week, 32,440 hours translates into 71.3 employees, a reduction of 21.7.

Task 2.2

REPORT

To: **George Phillips**

From: **Trainee Accountant**   **Date:**   **19 August 1998**

Subject: **Classification of labour costs, key factors and spreadsheet packages**

The following report is in response to your request for advice on the issues raised at your recent management meeting. The report follows the same sequence as the issues raised.

(a)   The decision on whether to reduce the workforce or not is a crucial one. The use of standards and estimates of 2.5 hours per unit for the Alpha and 2.785 hours per unit for the Beta, suggests that the labour costs are variable. This would be the case if the employees were employed on a piecework basis but most companies employ labour per week or per period and therefore the labour costs become a fixed cost in the short term. The effect on the cash flow should also be considered, i.e. the cost of redundancy, the cost of continued employment and the cost of recruitment and training.

For the longer term, all costs are variable and the company would not continue to employ staff if they were surplus to requirements. The production manager has a valid point in that the staff who have been made redundant may not be keen to be re–employed if there is a risk of them being made redundant again. The case for retaining them is also supported by the fact that they are stated to be highly trained staff and the training value lost may take some time to regain. Another factor to be considered would be the cost of recruiting new staff and the costs of training them and the potential increase in reject products. On balance it would probably be preferable to keep the staff as the problem appears to be a short term one.

(b)   The importance of identifying key factors or limiting factors in the preparation of budgets should not be undervalued. There are many key factors in an organisation and their ranking may change as time elapses. The key factors in most organisations are sales, stock, materials, space, cash, equipment, trained staff and cost of staff to name a few. It is true that key factors do change over time the secret is to establish what they are and what the implications are of solving them. For example, the company may not have enough machine capacity this can be solved by buying more machinery, but this decision may well impact on cash flow (insufficient cash to purchase the machinery), and labour (not enough trained staff to run the machine) and sales (the sales will not immediately increase to fill the capacity of the machine). Therefore the identification of key factors is important as is the implications for the company of any change in their ranking.

(c)   A relevant package here would be a spreadsheet package incorporating Profit and Loss statement, Balance Sheet and Cash Flow statement. The model could be set up using a data area for the key variables such as material usage per product, price per kilo of material, inflation, payment profiling and so on. The relevant relationships could then be input into the cells of, say, the Profit and Loss schedule eg, sales × selling price per unit. The model could be used to ask 'what if' questions and to illustrate the effect of changes in the figures on the three statements, with the recalculation of the figures being automatic. The figures could also be used to calculate key ratios. Constraints (eg, overdraft not to exceed £x) could also be built into the formulae. The benefits of using such a package are significant in terms of time and accuracy, particularly as the costs of such a package are relatively low.

UNIT 9 – SECTION 2 – DECEMBER 1998

SECTION 2

Task 2.1

(a)

Red Ltd – Analysis of fixed and variable costs						
	First budget a	Second budget b	Change in volume c=a–b	Unit variable cost d=c/2,000	Total variable cost e=d×20,000	Fixed cost f=b–e
Volume	Units 18,000	Units 20,000	Units 2,000			
	£	£	£	£	£	£
Material	180,000	200,000	20,000	10	200,000	nil
Labour	308,000	340,000	32,000	16	320,000	20,000
Power and maintenance	33,000	35,000	2,000	1	20,000	15,000
Rent, insurance and depreciation	98,000	98,000	nil	nil	nil	98,000
Total cost	619,000	673,000	54,000	27	540,000	133,000

(b)

Red Ltd – Revised performance statement – year to 30 November 1998						
	Unit variable cost £	Total variable cost £	Fixed cost £	Flexed budget £	Actual cost £	Variance £
Material	10	195,000		195,000	197,000	2,000 (A)
Labour	16	312,000	20,000	332,000	331,000	1,000 (F)
Power and maintenance	1	19,500	15,000	34,500	35,000	500 (A)
Rent, insurance and depreciation	nil		98,000	98,000	97,500	500 (F)
Total cost				659,500	660,500	1,000 (A)

Key: (A) = Adverse, (F) = Favourable

Task 2.2

M E M O

To: Tony Brown   **From**: Accounting technician

Date: 2 December 1998

Subject: ***Performance–related pay***

(a)   In order for performance–related pay to lead to improved performance, a number of conditions are necessary.

- Managers need to know the objectives of the whole organisation.
- Budgets need to be consistent with those objectives.
- Managers must want to achieve those objectives.
- Managers must feel that the objectives are achievable.
- Managers must feel they can influence the achievement of the objectives.
- The objectives should provide a challenge.
- The level of rewards – both financial and non-financial – should be sufficient to help motivate managers.
- Managers need to have the appropriate skills to achieve improved performance.

(b)   Given these conditions, it is not clear that the proposed scheme of performance–related pay will lead to improved performance.

- The level of production is not under the control of Red's managers. This is dictated by the needs of the Green subsidiary.

- One measure of performance is profit. Under the present accounting system, any profit generated towards Colour plc by Red Ltd is reported in Green's performance as the part is sold at cost.

- Some of the expenditure incurred by Red Ltd such as rent and insurance may not be controllable by its managers.

(c)   The proposed scheme is possibly open to misuse by the managers of Red Ltd.

- By simply focusing on costs, the managers of Red Ltd might use inferior materials.

- If Green requires a higher volume of parts from Red, then unit cost will fall because of the element of fixed costs being spread over a larger volume. The managers of Red Ltd will, therefore, achieve, an increase in their pay even though this will not have involved any effort on their part.

UNIT 9 – SECTION 2 – JUNE 1999

Task 2.1

(a)

<table>
<thead>
<tr><th colspan="5" align="center">Calculation of unit variable costs</th></tr>
<tr><th>High low method</th><th align="center">High</th><th align="center">Low</th><th></th><th></th></tr>
<tr><th></th><th></th><th></th><th align="center">Difference</th><th></th></tr>
<tr><th></th><th align="center">Original
budget</th><th align="center">Revised
budget</th><th align="center">Increase in
units</th><th align="center">Variable
unit cost*</th></tr>
</thead>
<tbody>
<tr><td>Fasta units</td><td align="center">24,000</td><td align="center">20,000</td><td align="center">4,000</td><td></td></tr>
<tr><td>Variable costs</td><td></td><td></td><td align="center">Increase in
cost</td><td></td></tr>
<tr><td>Material</td><td align="center">£216,000</td><td align="center">£180,000</td><td align="center">£36,000</td><td align="center">£9</td></tr>
<tr><td>Labour</td><td align="center">£288,000</td><td align="center">£240,000</td><td align="center">£48,000</td><td align="center">£12</td></tr>
<tr><td>Semi–variable costs
Heat, light and power</td><td align="center">£31,000</td><td align="center">£27,000</td><td align="center">£4,000</td><td align="center">£1</td></tr>
<tr><td colspan="5">Analysis of heat, light and power</td></tr>
<tr><td>Variable cost £1 per unit</td><td align="center">£24,000</td><td align="center">£20,000</td><td></td><td></td></tr>
<tr><td>Total cost</td><td align="center">£31,000</td><td align="center">£27,000</td><td></td><td></td></tr>
<tr><td>Fixed cost</td><td align="center">£7,000</td><td align="center">£7,000</td><td></td><td></td></tr>
</tbody>
</table>

* Unit variable cost is increase in cost divided by increase in the volume of output.

(b)

Rivermede Ltd – flexible budget statement for the year ended 31 May 1999

<table>
<thead>
<tr><th></th><th align="center">Revised
Budget</th><th align="center">Actual
results</th><th align="center">Variance
F = favourable
A = adverse</th></tr>
</thead>
<tbody>
<tr><td>Production and sales (units)</td><td align="center">22,000</td><td align="center">22,000</td><td></td></tr>
<tr><td></td><td align="center">£</td><td align="center">£</td><td align="center">£</td></tr>
<tr><td>Variable costs</td><td></td><td></td><td></td></tr>
<tr><td>Material 22,000 × £9</td><td align="center">198,000</td><td align="center">214,320</td><td align="center">16,320 (A)</td></tr>
<tr><td>Labour 22,000 × £12</td><td align="center">264,000</td><td align="center">255,200</td><td align="center">8,800 (F)</td></tr>
<tr><td>Semi–variable costs
Heat, light and power
(22,000 × £1) + £7,000</td><td align="center">29,000</td><td align="center">25,880</td><td align="center">3,120 (F)</td></tr>
<tr><td>Fixed cost
Rent, rates and depreciation</td><td align="center">40,000</td><td align="center">38,000</td><td align="center">2,000 (F)</td></tr>
<tr><td></td><td align="center">£531,000</td><td align="center">£533,400</td><td align="center">2,400 (A)</td></tr>
</tbody>
</table>

MEMO

To: **Steven Jones**   **From:**   **Management Accountant**

Subject: **Flexible budgetary control**

Date: **16 June 1999**

(a)   I note your comments on the performance of Rivermede for the year based on participative budgeting principles.

The original statement compares costs related to the production of 22,000 units with that of a budget for 20,000 units. This is not a 'like with like' comparison. However, the flexible budget addresses this criticism by comparing the actual performance for 22,000 units with the budgetary allowance for that level of output and sales.

The flexible budget recognises the distinction between variable and fixed costs and the effect on volume. The variances prepared are therefore based on meaningful comparisons.

(b)   There are a number of reasons why favourable cost variances could arise, other than through participation in the budgetary process.

- Some costs are outside the span of management's control. For example a favourable variance on fixed costs ie, rent, rates and depreciation is a typical example.

  A general fall in the price of a commodity on world markets can also create a favourable variance not influenced by the control mechanism exercised by management.

- Managers may have inflated budgeted costs as a result of participation thus distorting the true position on the under–spend.

- Managers may have reduced costs at the expense of quality and or safety levels.

(c)   A similar argument can be developed for the increase in sales volume.

- There may have been a general increase in the demand independent of the effort of sales management.

- The revised budget was significantly lower than the original plan. The original forecast may have been set too high, however the sales director may have deliberately set the forecast at that level to ensure that the actual results look better than they should.

  In future together with employing a participative approach we should plan to introduce a system of flexible budgetary control.

UNIT 9 – SECTION 2 – DECEMBER 1999

Task 2.1

(a)   (i)   Budgeted selling price
(£960,000 ÷ 20,000 units) = £48.00

(ii)   Budgeted material cost per unit
(£240,000 ÷ 20,000 units) = £12.00

(iii)   Budgeted marginal cost of light, heat and power per unit
([£68,000 − £20,000] ÷ 20,000 units) = £2.40

(iv)   Actual marginal cost of light, heat and power per unit
([£74,500 − £12,000] ÷ 25,000 units) = £2.50

(b)

HFD Processes Ltd: Flexible budgeting statement – year ended 30 November 1999						
Units	*Workings*		*Flexible budget* 22,000		*Actual* 22,000	*Variance* nil
		£	£	£	£	£
Turnover	(22,000 × £48,000)		1,056,000		1,012,000	44,000 (A)
Marginal costs						
Material	(22,000 × £12.00)	264,000		261,800		2,200 (F)
Light, heat and power	(22,000 × £2.40)	52,800		55,000		2,200 (A)
Fixed costs						
Labour		260,000		273,000		13,000 (A)
Light, heat and power		20,000		12,000		8,000 (F)
Fixed overheads		400,000		430,000		30,000 (A)
			996,800		1,031,800	
Operating profit/(loss)			59,200		(19,800)	79,000 (A)

Task 2.2

MEMO

To: **CEO**   **From:**   **Management**
               Accountant

Subject: **Flexible budgetary control**

Date: **2/12/99**

The flexible budgetary control statement differs from that prepared because:

- The original statement does not compare 'like with like' as budgeted sales level was 20,000 units compared with an actual performance of 22,000 units.

- The original plan did not account for stock levels whereas the actual performance included stocks valued on a full cost basis.

Although fixed overheads are essential to the production of stocks from a control perspective they are a period cost and should be on a period basis.

Stocks value accounted at marginal cost include those costs well within the 'span of control' of the managers.

In future reports on performance should be based on marginal costing principles.

UNIT 9 – SECTION 2 – JUNE 2000

SECTION 2

Task 2.1

(a)	Revised budgeted selling price (£1,760,000/11,000)	£160
(b)	Material cost per Raider in revised budget (£396,000/11,000)	£36
(c)	Variable cost of production and administrative labour	
	Increase in budgeted labour cost (£630,000 − £580,000)	£50,000
	Increase in budgeted volume (11,000 − 10,000)	1,000
	Variable cost of labour per unit (£50,000/1,000)	£50
(d)	Fixed cost of production and administrative labour	
	Total budgeted cost of labour	£630,000
	Total variable cost of labour (11,000 × £50)	£550,000
	Budgeted fixed cost of labour	£80,000
(e)	Variable cost of light, heat and power	
	Increase in budgeted light, heat and power (£164,000 − £160,000)	£4,000
	Increase in budgeted volume	1,000
	Budgeted variable cost of light, heat and power per Raider (£4,000/1000)	£4
(f)	Fixed cost of light, heat and power	
	Total budgeted cost of light, heat and power	£164,000
	Total variable cost of light, heat and power (11,000 × £4)	£44,000
	Budgeted fixed cost of light, heat and power	£120,000

Task 2.2

MEMO

To: **Mike Green**   From: **Management Accountant**

Date: **22 June 2000**   Subject: **Motivation and performance**

I attach a flexible budgetary control statement for Visiguard and my observations concerning motivation and performance.

(a)

Visiguard Ltd: Flexible budget statement for year ended 31 May 2000			
	Fixed budget	*Actual results*	*Variances*
Sales and production volume	11,600	11,600	nil
	£	£	£
Turnover (£160 × 11,600)	1,856,000	1,844,400	11,600 (A)
Variable materials (£36 × 11,600)	417,600	440,800	23,200 (A)
Production and administrative labour			
(£80,000 + [£50 × 11,600])	660,000	677,600	17,600 (A)
Light, heat and power			
(£120,000 + [£4 × 11,600])	166,400	136,400	30,000 (F)
Fixed overheads	240,000	259,600	19,600 (A)
Budgeted profit	372,000	330,000	42,000 (A)

(b)   It is assumed that participation in budget preparation improves motivation and increases performance, this is not always the case. There are a number of situations where an imposed budget may be more effective and includes where:

- there is sufficient urgency that there is not the time to allow participation
- managers would prefer not to set their own budgets and prefer set targets
- managers may not have the technical knowledge to set budgets
- managers' objectives may differ from those of the organisation.

(c)   Setting a budgetary target which cannot be achieved is often de–motivating. If it is too rigid, managers might recognise its impossibility and not even attempt to achieve the target. They might attempt to achieve the target but at the cost of ignoring other aspects of the budget. Setting impossible targets can be counterproductive and bring the whole budgetary process into disrepute as managers question the validity and usefulness of all other aspects of the budget.   This might possibly have been the case in terms of the desire to reduce material costs. If there is only a single supplier of material the managers of Visiguard may not be able to control the price.

(d)   It cannot be assumed that the improved performance compared to the original budget has arisen because managers were motivated by the revised budget.

- The actual sales demand was greater than the revised budget. This may have arisen as a result of increased motivation. However it may be factors outside the control of management such as a general increase in demand for the Raider, not influenced by the sales force.

- The only cost which shows a favourable variance is light, heat and power. This could have arisen for a number of reasons – all without any effort on the part of the managers of Visiguard. The power suppliers might have reduced their prices. Alternatively, the weather in the year might have been milder, requiring less heating and so reducing costs.

UNIT 9 – SECTION 2 – DECEMBER 2000

Task 2.1

(a)   **Budgeted data**

(i)   Budgeted cost of material per Delta: £600,000/100,000 Deltas = £6.00.

(ii)   Budgeted variable cost of light, heat and power (£200,000 – £40,000)/100,000 Deltas = £1.60.

(iii)   Number of budgeted production employees £120,000/£12,000 wages per employee = 10 employees.

(b)

Flexible budget statement for year ended 30 November 2000			
	Flexible budget	*Actual results*	*Variance*
Volume	125,000	125,000	nil
	£'000	£'000	£'000
Turnover	2,500	2,250	250 (A)
Material (125,000 × £6.00)	750	800	50 (A)
Light, heat and power (£40,000 + [125,000 × £1.60])	240	265	25 (A)
Production labour (13 employees × £12,000)	156	156	0
Rent, rates and depreciation	140	175	35 (A)
Administrative salaries and expenses	110	110	0
Profit	1,104	744	360 (A)

Key: A = adverse, F = favourable

Task 2.2

**The role of budgets, forecasting and variances at
Parkside Manufacturing Ltd**

**A report
Prepared by Management Accountant
For Judith Green, Production Director
Date: 7 December 2000**

Introduction

This report provides an overview and briefing on the subject of budgets and budgetary control.

(a)   **Types of budgets used in Parkside Manufacturing**

There are two types of budget used in Parkside Manufacturing Ltd. A fixed budget is essentially a planning device. This is predetermined in advance. It aids co–ordination of activities. In addition, once adopted, the managers are committed to achieving the budget as it compels achievement.

A flexible budget is a control device. It re–states the original budget to take account of what costs and revenues should match the actual activity achieved. This flexible, or revised budget, can be compared directly with the actual results on a like with like basis. As comparing like with like, the flexible budget is more meaningful for control purposes.

(b)   **General factors to be taken into account before investigating variances**

It is often not possible to investigate all variances. Exception principles are often applied either as a minimum absolute variance or minimum percentage variance before the variance is investigated.

A variance might also be worthy of investigation if it is part of a continuing trend. Waiting until a trend is established avoids investigating variances caused by random events.

Variances are often not analysed fully if the cause is already known or if the variance is not controllable, as in the case of local business authority rates. In addition, variances might not be investigated when they are compensated by opposite variances elsewhere.

In all of these, the essential point is that the benefits from analysis should be greater than the costs.

(c)   **Limitations to the use of linear regression in sales forecasting**

There are a number of limitations to the use of linear regression technique in sales forecasting.

Examples include:

- assumption of linearity. Sales demand might follow a clear but curvilinear pattern
- assumption that demand is simply a function of time. Demand is more likely to be based on consumer tastes and disposable income
- use of historical data. The past may not be a good guide to the future.

UNIT 16 – SECTION 1 – DECEMBER 1996

Task 1.1

WORKINGS:

Production volume (packs)	(i)	40,000	50,000	60,000	70,000
Average cost	(ii)	£430	£388	£360	£340
Total cost	(i) × (ii)	£17,200,000	£19,400,000	£21,600,000	£23,800,000
Cost per extra 10,000 packs	(iii)		£2,200,000	£2,200,000	£2,200,000
Unit variable cost	(iii)/10,000		£220	£220	£220

(a)   Total cost for 40,000 packs   £17,200,000
        Less: Variable costs (40,000 × £220)   £8,800,000

        Fixed costs   £8,400,000

(b)   Unit contribution = £420 – £220 = £200
        Total contribution = £200 × 65,000 packs =   £13,000,000
        Less Fixed costs   £8,400,000

        Profit   £4,600,000

(c)   Break–even point (packs) = Fixed costs/Unit contribution = £8,400,000/£200 = 42,000

(d)   Margin of safety = (65,000 – 42,000)/65,000 = 35.4%

Task 1.2

MEMO

◈ FOULKS*lynch*

To: Ben Cooper   **From:**   A Technician
                Marketing Director   Management Accounting Department

Date: 5 December 1996

Subject: Profitability of orders

Following our recent conversation concerning the possible export order, I have now evaluated the likely profitability. With a volume of 5,000 packs and a selling price of £330, the profits of our company would increase by £550,000. However, if the price increased to £340 and volume to 15,000, profits would fall by £200,000. My workings are enclosed below.

(a)	Volume	5,000	(b)	Volume	15,000
	Unit contribution (330 – 220)	£110		Unit contribution (340 – 220)	£120
	Total contribution from order	£550,000		Total contribution from order	£1,800,000
				less contribution lost	£2,000,000
				Loss from order	£200,000

(c) In both proposals, fixed costs are irrelevant as they will remain the same irrespective of any possible change in volume. This unusual result – that an increase in price and volume leads to a fall in profit – arises because production capacity is limited to 70,000 packs. The order for 15,000 units take demand beyond the capacity of the plant. As a result, the order can only be achieved by diverting production from existing sales with a higher unit contribution. Existing sales have a contribution of £200 per pack. Accepting the order for 15,000 packs involves giving up sales of 10,000 packs with a unit contribution of £200.

(d) Given the grounds for Dr Harper's suggestion – that the larger order would avoid losses – York should reject the option of selling the 15,000 extra packs. Although the smaller order does increase the company's profit, there are other, non–financial issues to consider before finally making a decision. The company should consider the effect on existing customers if they discovered our company was selling at a lower price to other customers. The existing customers might also demand the lower price. A similar problem might occur if the new customer is able to sell in our existing market at a lower price. Demand from current customers might then decrease, possibly causing company profitability to fall.

UNIT 16 – SECTION 1 – JUNE 1997

Task 1.1

Solution

(a)   Number of beds to be sold to avoid a loss
       Break–even point = £98,450/£11 = 8,950 beds

(b)   Turnover at break–even point
       Average unit selling price = £2,106,000/5,400 = £390
       Turnover = £390 × 8,950 = £3,490,500

WORKINGS

Contribution	£		Fixed costs	£
Turnover	2,106,000		Rates and insurance	8,450
Cost of beds	(1,620,000)		Light, heat and power	10,000
Commission	(210,600)		Assistants' salaries	40,000
Transport	(216,000)		Manager's salary	40,000
Total contribution	59,400		Total fixed costs	98,450
Number of beds sold	5,400			
Unit contribution	£11			

Task 1.2

Workings for information needed in letter

Required contribution

		£
Salary		36,550
Interest lost		15,000
(a) Required profit		51,550
Add fixed costs as above		98,450
Less Manager's salary saved		(40,000)
Total contribution		110,000
Unit contribution =		£11

(b)   Required sales volume = £110,000/£11 = 10,000 beds

(c)   Average life of a bed

Proportion	Life (years)	Expected value	
0.1	9	0.9	Population = 44,880 households
0.6	10	6.0	Expected life of bed = 10.2 years
0.3	11	3.3	Annual demand = 44,880/10.2 = 4,400 households
			Beds per household = 2.1
1.0		10.2	Annual demand = 4,400 × 2.1 = 9,240 beds

Solution

Smith, Williams and Jones
Accountants and Registered Auditors
Anytown

19 August 19X8

Ms Judith Howarth
Anytown

Dear Ms Howarth,

Possible acquisition of Brita Beds Ltd

At our recent meeting, you raised a number of queries concerning the potential profitability of Brita Beds Ltd. These are addressed below.

(a) **Required profit**

Currently you earn £15,000 p.a. interest on your savings and receive a salary of £36,550. Purchasing Brita Beds Ltd would require you giving up all your savings to pay for the company. In addition, you will no longer be in receipt of your salary if you take on the manager's role within that company. However, there will be savings of £40,000 from not replacing the current manager and so the minimum profit you will need to earn to compensate for giving up your salary and interest is £11,550.

(b) **Sales volume required to achieve a profit of £11,550**

With a required profit of £11,550 and fixed costs of £98,450, you need to generate a contribution of £110,000. The unit contribution per bed is £11 and so you will have to sell 10,000 beds each year.

(c) **Maximum demand**

According to market research, the average life of a bed is 10.2 years. With 44,880 households living in Mytown, this means that there will, on average, be 4,400 households changing their beds in any one year. As each household has an average of 2.1 beds, the maximum demand for beds in Mytown will average 9,240 beds each year.

(d) **Viability of the purchase**

With a maximum demand of only 9,240 beds per year and a need for you to sell 10,000 beds in each year to maintain your total income, the proposal does not appear profitable.

(e) **Limitations to the analysis**
This conclusion, however, has to be treated with caution for the following reasons:
(i)   The market research data may have been derived from a sample and so there might be a sampling error.
(ii)   The population of Mytown may not fit the population of the whole country. For example, Mytown might be a new town with new, young households. As a result, there may be a greater demand both because households are newly established and because those households might be starting families.
(iii)   The data is historic and does not allow for changes in tastes by the population nor technological changes which might cause demand to increase.
(iv)   The survey data takes no account of changes in demand if prices were to be reduced. Reducing prices might encourage customers from other towns.

I hope these observations help you arrive at a decision concerning Brita Beds Ltd.

Yours sincerely,
A Technician

Task 1.3

First we calculate the contribution earned from each model of bed:

Model	A £	B £	C £	Total
Selling price	240.00	448.00	672.00	
Unit cost	130.00	310.00	550.00	
Carriage in	20.00	20.00	20.00	
Unit contribution	90.00	118.00	102.00	
Square metres per bed	3.00	4.00	5.00	
Contribution per square metre	£30.00	£29.50	£20.40	
Ranking	(1)	(2)	(3)	
Maximum demand	35	45	20	
Storage requirement (square metres)	105	180	100	385

But current storage space is only 300 square metres.

(a)   **Monthly sales schedule – bed department**

	Units	Square metres
Available storage		300
Sales of model A	35	105
		195
Sales of model B	45	180
		15
Sales of model C	3	15
Surplus capacity		nil

(b)   **Statement of profitability – bed department**

	Units	Unit Contribution £	Total £
Model A	35	90	3,150
Model B	45	118	5,310
Model C	3	102	306
Total contribution			8,766
Staff costs		3,780	
Departmental fixed overheads		2,000	5,780
Profit directly attributable to the department		2,986	
General fixed overheads			2,520
Departmental profit after central overheads			466

UNIT 16 – SECTION 1 – DECEMBER 1997

Task 1.1

(a) **Budgeted sales volume in litres**   £'000

    Production fixed overheads absorbed   640
    Production fixed overheads unabsorbed   160
                                                                                              ─────
    Total production fixed overheads   800
                                                                                              ─────

    Maximum capacity = maximum sales (litres)   100,000
    Budgeted capacity = budgeted sales (litres) [(640/800) × 100,000]   80,000

(b) **Break–even point**
    Fixed costs   £'000

    Production fixed overheads (see above)   800
    Fixed selling expenses   600
    Fixed administration expenses   400
                                                                                              ─────
    Total fixed costs   1,800
                                                                                              ─────

    Contribution   £'000

    Turnover   16,000
    Variable material   (6,400)
    Variable labour   (3,200)
    Variable overhead   (1,600)
    Commission   (800)
                                                                                              ─────
    Total contribution   4,000
                                                                                              ─────

    Unit contribution   £50
    Break–even point (litres) [£1.8m/£50]   36,000

    Contribution percentage [£4m/£16m]   25%
    Break–even point (£)   £7.2m

(c) **Percentage decrease in budgeted sales to achieve break–even**
    Units
    Current sales (litres)   80,000
    Break–even sales (litres)   36,000
                                                                                              ─────
                                                                                             44,000
                                                                                              ─────

    Percentage decrease [(44/80) × 100]   55%

(*Tutorial note:* Alternatively:

    Value   £'000

    Current sales   16,000
    Break–even sales   7,200
                                                                                              ─────
                                                                                              8,800
                                                                                              ─────

    Percentage decrease [(£8.8m/£16m) × 100]   55%)

Task 1.2

Selling price = marginal cost per litre + contribution per litre = £60 + £40 = £100

MEMO

To:	Sales Manager, Colouring Division	**From:**	Assistant Management Accountant, Head Office

Date: 19 August 1998

Subject: Budget preparation

I note that you have not yet been able to prepare a budget for the year to 31 December 1998. In order to assist you, I have identified the budgeted sales and profit from existing customers and analysed the financial implications of the possible special order. Before deciding whether or not to accept the special order, the non–financial implications should also be considered.

(a)   **Budgeted turnover and profit excluding the special order**

	£'000
Turnover [100,000 litres × £100]	10,000
Marginal cost [100,000 × £60]	6,000
Contribution	4,000
Fixed costs	2,400
Budget profit before special order	1,600

(b)   **Evaluation of Special order**

(i)   *Without external sourcing*

Order volume (litres)	30,000
Unit contribution [£90 – £60]	£30
Gross contribution [£30 × 30,000]	£900,000
less contribution lost from existing customers [£40 × 10,000]	£400,000
Net contribution on accepting special order when sourced internally	£500,000

(ii)   *With external sourcing*

Contribution from internally sourced production [£30 × 20,000]	£600,000
Contribution per litre from external sources [£90 – £105 = –£15]	
Contribution from externally sourced production [–£15 × 10,000]	(£150,000)
Net contribution when partially sourced externally	£450,000

(c)   **Non–financial issues to be considered**

Although the best option appears to be to accept the special order and source all production internally, before making a final decision there is a need to consider the wider implications. These include:

- Loss of goodwill from failing to fully satisfy demand from existing customers if production of the special order is sourced entirely from within the division.
- The possibility of existing customers becoming aware of reduced prices and demanding similar terms whichever option is chosen.
- The effect of the reduced price on the Colouring Division's image.
- A possible lowering of overall divisional profitability if the new customer takes an increasing proportion of output at the expense of existing, more profitable customers.
- The supplier becoming aware of the Colouring Division's markets.

Task 1.3

The notes should include the following:

(a)   **The minimum contract price**

Proposed contract – revised cost		
	Notes	£
Material A	1	28,000
Material B	2	55,000
Labour	3	1,000
General divisional overheads	4	nil
Minimum price for the contract		84,000

Notes

		£	£
1	£1,000 kg × £28		28,000
2	500 kg	13,000	
	1,500 kg @ £28	42,000	55,000
3	900 hours	nil	
	100 hours @ £10	1,000	1,000
4	Overheads are not an incremental cost		

(b)   **The technique used to derive the costs of the contract**

The technique used to derive the minimum contract price is known as opportunity costing. This measures the cost of a resource as being its value in the next best alternative to its proposed use.

The 'real' cost of a resource is not necessarily how much it costs but, rather, its value to the business. This can often be measured by calculating how worse off the business would be if it was deprived of the resource.

(c)   **Justification for the cost of labour and divisional fixed overheads**

Using the information provided, the opportunity cost of the fixed overheads and the 900 hours of labour is nil if these are surplus and have no other possible uses. The amount of these expenses is the same whether or not the contract is undertaken. There is therefore no extra cost to the division if they are used in the contract. The only extra cost will be the 100 hours of overtime as this involves cash leaving the business as a direct result of accepting the contract.

UNIT 16 – SECTION 2 – DECEMBER 1996

Task 2.1

WORKINGS

Annual   growth   rate $= \dfrac{(132{,}000 - 120{,}000)}{120{,}000}$ $-$ 1 $=$ 10%

To: The Chief Executive   From: A. Technician
          Portsmere Hospital

Date: 5 December 1996

Subject: **Replacement of laundry equipment**

(a) I have evaluated the two options for replacing the laundry equipment. My detailed analysis is shown in the enclosed table.

Machine A

End of Year	Volume	Variable costs (£)	Fixed costs (£)	NCF £	Discount factors	DCF £
1	145,200	726,000	20,000	746,000	0.870	649,020
2	159,720	798,600	20,000	818,600	0.756	618,862
3	175,692	878,460	20,000	898,460	0.658	591,187
						1,859,069
Capital cost						60,000
Net present cost						1,919,069

Machine B

End of year	Volume	Variable costs (£)	Fixed costs (£)	NCF £	Discount factors	DCF £
1	145,200	755,040	38,000	793,040	0.870	689,945
2	159,720	830,544	38,000	868,544	0.756	656,619
3	170,000	884,000	38,000	922,000	0.658	606,676
3	5,692	56,920		56,920	0.658	37,453
Net present cost						1,990,693

(b)   On the information provided to me, and using the hospital's required return of 15%, the purchase of Machine A appears to be the more economic option. Machine A has a net present cost of £1,919,069 compared with a net present cost of £1,990,693 for the rental option, a saving in present value terms of £71,624.

An additional benefit from purchasing machine A is that it has surplus capacity. This provides an additional safeguard should the forecast growth in demand be under–estimated.

(c)   I have ignored the £10,000 residual value of the existing equipment. This is not a benefit derived from purchasing machine A or renting machine B. The residual value is merely a source of funds, similar to any other cash belonging to the hospital.

(d)   The technique used in the appraisal is known as discounted cash flow. Money has a cost even without inflation or risk. This cost arises because, in general, consumption now is preferred to consumption in the future. Because of this, investors demand a reward in the form of interest or some other return if they are to defer consumption. For borrowers, they have to pay this reward to investors in exchange for receiving cash today rather than in the future.

From this, it follows that the value of a pound in the future has less value than a pound today. The further into the future is the pound, the lower its present value.

UNIT 16 – SECTION 2 – JUNE 1997

Task 2.1

(Tutorial note: Because Sound Equipment Ltd (i) carries no stock, (ii) pays for materials immediately and (iii) receives cash on delivery for sales, then turnover, material and labour represent cashflows as well as elements making up profitability.)

Before starting the report, we need workings to calculate the tax payable in each year:

	Tax computation		
	Year 1 £	*Year 2* £	*Year 3* £
Turnover	180,000	180,000	180,000
Material and labour	100,000	105,000	110,250
Profit before depreciation	80,000	75,000	69,750
Capital allowances	37,500	28,125	84,375
Taxable profit	42,500	46,875	(14,625)
Tax @ 33%	14,025	15,469	(4,826)
Payable in year	2	3	4

Task 2.1 (cont'd)

Report on the viability of accepting the contract from JBZ plc

To: John Green   From: Assistant Accountant
         Financial Director

Date: 19 August 1998

Further to your request for a financial appraisal of the proposed contract with JBZ plc, I have evaluated the proposal using discounted cash flow techniques. My findings are that the proposal fails to add value to our company when discounted at our 18% cost of capital. The detailed analysis is given below.

(a)   **Financial evaluation of the contract**

Investment appraisal – proposed contract with JBZ plc

End of year	*0* £	*1* £	*2* £	*3* £	*4* £	*Net present value* £
Pre–tax cash flows	(150,000)	80,000	75,000	69,750		
Tax paid			(14,025)	(15,469)	4,826	
Net cash flow	(150,000)	80,000	60,975	54,281	4,826	
Discount factor	1.000	0.847	0.718	0.609	0.516	
Discounted cash flow	(150,000)	67,760	43,780	33,057	2,490	(2,913)

(b)   **The treatment of taxation**

Corporation tax is payable on taxable profits – not accounting profits. To derive taxable profits for the proposal involves the company depreciation being replaced by the capital allowances allowed by the Inland Revenue. These are at the rate of 25% per annum on the reducing balance. However, at the end of the third year, the asset has no further use and so there is a balancing allowance at the end of that year equivalent to the unclaimed amount.

Taxation is then payable on this revised profit at the rate currently in force of 33%. This is normally paid 9 months after the company's year–end but for the purpose of simplification, a one year delay has been assumed in the above appraisal. This delay in the payment of the corporation tax is important in investment appraisal as the timings of cash flows are central to the DCF approach to investment appraisal.

(c)   **Other factors**

Before finally deciding whether or not to accept the contract, there are a number of other points to be considered.

- If there is a subsequent contract, there will be no need to purchase a further machine and so any second contract may be much more valuable.
- The forecast of material and labour cost increases may be inaccurate. With a fixed price contract, this is a critical factor.
- There are no charges in the proposal for the use of Sound Equipment's premises or any other shared costs. This is only valid if there is spare capacity and no other worthwhile use for that capacity.
- The negative net present value is relatively small. Because of this, it might be worthwhile accepting the contract if other benefits result. These include the possibility of the second contract being awarded to Sound Equipment Ltd and an improvement in our reputation by being associated with a major multinational company.

UNIT 16 – SECTION 2 – DECEMBER 1997

Task 2.1

REPORT

To:　　　　Ann Spring　　　　　　　　　　　　　　　**From:**　Accounting Technician

Date:　　　19 August 1998

Subject:　　Investment proposal and the internal rate of return

(a), (b)　　　Calculation of net present value at 30% and 70% discount rates.

INVESTMENT APPRAISAL – CALCULATION OF NET PRESENT VALUES

End of year	Units	Cash Received £	Material £	Labour £	Rent £	Net cash flow £	30% factor	DCF £	70% factor	DCF £
1	10,000	420,000	200,000	150,000	20,000	50,000	0.769	38,450	0.588	29,400
2	11,000	462,000	220,000	150,000	20,000	72,000	0.592	42,624	0.346	24,912
3	12,100	508,200	242,000	152,000	20,000	94,200	0.455	42,861	0.204	19,217
4	13,310	559,020	266,200	176,200	20,000	96,620	0.350	33,817	0.120	11,594
								157,752		85,123
Initial cost								(100,000)		(100,000)
Net present value								57,752		(14,877)

c)　　Estimation of the internal rate of return

$$\text{Internal Rate of Return} = 30\% + \left(\frac{57,752}{57,752 + 14,877} \times (70\% - 30\%) \right)$$

$$= 61.8\%$$

(d)　　The meaning of the internal rate of return

The internal rate of return is the discount rate which reduces the net present value of a proposed cashflow stream to zero. For a traditional investment comprising an outflow followed by inflows, if the internal rate of return is greater than the required return then the proposal is worthwhile.

◈ **FOULKS**$lynch$

PRACTICE
ASSESSMENT ANSWERS

TECHNICIAN STAGE

NVQ/SVQ LEVEL 4 IN ACCOUNTING

PRACTICE CENTRAL ASSESSMENT

**CONTRIBUTING TO THE MANAGEMENT OF COSTS
AND THE ENHANCEMENT OF VALUE
(UNIT 8)**

SUGGESTED ANSWERS

◈ **FOULKS**_lynch_

SECTION 1

Task 1.1

(a)

20X7		Q1	Q2	Q3	Q4
Actual price		£20	£22	£32	£38
Seasonal variation		-£2	-£4	+£2	+£4
Trend		£22	£26	£30	£34

(b)

20X8		Q1	Q2	Q3	Q4
Trend		£38	£42	£46	£50
Seasonal variation		-£2	-£4	+£2	+£4
Forecast price		£36	£38	£48	£54

Task 1.2

Standard hours produced
$$1,150 \text{ tonnes} \times 1.3 = 1,495 \text{ standard hrs}$$

Standard hours in budget
$$1,200 \text{ tonnes} \times 1.3 = 1,560 \text{ standard hrs}$$

Actual hours worked = 1,600

(a)   Productivity measure:

Efficiency ratio

$$\frac{\text{Standard hours produced}}{\text{Actual hours worked}} = \frac{1,495}{1,600} \times 100$$

$$= \quad 93.4\%$$

(b)   Production volume measure:

Activity ratio

$$\frac{\text{Standard hours produced}}{\text{Budget hours}} = \frac{1,495}{1,560} \times 100$$

$$= \quad 95.8\%$$

(c)   Utilisation measure:

Capacity ratio

$$\frac{\text{Actual hours worked}}{\text{Budget hours}} = \frac{1,600}{1,560} \times 100$$

$$= \quad 102.6\%$$

The efficiency of labour in the month was adverse by 7%. However this was offset by a marginal increase in capacity ie, hours worked of approximately 3%, which resulted in the activity level of 96% ie, a fall of 4% in production volume.

Task 1.3

A = Adverse
F = Favourable

(a)   **Direct labour rate variance**

(Std rate – actual rate) actual hours	£
(£6 – £6.05*) 1,600 =	80A
* £9,680/1,600 hours	

(b)   **Direct labour efficiency variance**

(Std hrs produced – actual hrs worked) standard rate	
(1,495 – 1,600) £6	630A
* 1,150 tonnes of product × 1.3 hrs	
	710A

(c)   **Fixed overhead variance**

Fixed overhead recovery rate (FORR) : $\dfrac{\text{Fixed costs (budget)}}{\text{Standard hours in budget}}$

$= \dfrac{£4,500}{1,560} = £2.8846$ per std hour

Fixed overhead recovered in production achieved

	£
1,150 × 1.3 = 1,495 standard hours @ £2.8846 =	4,312
Actual fixed cost =	4,700
Under-recovery	£388 A

(d)   **Fixed overhead expenditure variance**

Budget fixed costs	4,500
Actual fixed costs	4,700
Over-spend	£200 A

(e)   **Fixed overhead volume variance**

Fixed overhead volume variance (standard hours produced – budget standard hours) × FORR

(1,495 – 1,560) £2.8846 = £188   A.

Volume variance	£188A	
Expenditure variance	200A	} £388A total fixed overhead variance

Reconciliation period 3 20X8

Standard cost of actual production:

	£
Direct labour 1.3 std hrs × £6	7.80
Direct material 1.1 tonnes × £25	27.50
Variable overhead 1.3 std hrs × £4 *	5.20
* £6,240/1,560 std hrs	
Fixed overhead 1.3 std hrs × £2.8846	3.75
Std cost per unit	44.25

	£
Actual production 1,150 × 44.25	50,887
Actual cost	53,194
Variance	2,307 A

Summary of variances:

	£	
Direct labour	710 A	
Direct material	789 A	
Variable overhead	420 A	} £2,307 A
Fixed overhead	388 A	

Task 1.4

BAY FEEDS LTD
Internal Memo

◇ FOULKS*lynch*

Period 3 20X8
To: Production Director

From: Accounting Technician

Re: Fixed overhead variances

I note your observation regarding the volume variances. Production volume or level of activity is affected by the two factors you mention: efficiency and capacity.

The under or over-recovery of fixed overhead due to changes in volume is the result of one of these factors or a combination of both.

The fixed overhead volume variance can be sub-divided into the fixed overhead efficiency variance and the fixed overhead capacity variance.

The volume variance for the period was £188 Adverse, as production volume was adverse by 50 units of output or 65 standard hours worth of production.

This adverse variance represents an under-recovery of fixed overhead.

The reason for the loss in volume was the adverse efficiency, which was highlighted in both the efficiency ratio and the labour efficiency variance.

The fixed overhead efficiency variance is thus:

(Standard hours produced – actual hours worked) × FORR
(1,495 – 1,600) £2.8846 = £303 A

The fixed overhead capacity variance is thus:

(Budget standard hours – actual hours worked) × FORR
(1,560 – 1,600) £2.8846 = £115 F.

This favourable variance is due to capacity being favourable ie, the capacity ratio was 102.6%.

	£
Fixed overhead efficiency variance	303A
Fixed overhead capacity variance	115F
	£188A

The total fixed overhead variance was shown in the report as £388 Adverse, representing an under-recovery of fixed overhead. £200 of this can be seen to be an expenditure variance; the balance as previously stated is due to volume, £188A.

In future reconciliations we will analyse fully the volume variance.

If, having considered my comments, you would like to discuss this matter further, please let me know.

SECTION 2

Task 2.1

(1)   Return on capital employed:

$$\frac{\text{Net profit before tax}}{\text{Capital employed}} \times 100 = \frac{0.39}{1.83} \times 100 = 21.3\%$$

(2)   Asset turnover

$$\frac{\text{Turnover}}{\text{Capital employed}} = \frac{3.30}{1.83} = 1.80$$

(3)   Net profit before tax to sales

$$\frac{\text{Net profit before tax}}{\text{Turnover}} = \frac{0.39}{3.30} \times 100 = 11.8\%$$

(4)   Current ratio

Current assets : current liabilities
1.24 : 0.85
1.46 : 1

(5)   Acid test

(Current assets − stocks) : current liabilities

= (1.24 − 0.30) : 0.85
= 0.94 : 0.85
= 1.11 : 1

(6)   Debtors collection period

$$= \frac{\text{Average debtors}}{\text{Turnover}} \times 365 \text{ days}$$

$$= \frac{\left(\dfrac{0.66 + 0.92}{2}\right)}{3.30} \times 365 \text{ days}$$

= 88 days

(7)   Cost of sales to finished stocks

$$= \frac{\text{Operating costs - dist and admin}}{\text{Finished goods stocks}}$$

$$= \frac{2.47}{0.22} = 11.2$$

(8)   Operating costs % of sales

$$\frac{\text{Operating costs}}{\text{Turnover}} \times 100 = \frac{2.91}{3.30} \times 100 = 88.2\%$$

(9)   Labour costs % of sales

$$\frac{\text{Labour costs}}{\text{Turnover}} \times 100 = \frac{0.62}{3.30} \times 100 = 18.8\%$$

(10)   Value added per £ of employee costs

Value added   =   Turnover less bought out materials and services
                     =   3.30 – 2.16 = 1.14

1.14 : 0.62   =   £1.84

(11)   Distribution and admin costs % of sales

$$\frac{\text{Distribution and admin}}{\text{Turnover}} = \frac{0.44}{3.30} \times 100 = 13.3\%$$

Task 2.2

Summary of performance ratios

Ratio	Bay Feeds	Sector	Comment
Return on capital employed	21.3%	26%	Return much lower than the sector as a whole.
Asset turnover	1.8	1.79	Creating slightly more turnover from the asset base than competitors.
% net profit to sales	11.8%	14.5%	Significantly lower return than industry average.
Current ratio	1.46	1.5	Marginally lower than industry average but good liquidity.
Acid test	1.11	1.03	Good sound level of liquidity.
Debtors collection period	88 days	83 days	Stricter controls required here, period slightly higher than industry average.
Cost of sales to finished stocks	11.2	8.1	Turning over inventory levels faster than competitors; holding approximately one months stock.
Operating costs % of sales	88.2%	85%	Problem lies here, operating overheads and other direct costs need tighter controls. Less efficient than competitors.
Labour costs % of sales	18.8%	18.1%	Slightly above average for industry.
Value added per £ employee costs	1.84	1.95	This is a measure of productivity; less productivity than industry as a whole.
Distribution/admin costs % of sales	13.3%	13%	In line with industry as a whole.

TECHNICIAN STAGE

NVQ/SVQ LEVEL 4 IN ACCOUNTING

PRACTICE CENTRAL ASSESSMENT

CONTRIBUTING TO THE PLANNING AND ALLOCATION OF RESOURCES
(UNIT 9)

SUGGESTED ANSWERS

SECTION 1

Task 1.1

(a)   Centred four-point moving average trend figures

Year	Quarter	Visitors	Moving annual total	Moving average	Centred average trend	Seasonal variation
20X7	1	6,000				
	2	9,200				
			36,700	9,175		
	3	15,000			9,275	+5,725
			37,500	9,375		
	4	6,500			9,475	-2,975
			38,300	9,575		
20X8	1	6,800			9,675	-2,875
			39,100	9,775		
	2	10,000			9,875	+125
			39,900	9,975		
	3	15,800				
	4	7,300				

(b)

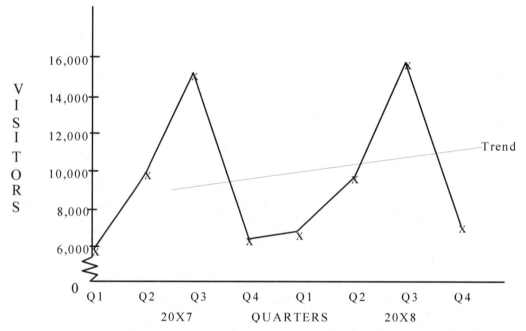

(c)   **Estimates of visitors per quarter 20X9**

20X9	Quarter	1	10,475 – 2,875	=	7,600
		2	10,675 + 125	=	10,800
		3	10,875 + 5,725	=	16,600
		4	11,075 – 2,975	=	8,100

(d)   (i)   A number of methods could be used to forecast visitor numbers using internal, external, primary or secondary data. The initial step is to gather the data used as input.

Internal sources are currently being used. Visitor numbers per quarter could be further analysed by month, week and date. The internal data can then be analysed using time series to establish the trend and seasonal variation.

However, this method assumes that the past will be repeated and ignores possible cyclical fluctuations. It also ignores the product life cycle and visitor needs and interests.

Primary and secondary data could be used in forecasting. Primary data has been referred to above.

Secondary data would include leisure based data, tourist data, etc.

(d)   (ii)   Selective sampling methods would include visitor questionnaire and telephone sampling.

Telephone sampling is considered more effective as:

- a higher response rate can be achieved
- all questions would be answered
- questions could be extended and adapted by the interviewer.

Task 1.2

MEMO

To: Owners of Bay Heavy Horse Centre
From: Accounting Technician
Date: November 20X8
Subject: Budgets

Following our recent meeting, I enclose my comments on the observations raised.

(1)   Do budgets motivate managers to meet objectives?

Motivation is the way in which a manager applies effort in attaining his or her objectives within the organisation. For budgets to motivate managers certain requirements must be met.

- Managers need to be fully aware of the organisations goals.
- Budgets must be consistent with the goals.
- Managers must need to achieve the objectives and believe that they are achievable.
- Managers must feel that they can influence the achievement of the objectives.
- Achievement of the objectives must provide a challenge.
- Rewards, either financial or non-financial, should be offered.

(2)   Do budgets lead to improved performance by managers?

If managers are motivated this will not always lead to improved performance. To achieve improved performance depends on the skills of the individual manager.

In turn this depends on factors such as training, education and inter-personal and managerial skills.

(3)   Does the current method of reporting motivate managers to be more efficient?

Issues to be addressed here are whether the statements are a valid measure of efficiency and how such statements might affect the behaviour of managers.

The budgets would need to identify both the fixed and variable costs. Fixed costs are usually less controllable, while those which vary with volume are more controllable.

Budgets need to provide a challenge if they are to encourage motivation.

To a point, budgets need to be demanding, but not too demanding as managers might then feel that they are not achievable. Variances between actual and budget figures will highlight areas for control.

If you wish to discuss these issues further please do not hesitate to contact me.

SECTION 2

Task 1.2

Note: Direct material £5 per unit variable
Direct labour £2 per unit variable

Indirect material (High-low method) for variable cost ie, $\dfrac{£36,000 - £16,000}{30,000 - 10,000 \text{ units}} = \dfrac{£20,000}{20,000 \text{ units}}$

$$= £1 \text{ per unit}$$

Fixed cost £16,000 – (10,000 × £1) = £6,000

PED plc

PM Ltd flexible budgets

Units of output	10,000	20,000	24,000	30,000
	£	£	£	£
Direct material	50,000	100,000	120,000	150,000
Direct labour	20,000	40,000	48,000	60,000
Indirect material	16,000	26,000	30,000	36,000
Indirect labour	24,000	24,000	32,000	44,000
Machine rental	8,000	16,000	16,000	16,000
Rent, rates etc	12,000	12,000	12,000	12,000
	130,000	218,000	258,000	318,000

Task 2.2

PED plc
PM Ltd Budgetary control statement period ended 31 March

Production level 30,000 units (full capacity)

Costs	Budget £	Actual £	Variance F/(A) * £
Direct material	150,000	154,500	(4,500) A
Direct labour	60,000	61,500	(1,500) A
Indirect material	36,000	36,100	(100) A
Indirect labour	44,000	43,900	100 F
Machine rental	16,000	16,000	–
Rent, rates etc	12,000	11,800	200 F
	£318,000	£323,800	£(5,800) A

* F = favourable   (A) = adverse variance

The two significant variances worthy of report and investigation are the prime cost variances of material and labour. The other variances are insignificant.

Direct material variance would have to be analysed for both price and usage, to identify the reason for the adverse overspend of £4,500.

Similarly, the direct labour needs analysis to labour rate and labour efficiency variances, to identify the causes of the excess of £1,500.

Once this analysis is complete then managerial action can be taken to improve the position in later budget periods.

356

TECHNICIAN STAGE

NVQ/SVQ LEVEL 4 IN ACCOUNTING

PRACTICE DEVOLVED ASSESSMENT

EVALUATING CURRENT AND PROPOSED ACTIVITIES (UNIT 16)

SUGGESTED ANSWERS

Task 1

Analysis of costs:

Costs	Division B budget £	Costs saved £	Costs not saved £
Turnover	950,000		
Variable costs			
Materials	570,000	570,000	
Labour	199,000	199,000	
Overhead	120,000	120,000	
	889,000	889,000	
Contribution	61,000		
Fixed overheads			
Rent	20,000		20,000
Rates	13,000		13,000
Heat, light	30,000		30,000
Depreciation	30,000	30,000	
Plant insurance	11,000	11,000	
Selling & Distribution Overheads			
Sales commission	19,000	19,000	
Sales expenses	32,000	32,000	
Central overheads			
Personnel	9,000		9,000
Finance	10,000		10,000
Administration	12,000		12,000
	186,000	92,000	94,000
Profit/(Loss)	(125,000)		

Effect on profitability if activities in Division B are discontinued

	£
Turnover lost	950,000
Variable production costs saved	889,000
Other costs saved	92,000
	981,000
Effect on profitability:	£31,000

Reconciliation:

	Division A £	Division C £	Total £
Turnover	800,000	750,000	1,550,000
Variable costs	466,000	278,000	744,000
Contribution	334,000	472,000	806,000

Fixed and other costs

Rent	60,000
Rates	40,000
Heat & Light	90,000
Depreciation	50,000
Plant insurance	19,000
Selling & Distribution	79,000
Central overheads	87,000
	425,000
Profit/(Loss)	£381,000

Recommendation:

- In the short term considering its variable costs, specific fixed costs and selling and distribution overhead, Division B is failing to contribute to the company's fixed overheads and thus profits. There is a shortfall of £31,000.

- The costs saved if the Division is closed include not only the direct variable costs, but specific fixed costs such as depreciation, insurance and sales and distribution expenses.

- The central fixed overheads are jointly incurred and have been apportioned and will still be incurred if Division B's activities are discontinued.

- Closing Division B would result in profits increasing by £31,000 and would increase the return on capital from 29% to 32%.

- It is therefore recommended that Division B's activities are discontinued.

- The report assumes that the plant can be disposed of and thus the depreciation charge and insurance can be saved.

- No consideration has been given to the possibility of using the spare capacity to expand the activities in Divisions A and B, particularly Division C which is highly profitable.

Task 2

Budgeted Operating Statement
Quarter Ended 31 March 20X9

Products	'SD'	'AH'	'JV'	'SH'	'JP'	'JJ'	Total
Production/Sales (Units)	960	900	825	900	930	1,050	5,565
	£	£	£	£	£	£	£
Turnover	38,400	33,750	29,700	29,250	29,760	31,500	192,360
Less Variable costs:							
Direct labour	14,400	12,150	10,395	10,800	11,160	11,970	70,875
Direct material	5,616	4,860	4,084	4,253	4,394	4,725	27,932
Variable overhead	4,876	4,114	3,520	3,657	3,779	4,054	24,000
	24,892	21,124	17,999	18,710	19,333	20,749	122,807
Contribution	13,508	12,626	11,701	10,540	10,427	10,751	69,553
Fixed Costs							45,000
Profit/(Loss)							£24,553

$$\text{Variable overhead recovery rate} = \frac{£24,000}{11,718 \text{ standard hours}}$$

$$= £2.03 \text{ per standard hour}$$

Contribution per unit of output

Products	'SD'	'AH'	'JV'	'SH'	'JP'	'JJ'
Contribution	£13,508	£12,626	£11,701	£10,540	£10,427	£10,751
Units/output	960	900	825	900	930	1,050
Contribution per unit	£14.07	£14.03	£14.18	£11.71	£11.21	£10.24
Standard hours per unit	2.5	2.25	2.1	2.0	2.0	1.9
Contribution per Standard Hour (limiting factor)	£5.63	£6.24	£6.75	£5.86	£5.61	£5.39
Ranking	4	2	1	3	5	6

Standard hours in budget	11,813
Shortfall: 90% capacity available due to breakdown	10,632
	1,181

	Hours
Production Schedule:	
Revised hours available	10,632
Products by ranking	
'JV' – produce	
825 × 2.1 hours	1,732
	8,900
'AH'	
900 × 2.25 hours	2,025
	6,875
'SH'	
900 × 2.0 hours	1,800
	5,075
'SD'	
960 × 2.5 hours	2,400
	2,675
'JP'	
930 × 2.00 hours	1,860
Balance to produce 'JJ'	815

The 815 hours available to produce 'JJ' will enable production of $\dfrac{815}{1.9}$ = 428 units of 'JJ'

Revised Production & Sales Schedule:

Products	*'SD'*	*'AH'*	*'JV'*	*'SH'*	*'JP'*	*'JJ'*	*Total*
Production & Sales (Units)	960	900	825	900	930	428	4,943
Contribution per unit (£)	14.07	14.03	14.18	11.71	11.21	10.24	
Contribution (£)	13,507	12,627	11,699	10,539	10,425	4,383	63,180
Fixed costs							45,000
Revised profit							£18,180

	£
Original budgeted profit	24,553
Revision	18,180
Shortfall due to reduced capacity	£6,373

- The revised mix is purely based on financial criteria.

  It may be that product 'JJ', which is the cheapest product in the range and subject to the greatest demand, need not bear all the shortfall. We must be careful not to upset our customers by reducing supply by approximately 60%.

  Perhaps we could consider spreading the shortfall across all products. We need to review this financially.

- The other option would be, in the short-run, possibly to contract out the shortfall on 'JJ'. We could buy in and label the cues with our logo.

  If we could take this action we may be able to avoid the profit shortfall in the period.

Task 3

- Breakeven point in sales value:

$$\frac{\text{Fixed costs}}{\left(\text{Contribution} \diagup \text{Sales} \right)}$$

$$= \frac{£4,500}{\left(\dfrac{69,553}{192,360} \right)} = \underline{£124,457}$$

- Breakeven point in units:

$$\frac{\text{Fixed costs}}{\text{Contribution per unit}}$$

$$= \frac{£45,000}{\left(\dfrac{69,553}{5,565} \right)} = \underline{3,600 \text{ units}}$$

-
Profit target	£40,000
Revised fixed costs	£50,000
Revised contribution required	£90,000

  If unit contribution is reduced by £1.00 to £11.50, then:

  Revised contribution
  = £90,000 / 11.50
  = 7,826 units

- Revised break-even point in units

$$\frac{\text{Fixed costs}}{\text{Contribution per unit}} = \frac{£50,000}{11.50}$$

$$= \underline{4,348 \text{ units}}$$

  Revised sales:

  Average selling price per unit was originally £34.57; if contribution per unit falls by £1.00 per unit due to selling price - then revised selling price is £33.57 per unit.

  7,826 units × £33.57 = £262,719

Break-even point in Sales Value:

$$\frac{\text{Fixed Costs}}{\left(\text{Contribution}\middle/\text{Sales}\right)} = \frac{£50,000}{\left(90,000\middle/262,719\right)}$$

$$= £145,956$$

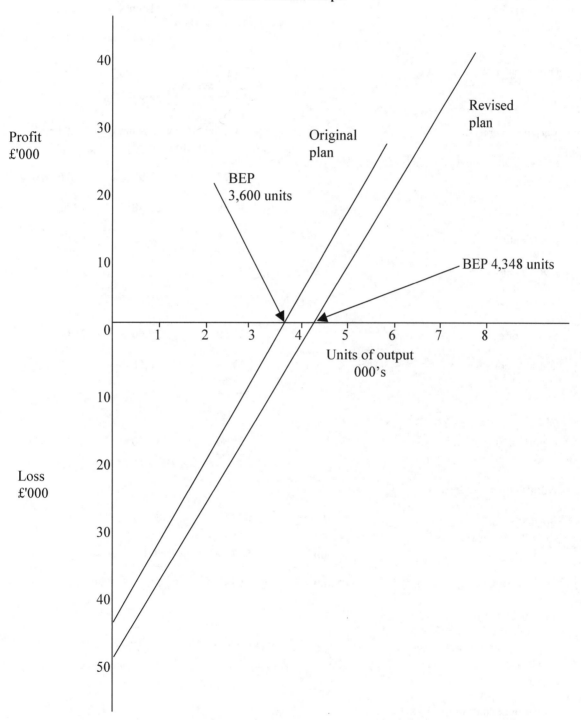

Cuescraft Ltd
Profit Volume Graph

Task 4

Option 1 – To produce in-house

Special order Year 1

Products	'SH'	'JP'	'JJ'
	£	£	£
Selling prices	27.50	27.00	25.00
Variable costs			
Direct labour	1.9 hrs	1.9 hrs	1.8 hrs
	@ £6.18 per hour		
	11.74	11.74	11.12
Direct material usage	1.05	1.05	1.00
	@ £4.64 per unit		
	4.87	4.87	4.64
Variable overhead	1.9 hrs	1.9 hrs	1.8 hrs
	@ £2.09 per Std Hr		
(*Note*: 20X9 budget is based on £2.03)			
	3.97	3.97	3.76
	20.58	20.58	19.52
Contribution	£6.92	£6.42	£5.48

Special order Year 2

Products	'SH'	'JP'	'JJ'
	£	£	£
Selling prices	27.50	27.00	25.00
Variable costs per unit	20.58	20.58	19.52
	+ 3%		
	21.20	21.20	20.11
Contribution per unit	£6.30	£5.80	£4.89

Additional contribution year 1

Products	'SH'	'JP'	'JJ'	Total
Contribution per unit (£)	6.92	6.42	5.48	
× Units	500	500	500	
	£3,460	£3,210	£2,740	£9,410

Efficiency gains
'SH' 1,100 × 0.10 Std hrs = 110
'JP' 1,150 × 0.10 Std hrs = 115   } 350 hours @ £6.18   £2,163
'JJ' 1,250 × 0.10 Std hrs = 125

£11,573

Additional contribution year 2

Products	'SH'	'JP'	'JJ'	Total
Contribution per unit (£)	6.30	5.80	4.89	
× 500 units	£3,150	£2,900	£2,445	£8,495

Efficiency gains

'SH'

'JP'   350 hrs @ £6.37   £2,230

'JJ'

                                                                       _____

                                                                       £10,725

Effect on profit

	Year 1 £	Year 2 £
Incremental contribution	11,573	10,725
Additional fixed costs	4,000	4,000
Additional profit	£7,573	£6,725

Option 2 – Years 1 and 2

'BUY IN'

Products	'SH' £	'JP' £	'JJ' £	Total £
Selling price	27.50	27.00	25.00	
Buy in price	24.00	23.50	21.50	
Logo/packing	0.60	0.60	0.60	
	24.60	24.10	22.10	
Contribution per unit	£2.90	£2.90	£2.90	
1,500 units @ £2.90				4,350

Additional profit per year is £4,350

The recommendation would be to produce the extra output "in-house" primarily due to the efficiency gains of using the new machinery.

Task 5

Pay-Back Period

	Cash Flow £	Cumulative £
Year 20Y0	11,600	11,600
Y1	10,700	22,300
Y2	10,500	32,800
Y3	10,350	43,150
Y4	10,210	53,360

$$\text{Pay-back} = \text{Year } 2 + \left(\frac{1,700}{10,500} \times 12 \right)$$

$$= 2 \text{ years } 2 \text{ months}$$

Capital allowances:

	Cost £	FYA/ WDA £	Tax WDV £
Year ending 20Y0	24,000	9,600	14,400
Y1	14,400	3,600	10,800
Y2	10,800	2,700	8,100
Y3	8,100	2,025	6,075

Balancing allowance calculation:

	£
Year end 20X4 proceeds	4,000
Tax written down value	6,075
Balancing allowance	2,075

Computation of tax payable or repayable:

		Incremental income £	Tax allowance £	Taxable income £	Tax rate	Tax payable £
Year	20Y0	11,600	9,600	2,000	25%	500
	Y1	10,700	3,600	7,100	25%	1,775
	Y2	10,500	2,700	7,800	25%	1,950
	Y3	10,350	2,025	8,325	25%	2,081
	Y4	10,210	2,075 *	8,135	25%	2,034

*Balancing allowance

Discounted Cash Flow

Year	Cash flow £	Tax £	After tax cash flow £	30% discount factor £	NPV £
20Y0		(24,000)	–	(24,000)	1.00 (24,000)
Y0	11,600	–	11,600	0.769	8,920
Y1	10,700	500	10,200	0.591	6,028
Y2	10,500	1,775	8,725	0.455	3,970
Y3	10,350	1,950	8,400	0.355	2,982
Y4	14,210*	2,081	12,129	0.269	3,263
Y5		2,034	(2,034)	0.207	(421)
				NPV	£742

* Includes sales proceeds

As the NPV is positive, the investment is achieving a return greater than 30%.

Discounted cash flow 35%

Year	After tax cash flow £	35% NPV factor £	NPV £
Year 20Y0	(24,000)	1.00	(24,000)
0	11,600	0.741	8,596
1	10,200	0.549	5,600
2	8,725	0.407	3,551
3	8,400	0.301	2,528
4	12,129	0.223	2,705
5	(2,034)	0.165	(336)
		NPV	£(1,356)

$$IRR = \text{Low Rate \%} + \left(\frac{\text{NPV at Lower Rate}}{\text{Range of NPV}} \times \text{Range of Rates} \right)$$

$$= 30 + \left(\frac{742}{2,098} \times 5 \right)$$

$$= 31.8\%$$

As the IRR is greater than the cost of capital, considered to be 30%, then the investment in new plant should proceed.

CLASS ACTIVITIES FOR COLLEGES

QUESTIONS

Chapters 1 – 2

INTRODUCTION PRINCIPLES

---

1 Activity

Task 1

Explain clearly the differences between financial accounting information and cost accounting information.

Task 2

Discuss one problem associated with production of

(i)   financial accounting information, and
(ii)   cost accounting information.

Task 3

How may a computerised integrated accounting system be used to provide information consistent with the needs of both financial accounting and cost accounting?

---

2 Activity

Task 1

Define the terms 'cost centre' and 'cost unit'.

Task 2

Distinguish between direct and indirect costs and discuss the factors which should influence whether a particular cost is treated as direct or indirect in relation to a cost unit.

Chapter 3

OVERHEADS

---

1   Activity

QRS Ltd has three main departments – casting, dressing and assembly – and for period 3 has prepared the following production overhead budgets for an output level of 110,000 units:

Department	Casting	Dressing	Assembly
Production overheads	£225,000	£175,000	£93,000
Expected production hours	7,500	7,000	6,200

During period 3, actual results were as follows for an output level of 117,500 units:

Department	Casting	Dressing	Assembly
Production overheads	£229,317	£182,875	£94,395
Production hours	7,950	7,280	6,696

Task 1

Calculate the predetermined departmental overhead absorption rates for period 3.

Task 2

Calculate the under/over absorption of overheads for *each* department for period 3 and suggest possible reasons for the value of under/over absorbed overheads you have calculated for the *casting* department.

Task 3

Analyse the values of under/over absorbed overheads you have calculated for *dressing* and *assembly* and briefly discuss whether the calculated values assist departmental management with the operations of their departments or in the control of their overheads.

---

2   Activity

The following data have been extracted from the budgets and standard costs of Hewitson Ltd, a company which manufactures and sells a single product.

	£ per unit
Selling price	45.00
Direct materials cost	10.00
Direct wages cost	4.00
Variable overhead cost	2.50

Fixed production overhead costs are budgeted at £400,000 per annum. Normal production levels are thought to be 320,000 units per annum.

Budgeted selling and distribution costs are as follows:

Variable   £1.50 per unit sold
Fixed   £80,000 per annum

Budgeted administration costs are £120,000 per annum.

The following pattern of sales and production is expected during the first six months of 20X3:

	January – March	April – June
Sales (units)	60,000	90,000
Production (units)	70,000	100,000

There is to be no stock on 1 January 20X3.

Task 1

Prepare profit statements for **each** of the **two** quarters, in a columnar format, using:

(a)   marginal costing, and
(b)   absorption costing

Task 2

Reconcile the profits for the quarter January – March 20X3 in your answer to Task 1 above.

Task 3

State and explain briefly the benefits of using marginal costing as the basis of management reporting.

Chapters 4 – 5

PRESENTATION OF INFORMATION

1 Activity

Briefly describe the following types of sampling AND indicate the circumstances under which they may be of value to management:

- simple random sampling
- stratified sampling
- quota sampling.

2 Activity

The following data shows a breakdown of two families' monthly expenditure:

	Expenditure	
Item	*Family 1*	*Family 2*
	£	£
Food and drink	540	180
Housing	730	370
Fuel and light	125	84
Transport	600	124
Other	315	32
Net monthly income	2,310	790

Task 1

Draw a suitable chart to represent the above data to enable a comparison between the two families' expenditure.

Task 2

Briefly compare each family's expenditure.

3   Activity

The managers of an import agency are investigating the length of time that customers take to pay their invoices, the normal terms for which are 30 days net.

They have checked the payment record of 100 customers chosen at random and have compiled the following table:

Payment in:	Number of customers
5 to 9 days	4
10 to 14 days	10
15 to 19 days	17
20 to 24 days	20
25 to 29 days	22
30 to 34 days	16
35 to 39 days	8
40 to 44 days	3

Task

Construct a histogram from the above data.

Chapters 6 – 7

TIME SERIES AND INDEX NUMBERS

1	**Activity**

You are employed by a major UK airline. The data below relate to the number of passengers transported on domestic flights by UK airlines on scheduled services, in millions.

UK Airlines: passengers carried

Average seasonal variation (20X0 – 20X5)

Year	Quarter	Value		Quarter	Value
20X1	Q_1	1.9		Q_1	−19%
	Q_2	2.6		Q_2	+3%
	Q_3	3.1		Q_3	+20%
	Q_4	2.5		Q_4	−4%
20X2	Q_1	2.3			
	Q_2	2.9			
	Q_3	3.3			
	Q_4	2.7			
20X3	Q_1	2.5			
	Q_2	3.1			
	Q_3	3.5			
	Q_4	3.0			
20X4	Q_1	2.8			
	Q_2	3.3			
	Q_3	3.7			
	Q_4	3.0			
20X5	Q_1	2.4			
	Q_2	3.1			
	Q_3	3.1			

(Source: Monthly Digest of Statistics, December 20X5, Table 13.9)

Task 1

Draw a time series graph of the data.

Task 2

By any method you consider appropriate, prepare forecasts for the numbers of domestic passengers flying on scheduled services with UK airlines, for the 3rd and 4th quarters of 20X6.

2   Activity

The managers of a company are preparing revenue plans for the last quarter of 20X3/X4, and for the first three quarters of 20X4/X5. The data below refer to one of the main products:

Revenue	April–June Quarter 1 £'000	July–September Quarter 2 £'000	October–December Quarter 3 £'000	January–March Quarter 4 £'000
20X0/X1	49	37	58	67
20X1/X2	50	38	59	68
20X2/X3	51	40	60	70
20X3/X4	50	42	61	–

Task 1

Calculate the four–quarterly moving average trend for this set of data.

Task 2

Calculate the seasonal factors using the additive model.

Task 3

Explain, but do not calculate, how you would use the results in Tasks 1 and 2 of this Activity to forecast the revenue for the last quarter of 20X3/X4 and for the first three quarters of 20X4/X5.

3   Activity

A company buys and uses five different materials. Details of the actual prices and quantities used for 20X5 and the budgeted figures for 20X6 are as follows:

Material	Actual 20X5 Quantity ('000)	Actual 20X5 Unit price £	Budgeted 20X6 Quantity ('000)	Budgeted 20X6 Unit price £
A	21	11	25	12
B	56	22	52	26
C	62	18	79	18
D	29	20	35	22
E	31	22	36	23

Task 1

Calculate the price relatives for each material separately, using 20X5 as the base year.

Task 2

Calculate a *Laspeyres* or base–weighted index for material prices based on 20X5 = 100.

Task 3

Explain (without calculation) the difference between a *Laspeyres* price index and the *Paasche* price index and what information such index numbers provide.

4   Activity

The following table shows data for gross domestic product (GDP), gross earnings and retail prices for the UK, 20X0–20X9:

	Gross domestic product (market prices, £ billion)	Average gross earnings (20X5 = 100)	Retail prices (20X5 = 100)
20X0	231	65	71
20X1	255	73	79
20X2	278	80	86
20X3	303	87	90
20X4	323	92	94
20X5	354	100	100
20X6	379	108	103
20X7	414	116	108
20X8	430	126	113
20X9	436*	136*	122*

* provisional

[Source: British Business, 1 September 20X9, and Economic Trends (various)]

Task 1

Convert the GDP series to index numbers with 20X5 = 100.

Task 2

Calculate deflated index numbers for GDP and average gross earnings, with 20X5 = 100.

Task 3

Plot the two deflated indicators against time on the same graph and comment critically upon the meaning of these data.

Chapters 8 – 10

BUDGETS

---

1   Activity

The following data and estimates are available for ABC Ltd for June, July and August:

	June £	July £	August £
Sales	45,000	50,000	60,000
Wages	12,000	13,000	14,500
Overheads	8,500	9,500	9,000

The following information is available regarding direct materials:

	June £	July £	August £	September £
Opening stock	5,000	3,500	6,000	4,000
Material usage	8,000	9,000	10,000	

Notes:

(1)   10% of sales are for cash, the balance is received the following month. The amount received in June for May's sales is £29,500.

(2)   Wages are paid in the month they are incurred.

(3)   Overheads include £1,500 per month for depreciation. Overheads are settled the month following. £6,500 is to be paid in June for May's overheads.

(4)   Purchases of direct materials are paid for in the month purchased.

(5)   The opening cash balance in June is £11,750.

(6)   A tax bill of £25,000 is to be paid in July.

Task 1

Calculate the amount of direct material purchases in EACH of the months of June, July and August.

Task 2

Prepare cash budgets for June, July and August.

Task 3

Describe briefly the advantages of preparing cash budgets.

2   Activity

JK Ltd has recently completed its sales forecasts for the year to 31 December 20X4. It expects to sell two products – J and K – at prices of £135 and £145 each respectively.

Sales demand is expected to be:

J	10,000 units
K	6,000 units

Both products use the same raw materials and skilled labour but in different quantities per unit:

	J	*K*
Material X	10 kgs	6 kgs
Material Y	4 kgs	8 kgs
Skilled labour	6 hours	4 hours

The prices expected during 20X4 for the raw materials are:

Material X	£1.50 per kg
Material Y	£4.00 per kg

The skilled labour rate is expected to be £6.00 per hour.

Stocks of raw materials and finished goods on 1 January 20X4 are expected to be:

Material X	400 kgs	@	£1.20 per kg
Material Y	200 kgs	@	£3.00 per kg
J	600 units	@	£70.00 each
K	800 units	@	£60.00 each

All stocks are to be reduced by 15% from their opening levels by the end of 20X4 and are valued using the FIFO method.

The company uses absorption costing, and production overhead costs are expected to be:

Variable	£2.00 per skilled labour hour
Fixed	£315,900 per annum

Task

Prepare for the year to 31 December 20X4 JK Ltd's:

(a)   production budget (in units)
(b)   raw material purchases budget (in units and £)
(c)   production cost budget
(d)   budgeted trading account.

Chapters 11 – 12

STANDARD COSTING AND VARIANCES

1	Activity

XYZ Ltd is planning to make 120,000 units per period of a new product. The following standards have been set:

Per unit

Direct material A	1.2 kgs at £11 per kg
Direct material B	4.7 kgs at £6 per kg
Direct labour	
Operation 1	42 minutes
Operation 2	37 minutes
Operation 3	11 minutes

Overheads are absorbed at the rate of £30 per labour hour. All direct operatives are paid at the rate of £8 per hour. Attainable work hours are less than clock hours, so the 500 direct operatives have been budgeted for 400 hours each in the period.

Actual results for the period were:

Production	126,000 units
Direct labour	cost £1.7m for 215,000 clock hours
Material A	cost £1.65m for 150,000 kgs
Material B	cost £3.6m for 590,000 kgs

Task 1

Calculate the standard cost for one unit.

Task 2

Calculate the labour rate variance and a realistic efficiency variance.

Task 3

Calculate the material price and usage variances.

Task 4

Describe the manufacturing environment in which labour variances can provide useful information.

---

2   Activity

The following standard costs apply in Company M which manufactures a single product:

Standard weight to produce one unit	12	kgs
Standard price per kg	£9	
Standard hours to produce one unit	10	
Standard rate per hour	£4	

Actual production and costs for one accounting period were:

Material used	3,770	kgs
Material cost	£35,815	
Hours worked	2,755	
Wages paid	£11,571	

The actual output was 290 units.

Task 1

Calculate relevant material and labour cost variances, and present these in a format suitable for presentation to the management of the company.

Task 2

Explain how standard costs for material and labour might be compiled.

---

3   Activity

The following details have been extracted from the standard cost card for product X:

	£/unit
Variable overhead	
4 machine hours @ £8.00/hour	32.00
2 labour hours @ £4.00/hour	8.00
Fixed overhead	20.00

During October 20X7, 5,450 units of the product were made compared to a budgeted production target of 5,500 units. The actual overhead costs incurred were:

Machine–related variable overhead	£176,000
Labour–related variable overhead	£42,000
Fixed overhead	£109,000

The actual number of machine hours was 22,000 and the actual number of labour hours was 10,800.

Task 1

Calculate the overhead cost variances in as much detail as possible from the data provided.

Task 2

Explain the meaning of, and give possible causes for, the variable overhead variances which you have calculated.

Task 3

Explain the benefits of using multiple activity bases for variable overhead absorption.

Chapters 13 – 14

IMPROVING PERFORMANCE

---

1 Activity

Task 1

Explain the differences between data and information.

Data

The following details have been extracted from the accounts of PQR plc for three years of recession. The company's year ends on 31 March.

	20X2 £m	20X3 £m	20X4 £m
Turnover (sales)	100	103	108
Gross profit	33.0	34.0	35.6
Net profit	15	15	15
Fixed assets	64	72	68
Stock	4	4	4
Debtors	8	11	15
Creditors	(5)	(6)	(6)
Cash at bank	5	–	–
Bank overdraft	–	6	5

Task 2

Calculate, for each of the three years:

- gross profit percentage
- net profit percentage
- quick ratio (acid test).

Task 3

Comment briefly on the ratios you have calculated.

---

2 Activity

You are considering the purchase of a small business, JK, and have managed to obtain a copy of its accounts for the last complete accounting year to 30 September 20X3. These appear as follows:

Trading and profit and loss account for the year to 30 September 20X3

		£	£
Sales			385,200
Less:	Cost of goods sold:		
	Opening stocks	93,250	
	Purchases	174,340	
	less Closing stocks	(84,630)	
			182,960
Gross profit			202,240
Less:	Expenses:		
	Selling and delivery costs	83,500	
	Administration costs	51,420	
	Depreciation	36,760	
			171,680
Net profit			30,560

Balance sheet at 30 September 20X3

		£	£
Fixed assets			
	Assets at cost	235,070	
	Less: Depreciation to date	(88,030)	
			147,040
Current assets			
	Stocks	84,630	
	Debtors and prepayments	36,825	
	Bank and cash	9,120	
		130,575	
Less:	Current liabilities		
	Creditors and accruals	(62,385)	
			68,190
			215,230
Financed by			
	Capital at 1 October 20X2		197,075
	Net profit for the year		30,560
	Proprietor's drawings		(12,405)
			215,230

Task

Calculate the following accounting ratios from the accounts as presented above:

(a)   net profit percentage
(b)   return on capital employed
(c)   current ratio
(d)   quick (acid test) ratio

Chapters 15 –16

DECISION MAKING PRINCIPLES

◈ **FOULKS**lynch

---

1   Activity

Task 1

Using the accountants' conventional breakeven chart as a 'model', explain how and why a breakeven chart drawn by an economist would differ. Illustrative diagrams should be adjacent to your answer and NOT on separate graph paper.

Data

PM Ltd owns the Premier Hotel which is on a busy main road near an international airport. The hotel has 40 rooms which are let at a rental of £35 per day.

Variable costs are £6 per room occupied per day.

Fixed costs **per month** are:

	£
Depreciation	9,000
Insurance	5,500
Maintenance	4,800
Services	2,700
Management	3,000

Business is not as good in the period October to March as it is in the period April to September. The figures below relate to the two six–monthly periods for 20X3/X4.

	April to September (183 days) £	October to March (182 days) £
Potential room lettings	256,200	254,800
Budgeted room lettings	218,400	165,200

Task 2

(a)   Calculate the budgeted room occupancy ratio to the nearest percentage figure for **each** six–month period.

(b)   Prepare a statement showing budgeted profit or loss for each of the two six–monthly periods.

(c)   State the number of room days per month which must be let on average each month to break even.

(d)   State with reason(s) whether or not you believe the hotel should be closed during January and February because in these two particularly poor trading months the fixed costs are not covered by the receipts from letting the rooms.

(e)   State briefly how you would investigate the costs for insurance and maintenance; the Manager of the hotel believes these two costs are too high and should be capable of being reduced.

2   Activity

The following details relate to a shop which currently sells 25,000 pairs of shoes annually

Selling price per pair of shoes	£40
Purchase cost per pair of shoes	£25

Total annual fixed costs

	£
Salaries	100,000
Advertising	40,000
Other fixed expenses	100,000

Answer each task independently of data contained in other parts of the requirement.

Task 1

Calculate the break–even point and margin of safety in number of pairs of shoes sold.

Task 2

Assume that 20,000 pairs of shoes were sold in a year.

Estimate the shop's net income (or loss).

Task 3

If a selling commission of £2 per pair of shoes sold was to be introduced, how many pairs of shoes would need to be sold in a year in order to earn a net income of £10,000?

Task 4

Assume that for next year an additional advertising campaign costing £20,000 is proposed, whilst at the same time selling prices are to be increased by 12%.

What would be the break–even point in number of pairs of shoes?

Chapters 17 – 18

DECISION MAKING TECHNIQUES

1	**Activity**

ABC Ltd makes three products, all of which use the same machine which is available for 50,000 hours per period.

The standard costs of the products per unit are:

	Product A £	Product B £	Product C £
Direct materials	70	40	80
Direct labour			
Machinists (£8 per hour)	48	32	56
Assemblers (£6 per hour)	36	40	42
Total variable cost	154	112	178
Selling price per unit	200	158	224
Maximum demand (units)	3,000	2,500	5,000

Fixed costs are £300,000 per period.

ABC Ltd could buy in similar quality products at the following unit prices:

A	£175
B	£140
C	£200

Task 1

Calculate the deficiency in machine hours for the next period.

Task 2

Determine which product(s) and quantities (if any) should be bought out.

Task 3

Calculate the profit for the next period based on your recommendations in Task 2.

2	**Activity**

A company produces a hard grade and, by additional processing, a soft grade of its product.

A market research study for next year has indicated very good prospects not only for both the hard and soft grades but also for a light grade produced after still further processing.

The raw material is imported and there is a possibility that a quota system will be introduced allowing only a maximum of £300,000 pa of material to be imported.

The company's marketing policy has been to sell 60% of its capacity (or of its allocation of material if the quota is introduced) in the most profitable grade. It has been decided that this policy should continue if it is to produce three grades, but that only 15% of its capacity (or material allocation) should be sold in the least profitable grade.

◇ FOULKS*lynch*

The budgeted prime costs and selling prices per ton for each grade are as follows:

	Hard £	Soft £	Light £
Selling price	70	95	150
Direct material cost	15	20	25
Direct wages (@ £2.50 per hour)	15	25	45

For next year the company's annual production capacity is 225,000 direct labour hours and its fixed overhead is £500,000. Variable overhead is 20% of direct wages.

Fixed overhead is at present absorbed by a rate per ton produced.

Task 1

State which of the three grades of product will be most profitable and which will be least profitable in the short term assuming that such volume as can be produced can be sold:

(a)   if the materials quota does not operate
(b)   if the materials quota does come into force.

Task 2

If the materials quota does come into force, calculate the budgeted profit for next year from the company's marketing policy if:

(a)   only light grade is produced
(b)   all three grades are produced in accordance with present policy.

Chapters 19 – 20

PRICING AND COST ESTIMATION

---

1 Activity

Watch–It–Go–Up Ltd has a contract for an office and leisure complex. Work is part complete at the year end on 30 June 20X3. The following information is available:

	£'000
Contract price	2,500
Direct materials:	
Issued	680
Returned to suppliers	30
Transferred to other contracts	30
On site at 30 June	40
Direct wages:	
Paid	440
Accrued	20
Direct expenses:	
Paid	50
Accrued	10
Value of work certified to date	1,500
Received from contractee	1,200
Plant installed on site:	
Cost	200
Valuation 30 June	150
Estimated cost to completion	700

Progress payments are based on architects' certificates less 20% retention.

Task 1

Calculate attributable profit for the year to 30 June 20X3.

Task 2

Prepare the contract and client ledger accounts.

2   Activity

You have received a request from EXE plc to provide a quotation for the manufacture of a specialised piece of equipment. This would be a one–off order, in excess of normal budgeted production. The following cost estimate has already been prepared:

		Note	£
Direct materials:			
Steel	10m^2 @ £5.00 per m^2	(1)	50
Brass fittings		(2)	20
Direct labour:			
Skilled	25 hours @ £8.00 per hour	(3)	200
Semi–skilled	10 hours @ £5.00 per hour	(4)	50
Overhead	35 hours @ £10.00 per hour	(5)	350
Estimating time		(6)	100
			———
			770
Administration overhead @ 20% of production cost		(7)	154
			———
			924
Profit @ 25% of total cost		(8)	231
			———
Selling price			1,155
			———

Notes:

(1)   The steel is regularly used, and has a current stock value of £5.00 per square metre. There are currently 100m^2 in stock. The steel is readily available at a price of £5.50 per square metre.

(2)   The brass fittings would have to be bought specifically for this job: a supplier has quoted the price of £20 for the fittings required.

(3)   The skilled labour is currently employed by your company and paid at a rate of £8.00 per hour. If this job were undertaken it would be necessary either to work 25 hours overtime which would be paid at time plus one half OR reduce production of another product which earns a contribution of £13.00 per hour.

(4)   The semi–skilled labour currently has sufficient paid idle time to be able to complete this work.

(5)   The overhead absorption rate includes power costs which are directly related to machine usage. If this job were undertaken, it is estimated that the machine time required would be ten hours. The machines incur power costs of £0.75 per hour. There are no other overhead costs which can be specifically identified with this job.

(6)   The cost of the estimating time is that attributed to the four hours taken by the engineers to analyse the drawings and determine the cost estimate given above.

(7)   It is company policy to add 20% on to the production cost as an allowance against administration costs associated with the jobs accepted.

(8)   This is the standard profit added by your company as part of its pricing policy.

Task 1

Prepare, on a relevant cost basis, the lowest cost estimate that could be used as the basis for a quotation.

Explain briefly your reasons for using EACH of the values in your estimate.

Task 2

There may be a possibility of repeat orders from EXE plc which would occupy part of normal production capacity.

What factors need to be considered before quoting for this order?

Task 3

When an organisation identifies that it has a single production resource which is in short supply, but is used by more than one product, the optimum production plan is determined by ranking the products according to their contribution per unit of the scarce resource.

Using a numerical example of your own, reconcile this approach with the opportunity cost approach used in Task 1 above.

Chapters 21 – 22

INVESTMENT APPRAISAL

---

1   Activity

Oracle plc invests in a new machine at the beginning of Year 1 which costs £15,000. It is hoped that the net cash flows over the next five years will correspond to those given in the table below:

Year	1	2	3	4	5
Net cash flow	£1,500	£2,750	£4,000	£5,700	£7,500

Task 1

(a)   Calculate the net present value assuming a 15% cost of capital.

(b)   Calculate the net present value assuming a 10% cost of capital.

(c)   Calculate the internal rate of return of the above project using the results of (a) and (b).

Task 2

An alternative machine would cost £17,500 but would produce equal net cash flows of £5,500 over the next five years. What cost of capital would produce a break–even situation on the project?

---

2   Activity

The cash flows for two projects are expected to be as follows:

	Project A		Project B	
Time	Cash flow £'000	Time	Cash flow £'000	
0	–25	0	–25	
1	10	1	0	
2	10	2	5	
3	10	3	10	
4	10	4	30	

Task 1

Use present value tables or first principles to compute the present values for each project at discount rates of 10%, 20%, 30% and 40%.

Task 2

Plot the two sets of points on a single sheet of graph paper, and join the two sets of points to produce two smooth curves.

Task 3

Use the graphs to read off the internal rate of return for the two projects.

◈ FOULKS*lynch*

AAT

FOULKS LYNCH
4 The Griffin Centre
Staines Road
Feltham
Middlesex, TW14 0Hs
United Kingdom

HOTLINES: Telephone: +44 (0) 20 8831 9990
Fax: +44 (0) 20 8831 9991
E-mail: info@foulkslynch.com

For information and online ordering, please visit our website at:
www. foulkslynch.com

PRODUCT RANGE

Our publications cover all assessments for the AAT standards competence.

Our AAT product range consists of:

Textbooks	£10.50	Workbooks	£10.50
Combined Textbooks/Workbooks	£10.50	Lynchpin	£6.25

OTHER PUBLICATIONS FROM FOULKS LYNCH

We publish a wide range of study material in the accountancy field and specialize in texts for the following professional qualifications:

- **Chartered Institute of Management Accountants (CIMA)**
- **Association of Chartered Certified Accountants (ACCA)**
- **Certified Accounting Technicians (CAT)**

FOR FURTHER INFORMATION ON OUR PUBLICATIONS:

I would like information on publications for: ACCA ❑   AAT ❑
                                                CAT ❑   CIMA ❑

Please keep me updated on new publications: ❑   By E-mail ❑   By Post ❑

Your Name...   Your email address...................................
Your address:...
....
....
....

Prices are correct at time of going to press and are subject to change